A Woman of EXCELLENCE

*Developing Your Special
Female Self*

L. Jane Mohline

FOREWORD BY DR. GARY R. COLLINS
A PERSONAL WORD BY DR. RICHARD MOHLINE

BROADMAN PRESS
NASHVILLE, TENNESSEE

© Copyright 1991 ● Broadman Press
All Rights Reserved
4260-34
ISBN: 0-8054-6034-9
Dewey Decimal Classification: 248.843
Subject Headings: WOMEN - RELIGIOUS LIFE // BIBLE. O.T. PROVERBS 31
Library of Congress Catalog Number: 90-35391
Printed in the United States of America

Library of Congress Cataloging-in-Publication Data

Mohline, L. Jane, 1937-
  A woman of excellence : developing your special female self / L.
Jane Mohline.
  p. cm.
  ISBN 0-8054-6034-9
  1. Women--Religious life. 2. Bible. O.T. Proverbs XXXI-
  -Devotional literature. I. Title.
BV4527.M58 1991
248.8′43--dc20

90-35391
CIP

*T*o Mom, my first example
of the Proverbs 31 woman

Contents

Foreword

I have a bias. I don't think men should write books about women. Solomon, of course, may have been an exception. He had seven hundred wives and three hundred in his concubine, so he must have known something about women. But the wives led him astray (1 Kings 11:3), and it seems unlikely that he knew any of these women very well.

But Solomon is known as the wisest man who ever lived, and his book of Proverbs ends with one of literature's most powerful and beautiful descriptions of women. The poem begins, "A wife [woman] of noble character . . . is worth far more than rubies," (Prov. 31:10, NIV). She is competent, diligent, and "clothed with strength and dignity," (v. 25, NIV). Little wonder the writer concludes that "a woman who fears the Lord is to be praised," (v. 30, NIV).

But many women don't feel very praiseworthy. Every day thousands face the trauma and indignity of abuse, violence, and harassment. Many carry the pain of childhood rejection, molestation, and failure. Some are treated as second-class citizens by church leaders who should know better. No estimate could predict how many struggle with poor self-concepts, insecurity, depression, and loneliness—sometimes brought on by the thoughtless words and actions of insensitive and self-centered men.

Jane Mohline knows about these rejections and insecurities, because she struggled with them for most of her life. Despite the gentle and sensitive support of a caring husband, she had come to view the woman of excellence in Proverbs 31 as an ideal that few (if any) ever come close to reaching. Most of the women she knew were like herself: "females who struggle with problems."

Over the years, however, Jane has learned that Proverbs 31 is a realistic guide for all women. In the following pages she shows how the disappointments and difficulties of life can be turned into realistic hope and genuine fulfillment. Step by step she takes us through the process of overcoming the effects of past or present hurts and moving into the realm of contentment, self-control, self-confidence, and true spirituality.

This book draws freely on the writings of others and weaves in the stories of women who, in various ways, have grown to maturity and excellence. Most impressive are the author's honest revelations about her own stresses and painful experiences. All of this is written with honesty and an obvious understanding of women, their struggles, their needs, and their potentialities.

I have known and respected Jane and Dick Mohline for many years. I have known, too, that this is not a book written carelessly or in haste. It has come from a lifetime of experiences, several years of painstaking work, and many hours of careful, clear thinking.

This is a book for women, but also for men who want to understand and encourage women. It is a book for parents who hope to see their daughters grow to become women of excellence. It is a book for church leaders who honestly care about the women in their congregations. It is a book that only a woman—a sensitive woman like Jane Mohline—could have written.

Dr. Gary R. Collins

A Personal Word

"See Dick run." "Run, Jane run." "See Dick catch Jane."
Little did I realize in first grade when I was reading about "Dick and Jane" that I would grow up and marry Jane and spend the rest of my life with her as my partner.

"An excellent wife, who can find,
For her worth is far above jewels."

As long as I have known Jane, she has driven herself to be an overcomer of the past and to pursue excellence in the Lord. This has not been without great pain and sacrifice in her own life.

This book is about excellence. It's about the Proverbs 31 woman, who fears the Lord. This book is about how an abused woman can become a woman of excellence. Above all, it shares the life experiences of individuals with whom Jane was acquainted and who were willing to share of themselves to help others. And finally, it records Jane's journey from her early childhood with many damaged memories to the present time and how she has worked on her own issues in life.

During the 33-plus years of our marriage, I have watched Jane's concern for the rearing of our four children, Faith, Lynn, Richard, and James, and that they be spared the pain which she experienced in her childhood. She has read literature extensively and searched inside herself intensively to understand her own thinking and feeling processes, always desiring to be a better person and please the Lord.

I have seen Jane do her homework for the writing of this book. Hundreds of hours were spent in the study putting together her understanding of Proverbs 31 and integrating hers and others' experiences in a meaningful and helpful way. Her library contains many books she has read and taken notes from.

Jane has run many risks in writing about her family background and disclosing her own struggles. She has shared with me again and again the hope that women would not feel guilty when they see such a perfect woman in Proverbs 31. She hopes this book will give permission for other women to be vulnerable and deal with the many issues in their lives which will help them to be the women God desires them to become.

I have been a therapist in private practice, a professor of psychology and theology, a military chaplain, a lecturer in Third World countries, and a graduate school administrator over a period of three decades. Often in my work, I have looked for a book to help women in the areas in which Jane has chosen to write. Rarely does one find a book by an author who has experienced abuses, researched the subject by reading and interviewing friends, and then written with the emphasis on **"how to"** overcome the hurts of the past. I realize that I am prejudiced, but I admire Jane for this endeavor.

Dr. Richard J. Mohline

Introduction

*M*ost of the books I've read about the Proverbs 31 woman picture her as ideal, perfect, and unattainable. At one time, I agreed with them. I thought the pictures of that special woman showed her spending almost twenty-four hours each day in the kitchen, dining room, or laundry—cooking, washing, and cleaning. I saw her as living in ideal circumstances; no major problems to cope with. Because I grew up in a troubled household, I couldn't see how this "perfect woman without problems" could help me. My emotions felt, "If she's perfect without problems, how can she model authentic womanhood for me? I need to see a woman who can face problems and cope with them."

I wanted to find an authentic model not just for me, but for all females who struggle with problems. Females supervising employees face problems like tardiness, laziness, and lack of job commitment. Females in the work force face personality conflicts and possible sexual discrimination, plus not enough pay. Those with husbands face changing personalities, emotional or physical tiredness, and sexual complications at times. Those parenting children face childhood illnesses, growing pains, and rebellious attitudes. The Proverbs 31 woman surely faced such problems, plus many more. So I discarded all overdeveloped pictures of a perfect, unattainable person and began taking new pictures. I used the best camera—God's Canon.

Instead of overdeveloped pictures, the Canon flashed clear pictures of an *attainable* special female self. I saw a person with a strong self-image showing me how to relate well with others, although she had to deal with relational problems. While there were difficulties with employees, she modeled reliable work ethics, realistic contentment, and competent career skills. Those pictures showed me this woman had developed those qualities through facing problems—not because she didn't have them. That gave me hope: hope that I, and all females who struggle with problems, could also develop her attainable qualities. Therefore, I chose the Canon's pictures showing how to face problems and cope with them.

In addition, I believe all women whether single or married can profit from Proverbs 31. My reasons rest on two suppositions. Verses 10 through 31, combined with four verses from Ephesians 5, present several pictures for developing both the inner and outer woman. Next, most of us—single or married—struggle with an ugly "caterpillar-like" self-image. That's why we need to develop our special female self to its fullest capacity. In doing this, our faulty self-pictures will disappear, and we will come to see ourselves as God's beautiful creations.

God provided females with power for personal development during the time that the Proverbs 31 woman lived. Similarly, today the Holy Spirit enables us to develop into women of excellence. During times when we feel too weak or discouraged to work on problems, we can receive Christ's strength from others' encouragement. Galatians 6:2 says to "bear one another's burdens." So I've listened while women shared struggles, and they have listened while I shared struggles. Bearing each others' burdens, we've helped each other to keep going and keep trying. Hoping to strengthen others, I'll share some of our struggles to show how God works "differentness" in our lives.

Writing about certain life experiences, I hope to help others who are hurting go through the process of stripping away emotional ugliness. Emotional ugliness says, "I'm dirty, a nothing, a worm." And yet the caterpillar, after weary, struggling work, strips away ugliness to develop into a beautiful flying butterfly. Myrna White, a friend we'll read about, still struggles with emotional damage suffered in childhood. In her latest album, she sings about that butterfly.

> The door has opened, I've stepped from my cocoon
> I'm pausing on this branch and I'm flexing my wings
> A wind is coming that will lift me away
> Up and higher I'm gonna fly, I'm gonna fly forevermore[1]

So whether you are single or married, suffer from an ugly "caterpillar-like" self-image, or struggle in other areas, there's hope. Rather than remain weak and underdeveloped in your inner woman, believe you can develop the fullness of your special female self. And, during the struggles to strip away emotional ugliness, you too will learn to fly. Together we will experience strength to become all we can be in Christ Jesus.

"A Woman of Excellence"

An excellent wife, who can find?
For her worth is far above jewels.
The heart of her husband trusts in her,
And he will have no lack of gain.
She does him good and not evil
All the days of her life.
She looks for wool and flax,
And works with her hands in delight.
She is like merchant ships;
She brings her food from afar.
She rises also while it is still night,
And gives food to her household,
And portions to her maidens.
She considers a field and buys it;
From her earnings she plants a vineyard.
She girds herself with strength.
And makes her arms strong.
She senses that her gain is good;
Her lamp does not go out at night.
She stretches out her hands to the distaff,
And her hands grasp the spindle.
She extends her hand to the poor;
And she stretches out her hands to the needy.
She is not afraid of the snow for her household,
For all her household are clothed with scarlet.
She makes coverings for herself;
Her clothing is fine linen and purple.
Her husband is known in the gates,
When he sits among the elders of the land.
She makes linen garments and sells them,
And supplies belts to the tradesmen.
Strength and dignity are her clothing,
And she smiles at the future.

She opens her mouth in wisdom,
And the teaching of kindness is on her tongue.
She looks well to the ways of her household,
And does not eat the bread of idleness.
Her children rise up and bless her;
Her husband also, and he praises her, saying
"Many daughters have done nobly
But you excel them all."
Charm is deceitful and beauty is vain,
But a woman who fears the Lord, she shall be praised.
Give her the product of her hands,
And let her works praise her in the gates
(Proverbs 31:10-31).

Section 1 *Developing a Strong Self-image*

*M*ost of my life I've struggled with feelings of weak self-identity, guilt, and depression. Those feelings crippled every area of my life. Because of a fuzzy, underdeveloped self-picture, I didn't know that within me a special female self, full of God-given gifts and abilities, lay dormant. Therefore, neither my inner woman nor most of my outer qualities had been developed. As a result, I suffered from an ugly "caterpillar-like" self-image.

Webster's New Dictionary of the English Language defines *self-image* as a concept or idea of oneself. Separating the words, it defines *self* as having its own nature, characteristics, and *image* as an exact likeness. Thus, none of us share the same likeness; we don't look alike on the inside or the outside. Since God designs us with individuality, we're different in nature and characteristics with our own likeness. Whether we look into our mind's mirror or look into a wall mirror, we see our likeness. Putting that all together, I define self-image as "how we picture ourselves." We interchange a collection of words—*self-picture, inner woman, self-concept, self-esteem, self-worth, self-acceptance*. These words help us understand different aspects involved in developing a strong self-image.

There's an important truism about self-identity. Our self-picture determines the way we *feel* about ourselves and others. In addition, females who feel self-acceptance picture themselves with a strong self-concept. They feel more healthy emotions than women who struggle with a weak self-concept.

They have developed their gifts and abilities, which helped them strip away emotional ugliness to develop a special female self.

In this first section we'll look at how to develop a strong self-image. We will learn that our self-worth is a free gift from God.

1 Self-worth: God's Free Gift

She feels self-worth . . . "For her worth is far above jewels"
(Prov. 31:10).

Wearing light coats over winter clothing, Dick and I shivered on our way to the First Baptist Church in Wheaton, Illinois. Sun rays gave some warmth to the cool, crisp spring air that April 1959 afternoon. With the snow melted, we could see a few flowers peeking up from the brown grass. A fresh vibrant green would soon replace the brown—a new beginning. *A new beginning for us too,* I thought. *Dick an ordained minister; me an ordained minister's wife. I wish Mom could be here to share this special time with us.*

Inside the sanctuary, holding our eleven-month-old daughter, I listened while pastors questioned Dick regarding his doctrinal beliefs. For years he had studied with the Navigators, a Christian organization that emphasizes Scripture memorization. In addition, he had graduated from the Moody Bible Institute and Wheaton College, both in Illinois. So, I believed his knowledge of Scripture adequate, and doubts about ordination approval never entered my mind. Through teaching the Bible and counseling others, Dick learned to express himself well. He seemed calm and confident.

Inside me, however, an emotional battle warred. On the one hand, I felt excited about his ordination; my self-worth depended upon Dick's achievements. Dick's becoming a minister and me becoming a minister's wife, I hoped, would strengthen my self-concept. On the other hand, thoughts of becoming a minister's wife tied my stomach nerves into small knots. For an ugly "caterpillar-like" self-image took away my "feelings" of self-worth.

How could I, a twenty-two-year-old country girl with only three college semesters and no Bible training, minister to others? Similar questions crowded my mind: *How can I help others when I have many problems that need solving? Will church members find out I grew up in a troubled household, resulting in emotional losses? Will they accept me, or will I just receive more rejection?* These questions show some of my emotional pain and fear. Pain and fear from underdeveloped, fuzzy self-pictures. I felt bound up in a cocoon but didn't have the knowledge or courage to break out.

In contrast, the Proverbs 31 woman evidently broke any cocoon strands that might have bound her. She models how to develop a special female self, filled with God-given gifts and abilities. Since the woman felt a strong self-concept, she could relate to family, employees, or customers with respect and concern. That balance connected to verse 10 shows she developed a clear self-picture, "her worth is far above jewels." Have you wondered how she developed a clear self-picture and a strong self-concept?

The field of psychology gives us insights into how our personalities develop. Many say that within each of us lives a parent-adult-child concept (PAC) from the past. Ira J. Tanner believes that concept forms like this. From birth until death, everything learned and experienced is stored in the mind, which becomes a storehouse filled with "do and don't" messages. That's the "parent" concept. While becoming an adult, we learn to evaluate and test reality. This trial and error procedure becomes a seat of choice or the basis for our decision making. That's the "adult" concept. Children, unless inhibited through abusiveness, feel inquisitiveness, adventurousness, spontaneity, and curiosity. These inclinations become a seat of feelings. That's the "child" concept.[1] This parent-adult-child concept continues throughout our lifetime. How well this concept develops rests on the type of relationship we had with parents (or other authority figures) during our formative years.

While reviewing old mind-messages collected in my "storehouse," I saw numerous emotional responses and mental stimuli received from my parents, teachers, pastors, or peers—authority figures that were significant to me. Scenes of emotional struggles, rejection, and other losses from my formative years flashed on my mental screen. Those losses caused my "parent" to develop an inadequate self-identity. During childhood, I couldn't separate myself from others' critical attitudes, responses, or actions toward me.

Childhood holds another important feature. When parents nurture their children's self-esteem with loving and healthy relationships, they build into those children a strong self-identity. But, some of my friends' parents neglected to establish meaningful relationships with them. They received as much damage to their self-identity as I did in growing up in a dysfunctional household. Since their parents didn't spend time being, playing, or talking with them they got the message, "I'm not important!" Children don't understand when their parents are too busy with work or others to take time for them. Therefore, their "storehouse" develops messages like, "They spend time at work; work's important to them. They spend time with others; others are important to them. They don't spend time with me; I'm not important to them." These mind-messages—whether perceived correctly or incorrectly—damage the "parent." As a result, fuzzy, underdeveloped self-pictures of the inner woman develop and carry over into adulthood.

In talking with friends, I've learned that their "adult" (like mine) was underdeveloped and stifled by uncaring, overprotective, and untrusting parents. Those parents failed to supervise our decision making with care, respect, and trust. Consequently, we were kept from experiencing choice or evaluating reality in a safe atmosphere. Decision making, then, for our "adult" became an overwhelming and frustrating experience because children can base self-worth only on feelings.

One friend's *uncaring parents* crippled her childhood emotions. Many Saturday afternoons when Jamie was only five years old, she would walk several blocks alone to attend the movies. Although she had two older sisters, her busy parents neglected to have them walk with her too for protection and supervision. At age nine, she started smoking and going further from home—unattended. At thirteen, she began drinking with friends and skipping school. Since the parents were too busy to supervise Jamie, decisions became overwhelming for her. She learned to procrastinate in taking care of responsibilities rather than committing herself to them. Because of her parents' obvious lack of care, my friend grew up feeling unimportant, uncared for, and unloved.

My *overprotective parents* stifled my decision making. They evidently had not worked through unproductive decision making and feared I would make the same mistakes they did. In their panic, they believed I would either hurt myself or embarrass them. Mom and Daddy, then, insisted on controlling my decision making instead of allowing me to learn through making small errors. For example, while in seventh grade, I wanted to make an apron and enter it in the 4-H county fair. Mom finally agreed; nevertheless, she made the entire apron "so I wouldn't err wasting the material." Feeling embarrassment and frustration, I complied and entered it under my name. I carried that inhibiting behavior into my adult life—frustrating my decision making.

Another friend's *untrusting parents*, because of their behavior pattern, believed she made wrong decisions deliberately. Because the parents didn't accept their past, they hadn't forgiven themselves. It was difficult for them to believe their children could live differently. So during Mary's teen-dating years, her mother often accused her of promiscuity. The suspicions were false; yet, because of her mother's past behavior, she had difficulty trusting Mary. Since my friend's mother didn't give her trust, Mary's feelings of self esteem and "seat of choice" were damaged, This kept her from being able to see herself as a person of worth. Mary developed rebellious and self-destructive patterns in her decision making, and she birthed a child while single. In contrast, when parents relate to their children through trust and acceptance, strong feelings of self-worth cover the children. As adults, they in turn can build relationships through trust, risk, and acceptance.

Our "inner-child" concept is like a three-room house. One room holds the **natural** child; one, holds the **adapted** child; one, holds the **professor** child. The "natural-child room" houses a child's caring and fun-loving spontaneity. With Daddy's volatile anger, our home atmosphere held continual change. As a result, an unhealthy fear wrapped its strands around me, and my fun-loving spontaneity disappeared. My damaged inner child found crawling into a compliance cocoon the safest way to cope.

The "adapted-child room" houses a child's ability to learn obedience. Because of her father's lack of healthy affection, Delores felt isolated and learned to withdraw from him in fear. Her damaged inner child found climbing into a silent-withdrawal cocoon the safest way to cope. That also gave her the safe appearance of obedience.

The "professor-child room" houses a child's ability in learning to relate through using manipulation, either for helping or hindering others. When Helen's parents failed to meet her need for loving acceptance, she felt unloved like an ugly caterpillar. She learned to manipulate her parents under the guise of noncaring uncooperation. As a result, her frantic inner child found slipping into a rebellious-behavior cocoon kept her at a safe emotional distance.

While we were children, Delores, Helen, and I were deprived of parental loving relationships. Instead, we lived with unloving attitudes that told us, "You're a nuisance, inferior, and unlovable." Those attitudes, which built our self-concept, also convinced us of our unimportance. Since our "inner-child rooms" did not receive loving care, serious problems developed in each of us. That's because our self-concept reveals feelings, moods, relationships, and values. In the formative years, therefore, the way our "parent," "adult," and "child" develops in us builds either feelings of worth or worthlessness. While we experienced different limitations, all three of us felt worthlessness. This inhibition causes us to struggle with an ugly "caterpillar-like" self-identity. On the other hand, healthy affection, fun times, and loving acceptance would have developed in us feelings of worth and self-esteem.

We don't know what kind of parents she had, but the Proverbs 31 woman developed a balanced parent-adult-child concept. She felt a strong self-concept and radiated self-worth, rather than worthlessness. Using a well-developed self-picture, she related to others with concern and respect. Self-identity also includes three functional aspects: Appearance, "How do I look?"; performance, "How am I doing?"; and status, "How important am I?"[2] Seeking importance and worth through an imbalance of these aspects only brings feelings of disappointment. However, balanced attention to these areas helps us develop a sense of worth and contentment.

The Aspect of Appearance

Most of us will agree with this statement, "Appearance is a functional aspect of self-concept that relates to how we view our bodies, our dress, and our personal grooming."[3] Because of society's craze over physical beauty, many of us struggle with feelings of inadequacy and inferiority. About 85 percent of us do not fit the perfect "ten" body. Consequently, we picture our bodies with many flaws and have difficulty accepting them. For that reason, society's body craze bothers us just as it bothers my friend, Ann.

She's a 31-year-old mother of 3 and carries gracefully her trim 5 feet 7 inches and 115 pounds. Her attractive oval face, blue-green eyes, and dark-blond hair enhanced by tailored clothing give her a striking appearance. But turbulent junior-high-school years made shambles of her self-esteem. She learned that a "curvy" female figure was of uppermost importance to most boys. "I felt like an ugly duckling," Ann says, "because most guys, even Christians, liked only 'busty' girls." While that adjective did not describe her, she related through grace, poise, and a pleasing personality. An extrovert, she enjoyed high school extracurricular activities including performing in the "swing choir."

In college she involved herself in many activities like Associated Student Body. Ann's life revolved around reaching out to others, showing concern. Yet, she found many men preferred a "curvy" figure to a good personality, even on Christian campuses. Her weak self-concept worsened. After eight years of marriage, it's hard for her to believe her body is attractive to Roy, although he often reassures her. Ann told me, "If I could change just one thing about me, it would be my bustline." Since society's body craze grades our acceptance by bust size rather than by self-worth, many of us can relate to Ann's frustration.

Yes, others' unkind, critical attitudes often damage our inner woman. And most of those attitudes we've heard since childhood. "It is surprising just how effectively we teach our . . . children to appreciate the beauty cult. . . . early in life, a child begins to learn the social importance of physical beauty. . . . Because in our society, a beautiful baby is much more valuable . . . than an unattractive one."[4] It's sad that these damaging attitudes exist in the Christian community, but society's appearance infatuation has discriminated against most of us. Yet, with hard work, we can help replace those attitudes with loving expressions of acceptance for children (or adults)—not emphasizing appearance.

The Aspect of Performance

Many tell us that ". . . performance is a functional aspect of self-concept that relates to how we view our abilities, our skills, our knowledge, and our sense of responsibility."[5] That's why the way we picture our performance depends on how we picture ourselves. Some of us base self-worth on our performance with friends or job or family. Others base self-worth on how well they teach the Bible and how many they lead to the Lord. These strong urges come from being performance-oriented, which may have begun at birth. Our parents cajoled and cooed, trying to make us smile; frantically taught us to walk by nine months; and spent hours reading to us so they could build in word concepts. They wanted us to smile, walk, and talk before other babies. They saw these pressured performances as a back door to gain feelings of self-esteem.

For some, this "performance demand" carried over into school, where parents urged them to make grades higher than their capabilities. At home, many of us labored under conduct or chore expectations for which we hadn't been trained. Not realizing we had become our parents' puppets, the performance demand carried over into adulthood. Our parents couldn't give unconditional love—just for us. So, the only *felt* approval came when some performance happened to please our parents. This damaged our self-concept and kept us from feeling good about ourselves; it's the wrong foundation for self-worth.

"Our self-image does not have to rest on the shifting sand of our performance and it does not have to rely on the judgments and evaluations we receive from others. . . . This shifting foundation for self-esteem can have serious consequences, for unless we live up to our inner expectations, we cannot really be content with ourselves."[6] Patti Roberts, former daughter-in-law of evangelist Oral Roberts, agrees with that concept in her recent book, *Ashes to Gold.* She tells about the performance pressures she and Richard Roberts experienced during their ten-year marriage. On stage and television they sang before millions. Audiences identified them and their two little girls with success, happiness, and fulfillment. But in trying to carry out others' expectations they neglected their marriage, and it fell apart.

> Our divorce was a direct result of the lives we lived. . . . We lived luxurious, storybook lives, but all of our acquisitions and acclaim still left us very lonely and tired and spiritually hungry . . . . No one loved us enough to hold us accountable. No one looked beneath the glitter to see if our lives matched our performance . . . . I tried to be the TOTAL WOMAN, but all my efforts only left me nervous, exhausted, depressed, and no closer to my husband than before . . . . We were roommates and stage partners.[7]

Performing for self-worth is like being bound up in a cocoon and leaves us feeling frustrated rather than fulfilled.

The Aspect of Status

"Status is the functional aspect of self-concept which relates to how we view our relative importance among people—our family name, wealth, education, position, or social rating."[8] Some of us felt a sense of acceptance, importance, and worth from our parents, while others were left with gnawing feelings of worthlessness and inadequacy, which caused many emotional struggles. Because of the latter, many of us—even in adulthood—struggle for an unattainable status.

That was Joan's struggle. Through a series of damaging disappointments, she began working toward a hoped-for-status that would give her self-worth. When Joan was four, her mother died giving birth. After that, she lived either with her aunt or grandmother, usually seeing her father only on weekends. At age twelve she won her first bronze dance metal. Her father couldn't share her excitement though, because he choose that day to remarry. At nineteen she got her first job as understudy and assistant stage manager. What's more, she took over the role before opening day to appear in "But for the Grace of God." They toured several weeks in Wales and Scotland and performed at the Wimbledon Theater.

She went on to other plays "rubbing shoulders with London's society and celebrities." The Queen and Prince Philip, Princess Margaret, and Queen Mary were among those attending the two-year run of "The Chiltern Hundreds." Soon, the strenuous emotional and physical effects of stage life proved too great for Joan. First, she began forgetting her lines; next, she began using phenobarbital. Then came the ultimatum of a month's complete rest. William Douglas Home, the play's author, arranged for her to stay at his Scotland estate. There she met royalty like the Duke and Duchess of Buccleuch, Drumlanrig Castle.

Joan also met famous Americans during her acting career. Probably the one who had the greatest effect on her life was Robert F. Kennedy. Bobby, a law student at the University of Virginia, spent part of his summers in Europe. His sister Kathleen married Lord Hartington, the Duke of Devonshire's son, and Joan visited them with Bobby. Later, she met Ethel Skakel, who became Ethel Kennedy. Although many famous people socialized in her circle, she didn't feel a "belongingness" with them, and doubts about her acting ability surfaced. Depression followed depression. "I felt locked inside my body and desperately wanted to free myself of all everyday responsibilities. . . . My confidence was gone. I dreaded getting out of bed in the morning and having to face people. The thought of even crossing a street would send fear running through me."

Wanting to get away from people, Joan took a bus to her grandmother's house. Just then, her filled-up emotions spilled out. She couldn't control her speech—she could only cry. Some thought she was drunk. "I felt naked as they stared . . . all I could utter were unintelligible sounds. I had no control over my mouth and what came out was a deep cry for help; an agonizing moan." Many months later, Joan felt strong enough to return to London and work; again, she found success on the stage. Instead of excitement, though, she felt emptiness. But she didn't dare let family or friends know of her struggles.

Then, she felt her health weakening again. She couldn't face another breakdown—not just for herself, but for her family. "I was a virtual prisoner—in my mind . . . . Finally, I became obsessed with the thought of ending my life." At that time, a friend invited Joan to attend a Billy Graham Crusade at the Harringay Arena in London. Listening intently while Dr. Graham explained God's plan for salvation, her inner struggling stopped. "As I stood by the platform along with so many others, I had finally reached a decision. I was no longer tossed in my mind as to what the future held. . . . I had simply given everything over to Christ—all my heartaches, longings, and ambitions."

Following that night, with Mrs. Ruth Graham's help, she began reading and studying the Bible. Learning and applying truths from God's Word, a dramatic change came into her life. "I felt His presence with me and rejoiced in my heart that no longer was my life filled with despair."[9] She discovered that regardless of its greatness, status can't give peace, belonging, or self-worth. Only God can give these. I've been acquainted with Joan for many years and have witnessed the beautiful change that lives within her today.

The Aspect of God's Image

The three aspects of appearance, performance, and status are significant to self-concept. And it's clear that the Proverbs 31 woman possessed a balanced self-picture developed from these. But self-image does not rest on these areas alone. "And God created man in His own image, in the image of God He created him; male and female He created them" (Gen. 1:27). The basis for self-worth doesn't rest on works. It rests on the truth that God created female and male in His image with mind, soul, and emotions. To all other information about self-image, *that truth stands paramount*. In addition, "To be in the image of God means to be in a complementary (not competitive) relationship to him, to be in correspondence."[10] Being in correspondence with God means *accepting* His free gift of self-worth, whereas, competing with Him means *working* for self-worth.

For example, working for status or position to enhance ourselves equals working for self-worth, like, "Doing unto others" just to impress them. "Continuing to try to build ourselves is actually based on flight from accepting what we are . . . . But the simple good news is that the search is already ended. We are already accepted, right where we are, as we are."[11] Paul says we can't work for salvation, neither can we work for self-worth. Just as salvation is received (Eph. 2:8-9), self-worth is also received. Yet, both remain God's free gift. When God created humanity, He could have created us as inanimate objects rather than animate beings. But because God is love, He's motivated by love. Exercising His first act of love, then, He created male and female in His image. Creating humanity in His image gave us self-worth based on *God's worth*.

We cannot measure God's worth. It's immeasurable! Therefore, our human worth is immeasurable. We can never do anything to make us "worthy" of God's love and worth. But being worthy and *feeling* God's worth are not the same. Feeling worth relates both to belongingness and to love, two primary elements in developing self-concept. From feeling loved, we feel a "belonging to." Therefore, we're both loved by God and belong to God through His creative acts of creation and salvation. That's why Joan felt belongingness after she came to know God through Christ.

Conclusion

Though we may not have developed a strong self-image in childhood, we can work on changing the way we see ourselves now. Part of that change comes as we learn to hear positive messages from inner parent, adult, and child. Change also comes as we bring a balance to measuring our appearance, performance, and status.

Parents, overall, want to give their children a feeling of wholeness and belonging, but most of us struggle with imperfect pasts and personalities. Following God's parenting model, however, can help us rear our children with a healthy self-concept. Parental acceptance and patience help children develop an accepting "inner parent" rather than a critical one. Encouraging children to evaluate and test reality under parental guidance helps children develop an "inner adult" with healthy, realistic decision making. Taking time for games, picnics, reading stories, and other fun activities helps children develop a healthy, uninhibited "inner child." Those choices build strong feelings of self-worth and a positive PAC self-concept. From there, children can develop clear pictures of performance, appearance, and status.

Martin Luther once said, "God's love does not love that which is worthy of being loved, but it creates that which is worthy of being loved." (Thus, human life both before or after birth remains valuable and precious.) That's why in the instant of physical conception, we are gifted with His worth. And no amount of disappointment or emotional losses can take away our self-worth.

God, therefore, doesn't want us to compete through *working* for self-worth. Rather, He wants us through cooperation to *receive* His worth. A dramatic difference develops in us when we stop working to receive. Along with Joan, we learn that God gives us belongingness and love through self-worth: His free gift.

2 Putting God in Proper Perspective

She puts God in proper perspective . . . "Charm is deceitful and beauty is vain, But a woman who fears the Lord, she shall be praised" (Prov. 31:30).

During the six days of creation, when finished with work each day, God looked at all He had created. Each time, He "saw that it was good." After creating female and male on the sixth day, God again looked at everything He had created "and behold, it was very good" (Gen. 1:1-31). We see that God *felt* good about Himself and all He created. That means He feels good about us, even with all our emotional struggles. In contrast, while Adam and Eve resided in their God-created garden they lived without struggles. God, however, knew coping with responsibility would be good for them to learn; thus, He told Adam to name all the birds and animals. Then He told him to cultivate the Garden of Eden, designed especially for his and Eve's needs.

God created a variety of fruit for their food, but He gave Adam one limitation, ". . . from the tree of the knowledge of good and evil you shall not eat, for in the day that you eat from it you shall surely die" (Gen. 2:17). And yet, later on we see that one day both Adam and Eve chose to go against God's command and ate fruit from the Knowledge Tree. In going against God's limitation, they violated His standards and estranged themselves from Him. Their choice broke relations with God, cut communications with Him, and introduced sin to humanity. Many describe sin as missing the mark, coming short of God's standards, or any act that violates His moral standards. Some ask, "What's so bad about sin?" Sin alienates us from God and causes a lonely emptiness. That's why loneliness, rather than God, became Adam and Eve's companion.

Using Memories' Power

When Adam and Eve put their own choice before God's command, they failed to put Him first in their lives. In short, they sinned, but sin did not destroy human self-worth. While salvation and self-worth are separate, many believers confuse them as being the same. God gave us self-worth when He created humanity in His image. And nothing can take away our worth to God—not emotional struggles or even sin. Sin, however, placed humanity in need of something to "wash out sin effects" and restore a relationship with God, putting Him first. The Proverbs 31 woman put God first in her life. She realized that charm or beauty can't give security, for they can be deceitful and vain (v. 30). In contrast, fear of the Lord (a reverential trust with hatred of evil) can bring praise—the praise that bestows commendation on us for putting God first. And we're able today—through Christ—to put God in proper perspective, like this.

> Before anything else existed, there was Christ with God. He has always been alive and is Himself God. He created everything there is—nothing exists that He didn't make. Eternal life is in Him, and this life gives [spiritual] light to all mankind (John 1:1-4, TLB).

> Christ died for our sins, . . . he was buried, . . . three days afterwards he arose from the grave just as the prophets foretold . . . now there is the resurrection from the dead. (1 Cor. 15:3,20,21, TLB).

> All those who believe this are reborn!—not a physical rebirth resulting from human passion or plan—but from the will of God . . . Unless you are born again, you can never get into the Kingdom of God (John 1:13; 3:3, TLB).

Christ's death and resurrection became the something needed to "wash out sin" and restore humanity's relationship with God. He wanted us to understand that our only entrance into heaven is through spiritual rebirth. Thus, *Christ's work in salvation covers our sin, and God's worth covers our inferiority.* But we must do more than just "know about" Christ's death and resurrection. As Corrie ten Boom once stated, "Going to church doesn't make you a Christian any more than going to a garage makes you an automobile." At age nineteen, I realized I didn't know Christ; I had been only "going to church."

During the 1956 Oklahoma City Billy Graham Crusade, I sang in the choir. One night Dr. Graham said, "Christ gave His life for you; what have you done for Him? Have you believed in Him as your Savior and Lord?" Those questions made me realize that even though I had gone to church all my life, I hadn't believed *in* Christ—just *about* Him.

As I started to walk forward, a voice whispered, "Eleven years ago you professed to be a Christian and were baptized. If you go forward, your parents and friends will think you're confused; that could embarrass the Lord. Maybe you should just keep this private." Fear of ridicule paralyzed my decision making.

Struggling with my thoughts, I feared going forward, and I feared not going forward. Finally, I decided that believing *in* Christ was more important than others' reactions. So, I walked forward with hundreds of others proclaiming my belief in Christ's death and resurrection. My act of faith "put God in proper perspective," giving me His acceptance and inner peace. Since my brother's death when I was eleven, I had feared death. Often at night I would awaken, gasping for breath. I thought I was dying. But that night, for the first time in many years, I slept in peace. My fear of death was gone. During the following months and years, other areas of my life also changed—especially my memories.

Since God created humanity in His image, we have spiritual awareness (a soul), feelings (emotions), and memories (mind). Our storehouse for memories, the brain, weighs about three pounds and is made up of the finest fibers which are connected to all the nooks and crannies of our body. Of all creation, a human brain contains the most elaborate communication network—some thirteen billion nerve cells. God created quite a brain for us.

The Bible gives little space to describing or discussing memory. David Seamand's research in *Healing of Memories* shows that Scripture uses memory (the noun) less than 6 times. It uses the verbs "remember" or "remembrance" over 250 times. About 75 of these refer to God and His memory. The remaining 175 describe human memory or forgetfulness. Our memory can either work for us or against us. Although we are forgiven, Satan often brings up the past to attack and accuse us. He tries to make us doubt God's forgiveness and whispers things like, "God doesn't want you. You're inferior to others and cannot compare to them; you're not important." Satan attacks memories since they accumulate all our experiences and feelings from the past.

Many wonder if putting God in proper perspective (believing in Christ as Savior) gives freedom from memories' painful hurts. God says, "[Yes], a new life has begun" (2 Cor. 5:17, TLB). We're not the same when we become a believer; a brand new Person comes to live within us. On the other hand, many of our actions say "no." Even Paul wrote about his struggles with the old self versus the new self (Rom. 6:5-7; Eph. 4:22-24; Col. 3:9,10). And these struggles, of course, included his memories. He found putting off the old and taking on the new to be quite difficult. Most of us struggle in this old-memories battle.

Others wonder if God's creativeness in sharing self-worth and salvation take away self-initiative, causing spiritual weakness. They wonder if our belief in Christ causes us to suffer from an "illusion" like Sigmund Freud suggested many years ago. An illusion deceives through producing a false impression or belief. It gives qualities not present in reality. But, neither Christ nor His qualities give us false impression or belief. With established reality He says, "I am the way, and the truth, and the life; no one comes to the Father, but through Me" (John 14:6). After that, our spiritual growth happens as we read and study God's Word and submit to His instructions. That requires from us initiative and commitment plus inner strength—not weakness. Since Freud based his life on false impression or belief rather than the reality of Christ, he's the sufferer of illusion—not believers. Here's one of his viewpoints on Scripture.

> The proofs they have left us . . . are full of contradictions, revisions and falsifications, and where they speak of factual confirmations they are . . . unconfirmed. It does not help . . . to have it asserted that their wording, or . . . content only, originates from divine revelation; for this assertion is . . . one of the doctrines whose authenticity is under examination. . . . But scientific work is the only road which can lead us to a knowledge of reality."[1]

This illusion can be seen throughout Freud's writings. He neither put God in proper perspective nor believed in Christ's salvation plan. His thoughts or memories, therefore, were not affected by God's power. Believers, on the other hand, have God's power through the Holy Spirit to affect their memories. His power produces a healthy interdependence between believers and God for the present, future, or past.

Besides storing past experiences and feelings, the brain also stores a developed self-picture of our inner woman. The Bible infers female and male are *whole beings*. "Nowhere does it isolate a person's brain from the rest of the personality, any more than it isolates the body or the soul. . . . Memories are the experiences of whole persons as they remember something, and not simply brain-stored pictures of the past."[2] Thus, our memories can either bring us much joy or great pain. Our ability to recall both happy and sad memories, therefore, includes the ability to *feel* both happy and sad memories. And both produce stress in our bodies.

Feeling Memories' Stress

All of our emotions, tissues, bones, and organs are affected greatly through happy or sad memories. The Bible says they're a joyful heart, good medicine; yet, a broken spirit drying up the bones (Prov. 15:13; 17:22). Happy memories, light, come up easy; whereas, sad memories, heavy, come up hard. Many of us often "block out" sad memories, trying to avoid dealing with emotional pain. Even if we block memories, our bodies still feel the stress. Dr. Hans Selye, a biologist known for his stress-effects research, calls stress the "wear and tear of living." Both good stress (what we enjoy and look forward to) and bad stress (what we don't enjoy or look forward to) use emotional and physical energy. That's why both experiences "stress out" our emotional system.

Dr. Gary Collins, author, lecturer, and teacher, has also researched and written about stress. He describes it as "A force which creates upset stomachs, gnawing fear, splitting headaches, intense grief, excessive drinking, and violent arguments. Stress dulls our memories, cripples our thinking, weakens our bodies, upsets our plans, stirs up our emotions, and reduces our efficiency."[3] Feeling a few short-duration stressors may not cause us to feel overwhelmed. On the other hand, feeling many long-lasting stressors overwhelms us, causing severe damage to our emotions and bodies. And the reasons for experiencing stress are numberless! *One main reason* for stress comes from painful, unhealed memories hidden within our inner woman.

My stressful memories span back to age five. While my dad was a believer, he didn't allow Christ to control many of his life areas. Since I didn't know him very well, insight into his stress areas isn't plentiful. But there were seasons in his life when rage covered and controlled him. During some of those times, he would beat my mom—sometimes almost killing her. Other times, he would hit her with angry, vulgar, accusing words. Being forced to become a part of those degrading times dumped much stress on me and damaged my feelings of self-esteem. In addition to those frightening, out-of-control scenes, I was exposed to some of their bedroom behavior for many years.

Those bedroom exposures robbed me of an innocent childhood and built into my mind a mental incest, which damaged me greatly. Even when parents feel love and respect for each other, children cannot be exposed to their bedroom behavior without receiving emotional harm. Damage from the exposure travels first to the mind, then a "mental incest" develops since both the mind and emotions are violated. These violations give as many problems as do physical incest or other sexual intrusions. (Films, books, or magazines showing explicit sexual material also violate minds and emotions.)

Since I lived with those overwhelming stressors for so many years, my body and emotions received great harm. As a result, I've suffered for fifteen years from an ulcerated colon. Whenever we feel prolonged stress, both our physical and emotional health must adjust to the harm done. For example, children and most teens can't protect themselves against parents' irresponsibility, anger, and critical responses toward them. They can't stop parents or significant others' unwanted physical or sexual intrusions. As a result, they suffer losses through damaged emotions and scarred bodies. That's why, even when abusive situations end, *it takes years for the memories to heal totally*.

"Memories include feelings, concepts, patterns, attitudes, and tendencies toward actions which accompany the pictures on the screen of the mind . . . not simply brain-stored pictures of the past."[4] That is why we need to talk about stressful memories rather than keep them stored in memory. Storing them in the subconscious requires continual use of our spiritual and emotional energy. Releasing memories through talking to a nonjudgmental friend, competent pastor, or trained counselor can help us facilitate healed memories. Letting out stored-up mental poison brings emotional release, and this release enhances healing. In turn, healed memories free our energies to healthy creativeness, like building friendships and meaningful careers or performing helpful community services. Yet, before the damage is healed, God's love often becomes distorted with Satan's successful use of "memory stress."

Receiving Memories' Healing

Unhealed memories hold emotions like anxiety, fear, hurt, anger, guilt, shame—plus unforgiveness. Sometimes it's difficult working through these emotions because of the attitude, "Christians are not supposed to have problems." This harmful illusion makes some ask, "Can healed memories reduce our stress level, and if so, will we continue to remember stressful experiences?" There are differences of opinion about healing of memories. Some say it isn't necessary to examine the past, just to go on from the present. Yet, others say we must examine the past to help release unhealthy conduct patterns in relationships. Regardless of viewpoint, hard work and prayer help facilitate the emotional healing of our memories. While we do continue to remember, forgiveness takes out the pain and helps reduce our stress levels.

And, forgiveness is the hard work. *Forgive (aphiémi)* means to send away or to let go, yet we must first learn how "to send away or let go." There are four choices involved in the forgiveness process. These are not simple or easy choices, but they are necessary. A time frame required for the forgiveness process depends on the depth of our emotional losses, how long ago they began, and how often the hurts were repeated.

Accepting our memories' reality begins the process. Accepting reality, though, proves stressful. When old memories of Daddy's rage or bedroom behavior flashed across my mind, I stuffed them back quickly into the subconscious. I kept them stored there so I wouldn't have to deal with them. But in my mid twenties, an insightful person helped me understand that storing old memories *denies* their reality. Denial kept me from accepting their reality, but I needed to *accept* them before I could forgive and move away from distorting reality. When we distort reality, we're more susceptible to building in relational patterns called defense mechanisms. Defense mechanisms are neither good nor bad; it depends on the way we use them. Unfortunately, most use them in unhealthy ways to relate to others. They don't change our reality; they only change the way we look at it. We generally use three primary defense mechanisms to distort reality in trying to cope with our losses.

- Denial—Refusing to acknowledge, lying about, or denying something we don't want to look at or accept. "If we say that we have fellowship with Him, and yet walk in the darkness, we lie and do not practice the truth" (1 John 1:6).

• Rationalization—Justifying wrong behavior, deceiving ourselves often through unrecognized motives. "If we refuse to admit we are sinners, then we live in a world of illusion and truth becomes a stranger to us" (1 John 1:8, Phillips).

• Projection—Projecting attitudes, feelings, inadequacies or failures onto others. "If we say we have not sinned, we make Him [God] a liar and His Word is not in us" (1 John 1:10).

"Because a lot of specifics are protected by our defense mechanisms and hidden in our buried memories, we cannot find emotional and spiritual relief from their onslaughts. . . . We cannot confess to God what we do not acknowledge to ourselves."[5] That's why defense mechanisms—when used in the wrong ways—will distort prayer life and influence our behavior negatively. Through denial, many transgressors refuse to acknowledge their guilt. When Mom tried to talk about his abuse, Daddy denied everything and said she imagined it. Those sinning against others learn quickly to rationalize wrong behavior. Daddy felt justified in beating Mom, since he was "teaching her a lesson." Both irrational behaviors kept him from healthy relationships.

Projecting inadequacies or failures onto others also becomes a way of life. When blinded by reality distortion, we feel justified in taking out our frustration and selfishness on others. Daddy vented his rage on Mom rather than face and deal with his reality. He also decided satisfying his sexual urges took precedence over protecting his family's privacy. On the whole, misusing defense mechanisms harms our emotional health. Reality distortion denies the Holy Spirit's power and prevents our memories from being healed emotionally.

To help facilitate our healing, each time an "old memory" comes flying through, we can pray something like this: "God, help me stop denying those hurtful, mean things. Help me accept their painful reality. And please help me forgive him for his sins against me." Those are small, quick prayers. But they will give courage to examine our emotional losses. Although it may take a long time, identifying the areas of damage shows us where we need emotional healing. As a result, many months later we can deny less and accept more of our reality. When we're able to *accept* our memories' reality, we can move on with the forgiveness-healing process.

Placing guilt where it belongs moves us further along in the forgiveness process. All of life's experiences are stored in the brain. As years pass those experiences add up to lots of brain space. It's like they stack up—layer on layer. At times we think we've worked through and forgiven others' hurts only to find similar memories took their place. That's because when we do work through the process and forgive, our conscious opens up brain space so our subconscious can release more old memories. When these memories and their feelings surface, the tendency is to stuff them back quickly into our subconscious. While looking at or examining them feels too threatening, that will provide us with needed insight to place guilt where it belongs and forgive.

Since Christ says to forgive seventy times seven, we may need to use this equation many times before all is worked through (Matt. 18:22). That's OK, and there's no need to "feel" guilty. Because *the deeper* our hurt and *the more often* it happened, *the longer* it takes to complete the forgiveness process. In addition, Satan often attacks us with false accusations, such as: "The Lord can't use you. You're a failure. You still struggle with forgiving your transgressors. You can't live a good Christian life like others." Believing Satan's attacks keeps us from placing guilt where it belongs.

Yet, we must discern between forgiveness and defense mechanisms. They mimic forgiveness and distort reality with thoughts like: "He didn't really mean to hurt me. He said he's sorry. She's really a good person. Her sharp, cutting words weren't at all what she meant to say." Rather than forgiving them, that excuses others' transgressions. And regardless of the type, transgressors always cause emotional thorns for others. While God has not promised a thornless rose garden, He's promised His presence when the roses' thorns prick. "Here on earth you will have many trials and sorrows; but cheer up, for I have overcome the world" (John 16:33, TLB). "I will never, never fail you nor forsake you" (Heb.13:5, TLB).

In order to take advantage of His provision, though, we cannot excuse or deny others' pricks. When we fail to identify and work through a damaged past, we often try to change it. "If only I had . . ." "If she had only . . ." "Why didn't he . . ." Yet, we can't change the past. Furthermore, trying to *change* the past rather than *accepting* it may freeze our feelings in unforgiveness. The past is the past. It cannot be changed. Trying to change it, to get rid of painful memories, doesn't work. We can forgive the past, but we cannot change the past. It's unchangeable!

Therefore, we must place guilt where it belongs rather than denying others' transgressions. We must recognize others' thorns pricks and hurts, for ignoring or refusing to deal with others' sins only mimics forgiveness. That identification helps us accept reality and place guilt where it belongs—on the transgressor. When we're able to do that, we can move on to the next forgiveness choice.

When we can turn loose of painful experiences, our hard work is almost completed. Most of us live with emotional losses, some spanning many years. They seem so much a part of us that letting them go feels overwhelming, but turning loose determines whether or not we can make a "clean break" with past hurts. While hanging on to past hurts, we can't live in the present free of old memories. Neither can we feel free from them in tomorrow.

Before turning loose my past, I tortured myself with many unanswerable questions. Often I asked, "Why did Mom and Daddy have me sleep in their bedroom instead of in my sister's bedroom? How could they have been so blind to the emotional damage done to me? Why didn't they care?" Each time I tried to find some answers for those questions, more anger and frustration built up inside me. Finally one day, after asking such questions, the Holy Spirit whispered softly, "You will never understand why, because you can't ask your parents since they are dead." Realizing I will never know the "whys," my eyes spilled out rivers of tears. They flooded over my face soaking many tissues, while I heaved convulsive sobs.

Later on, I understood there were two choices before me. I could continue the anger and frustration or I could accept the past and let it go. In agony I cried out, "God, I can't understand why my parents exposed me to their sexual behavior, and the pain hurts so bad. Somehow help me accept their faults and forgive them. And please release me from the pain." Gently, the Holy Spirit reached down through my tears and pain, touching me with peace—the "peace of God which passeth all understanding" that Paul talks about in Philippians 4:7 (KJV). God's peace enabled me to accept and turn loose of my parents' mistakes and poor judgments. I felt a calmness take over my frustration, and the intense anger towards my dad began melting away. Although this turning loose took just a few minutes, more time had to pass before I could work through complete forgiveness toward them.

Another threatening issue involved in turning loose is **accepting a future** without trying to control the outcome. When we grow up with emotional losses, we live with a "strong urge" to control our future. We feel that urge first in working hard to offset the transgressor's imperfection with our perfection. As an adult, an inner voice often whispered, *You must not be like your parents. Whatever you do you must act better than they did.* We feel that urge next in feeling overly responsible for others' happiness. My natural response said, "Keep your children from pain. Don't let them feel hurts like you did." So, during their growing-up years, I often overprotected my children in trying to keep them from painful hurts. But I found that in trying to protect them from pain, they got hurt. **It's in living life—not hiding from it—that we grow and mature in emotions.**

Through the understanding that only He can control my future, God **freed** me gradually from those misconceptions (Ps. 37:3-5; Prov. 3:5-6; Heb. 13:5-6,8; Jas. 1:2-6). Accepting the future without trying to control its outcome still presents a struggle at times. But I feel I'm a richer person in my emotions for the times I've turned loose, rather than controlled. *Putting aside* a fearful control of the future encourages us to live out these instructions. "Be kind to one another, tender-hearted, forgiving each other, just as God in Christ also has forgiven you" (Eph. 4:32). Sound easy? It isn't! Forgiving others depends on whether or not we "feel" motivated to obey God's instructions. We can't guarantee hurt won't come again from a transgressor—somewhere.

Turning loose of past losses proves essential to healing our memories. Some months after God enabled me to turn loose, I began feeling less anger in dealing with stressors. I felt less frustration in misunderstandings with Dick, my children, or others. With the passing of time, my anger fuse has shortened while my anger control has lengthened. Turning loose of the past, moves us *closer* to forgiveness and healed memories.

When we can give up punishing others for their transgressions, our hard work is finished. Sometimes, since we allow painful and unresolved memories to control us, we strike out in revenge. At times we hit others with loud, angry, hate-filled words because of the emotional pain they inflicted on us. Or we ignore and refuse to communicate with them. Or, slanted to our view, we tell others about their faults. That punishes them, and punishing can feel good for awhile. But rather than continue that harmful behavior, we must learn to give it up. Forgiveness clears out a layer of old losses, words, or feelings and opens up more brain space. The subconscious can then release up other content to the conscious. While this process takes time, it helps us progress to where we can give up punishing those who've sinned against us.

Christ gives us a choice. We can forgive or not forgive, but we must take the consequence of our choice. If we don't forgive, then God will not forgive us (Matt. 6:14-15), and the transgression effects control us. But if we "work out" forgiveness, Christ forgives us and the Holy Spirit, rather than the transgressor, controls us. Deep emotional hurts may take several times of remembering, accepting, and forgiving before we're ready to give up punishing others. At the time, giving up punishment to forgive others may "feel" unfair or impossible. It's difficult to believe our pain will be resolved. If it gets resolved, we have even more difficulty feeling vulnerable again to the same, or a similar, risk. Once we've felt emotional loss, we don't want to risk more.

Some say that intertwined with solutions to life problems sit two needed ingredients, the "twin tensions of trust and risk . . . . Life is a series of trust ventures: it is trust risked, risk rewarded; new trust ventured, and new risks taken."[6] Since life is a series of trust ventures, some risks prove rewarding while others prove unrewarding. For example, marrying and birthing babies carries both rewarding and unrewarding experiences. And in the risk of giving up punishment, we may develop three particular unrealistic demands. Perfection says, "I won't be hurt again." Revenge feels, "Appease me by suffering like I did." Impossible demands, "Make life like it was before."

These demands become a "security blanket." The only way we can turn loose of them is through trusting and risking in our relationships. When they bombard us, we can pray something like, "Well Lord, here's some memory pain I didn't know still lived in there. Although it's painful, help me look at the content rather than hold it in. Help me cope so I can forgive my transgressor. My Father, thank You for loving me enough to release the memories from my subconscious. And thanks for motivating me toward forgiveness; giving me the power to forgive."

Conclusion

For our emotional healing, there's **reality**, identifying hurt; there's **help**, seeking solution; and there's **hard work**, using the information. These ingredients give us a cooperative attitude with God that helps us *believe* "[we] can do all things through [Christ] who strengthens [us]" (Phil. 4:13). In becoming "healed helpers," we can help others in their emotional pain. Helping others nurtures their self-esteem and enhances our self-concept, which says we can feel good about our inner woman, and we can feel good about believing in Christ as our Savior and Lord. That puts God in proper perspective and gives us hope.

3 Feeling Hope that Doesn't Disappoint

She feels hope . . . . "And she smiles at the future" (Prov. 31:25).

*M*any of our experiences bombard feelings of hope. Yet, we cannot live without hope; it's another important dynamic in developing a strong self-image. Webster defines hope as that which gives hope. There are many different kinds of hope. But our foundation rests on the fact we're accepted in the Beloved (Eph. 1:6). This hope has nothing to do with our appearance, performance, or status. It has to do with whether or not we have believed in the *Beloved.* God accepts us through Christ, and His acceptance nurtures our self-esteem.

Earlier we talked about God placing the basis for our self-worth on His immeasurable worth. The definition I use for worth is *equal in value to.* That equality wipes out both superiority and inferiority. Even when we suffer emotional losses and feel we're lacking in status, performance, or appearance, God doesn't see us as inferior. God "blueprinted" all of us. Therefore, there's no inferiority in God's family. We're all copartners in self-esteem and "equal in value to." This truth gives us hope.

Hope as well as a strong self-esteem must play a significant role in our feelings. Hope helps us risk and trust in relationships, endure emotional pain, and keep going. The Proverbs 31 woman feels hope for "she smiles at the future" (v. 25). The writer doesn't tell how she developed hope, but here's a possibility. In developing a self-identity with hope, some sources work for us giving hope, while others work against us destroying hope. We must learn to discern between these sources.

Abuse from Outer World Damages Self-esteem

The first source "the outer world . . . includes all the factors that have gone into your makeup—your inheritance and birth, your infancy, childhood, and teen years . . . right up to the present time."[1] Many child psychologists believe that a child's basic personality forms by age six. Nonetheless, since we need feelings of self-esteem and hope at any age, children need ongoing, nurturing, loving relationships during their maturing years. Caring guides them toward emotional maturity. James Dobson, parent and psychologist, writes that "The art of good parenthood begins with the fundamental skill of being able to get behind the eyes of the child, seeing what he sees, feeling what he feels, hoping what he hopes."[2] Parental caring lays a foundation of hope within children.

But Esther, a petite and pretty twenty-eight-year-old, didn't receive a foundation of hope. As a toddler, her father's physical intrusions started. Often her father came home in a drunken stupor, hitting her with his anger, fear, and frustration. Her fear and hatred of him grew in intensity, and in her teens, she related to all males with difficulty. Males' impatience or anger gave her the feeling they did not like her, and she feared they also might overpower her. Esther now sees the need for a new self-picture and is working on accepting memories of her father's cruelty.

Through a young Christian man's friendship, she's building hope and trust with role playing. While he's her "sounding board," Esther says to him the words she would like to scream at her father—words of anger, hate, and frustration for the years he took out his emotional problems on her. Books on forgiveness, emotional growth, prayer, and perspective from God's Word have brought inner growth. Esther holds a responsible job with a Christian organization and finds relating to males has become easier. She can look into men's eyes and talk with them now without fear; even talking with God has become easier. Her damaged emotions are changing slowly into healed emotions. Esther sees she can, with God's strength, take charge of her life. She's finding that "hope [in Christ] does not disappoint" (Rom. 5:5).

Esther has learned that when children receive parents' violence, particularly from their fathers, it's difficult in adulthood to relate to a Heavenly Father. Since she thought of Him like her earthly father—unfair and cruel—Esther had problems seeing God as kind or merciful. Thus, she feared acknowledging sin. Feeling loving care from God through a friend is helping her "see" God as kind and merciful. Her father destroyed her feelings of hope; whereas, with brotherly kindness (*phileo*, 2 Pet. 1:7), her friend nurtures her self-esteem. Significant others affect greatly our self-concept during the formative years. We receive from them both emotional feelings and mental perceptions about ourselves. Because children tend to believe what they hear and feel (perceptions and feelings), those of us who lived with criticism and other unwanted intrusions have felt damaged hope.

Nurturing Restores Self-esteem

The second source, the inner world, "includes our senses, our nerves, our capacity to learn, to register, to respond. For some of us . . . handicaps, deformities, and defects"[3] not only physically, but emotionally. In other words, the physical, emotional, and spiritual make up our inner world, which needs tender loving care (TLC). Yet, many of us didn't receive TLC. At times, plants and pets seem to receive better care than some children. David Seamands, teacher and counselor, often tells his clients that children are the world's greatest recorders but the world's worst interpreters. So, even if some of us had parents who gave loving care, we may have misunderstood their motives and intentions. Those misunderstandings damaged our self-esteem; they also limited our hope, cutting off emotional nurture.

From conception until birth, babies receive nourishment from their mother's body. After birth, they learn quickly that *nourish* means to feed and cause to grow, encourage, and comfort. Then, they learn that *nurture* means to nourish, educate, train, or bring up; therefore, babies receive nurture from many individuals. Most of us may feel "a mother's love" represents unconditional acceptance for children's needs, but we also know mothers can't always give children unconditional acceptance, since *they* did not always receive that from *their* parents. Consequently, they can't always nurture their little girls' or boys' feelings.

Important, too, but often overlooked, is fathers' loving nurture for their children's inner world. Our society's discomfort with healthy, male *phileo* friendships keeps some fathers from giving affectionate hugs to their sons. But sons feel the need for nurturing affection from their fathers as much as from their mothers. In fact, some say males choose homosexual life-styles because their fathers didn't show them affection or give acceptance. So boys, not just babies, need their father's healthy, affectionate hugs saying they're OK.

Through default, many of us have learned yet another important truth. One reason wives can't respond to their husbands' affection rests on not receiving their fathers' affection. Delores, mentioned earlier, has two sisters. Her father worked hard to provide well for the family. While he showed his wife affection, he never hugged his daughters or gave them encouragement. His lack of sensitivity built in silent messages telling them, "You're unimportant and not special." Consequently, they felt isolated from him and did not feel attractive to men. Even in adulthood, it's difficult to feel they're attractive to their husbands. Yes, girls, too, need their fathers' healthy, affectionate hugs saying they're OK.

Parents' imperfections, though, make it difficult to always choose mature, loving ways of rearing children. Many believe parents' main responsibility is nurturing their children's often-changing needs. Blame for their mistreatment or lack of love, though, is placed more often on mothers. Heavy responsibilities rest on their shoulders—especially single mothers—often overloading them and making it difficult to care properly for their children. But many children don't understand those problems and feel uncared for. In contrast, if parents are able to meet their children's needs, the children usually feel nurtured rather than damaged.

Helen, also mentioned earlier, lives with damaged self-esteem feelings. Since neither of her parents grew up with nurture and approval, they didn't understand how to help Helen develop a healthy self-esteem. They worked hard at caring for Helen, but couldn't give much affection or praise. Counseling has improved their relationship. They now feel better about themselves and are getting beyond emotional losses.

It has been said that "one negative" spoken to children requires "ten positives" to offset it. In addition, traumatic, unkind, unloving experiences stay longer and are remembered more easily than pleasant times. "It is easier . . . to remember the traumatic times, for during those times our bodies were mobilized with either anger or fear against the trauma. Our memories record stronger impressions of those uncomfortable . . . traumatic events than of the neutral and pleasant ones."[4] Helen, Delores, and I agree that's another reason why we need to receive the hope of inner-world nurture.

My husband Dick has taught counseling to college, seminary, and graduate students for more than twenty-five years. One subject of emphasis is a Christ-designed community providing inner-world nurturing for all ages. He says Christ designed the New Testament community model from *agape, koinonia,* and *ekklesia. Agape* (caring concern for one another) gives the foundation of love to community. *Koinonia* (fellowship, joint participation or sharing together) gives strength to community. *Ekklesia* (a called-out group of people, an assembly, or a gathering together) gives uniqueness to community.

Dick describes community like this. "These three concepts characterizing the body of Christ can be expressed in this way. The Body of Christ gets together (*ekklesia*) to share their lives (*koinonia*) because they are concerned for each other (*agape*)."[5] When we're ignorant of or ignore these three concepts, the body of Christ suffers because we fail to nurture and encourage each other. Christ designed "community" and placed on believers' shoulders the responsibility of living out His design. That's one way to help offset parents' imperfections. So where parents—both non-Christian and Christian—failed to nurture, concerned believers can nurture and build up the hurting members with hope.

Satan Uses "Old Tapes" Against Believers

But many of us have found that the third source, Satan, bombards our feelings of hope continually. "Satan with all the forces of evil . . . plays three roles as a liar (John 8:44), the accuser (Rev. 12:10), the one who blinds our minds (2 Cor. 4:4),"[6] using feelings of "caterpillar-like" self-esteem as a terrible weapon against us. Through environment (the outer world) Satan puts great pressure on our self-concept. Since we are born without any sense of right and wrong, our conscience shapes very slowly. Depending on what our inner world receives from the outer world, we develop either a strong or weak self-concept. Weak self-identity and a faulty self-picture make us *feel* like a bound-up cocoon.

Many minimize the significance of feelings that stem from childhood. But when the outer world of children gives only repressive response or reaction, they develop one of three personality types. The defiant personality is independent, critical, controlling, seldom critical of herself, and more or less insensitive to others' feelings. Through the defiant personality, Helen discovered a sense of autonomy in overpowering people who tried to govern her. But defiance destroys closeness, building in divisions and distance between individuals. Because she didn't feel a sense of worth and approval from her parents, defiance felt safer for Helen.

The compliant personality is more or less dependent, passively manipulative, often critical of self, tends to subjugate self to others, and has the facade of caring for others' feelings. Through the compliant personality, I discovered a sense of worth in winning parental approval by complying with them. But compliance calls for denying wishes and feelings to "feel" acceptance. While compliance is an anger builder, it felt safer for me than trying to reason with a revenging and ridiculing father.

The withdrawing personality develops when defiance doesn't work or fear of parents' wrath becomes too great for compliance. Through the withdrawing personality, Delores found she could hide "feelings" from her parents to keep them from bothering her with their wishes or demands. She feared them too intensely to want their love but remained dependent on them for essential needs. She complied to get basic needs, then retreated to herself or her fantasies for a sense of being somebody.[7] Withdrawal felt safer for Delores than trying to cope with an inattentive, uncomplimentary father.

Using defiance, compliance, or withdrawal—or a mixture of them—children try to capture some sense of worth from their parents and others. Regardless of their personality, they develop damaging mind-messages. These mind-messages, like *cassette tapes*, play on and on. "I can't do things right. My decisions are always wrong. I can't do things like others; I'm a failure. I'm a nothing—a nobody." Satan, author of weak self-esteem, uses these "old tapes" against us, destroying feelings of self-esteem. Therefore, we feel like an ugly caterpillar. That's why damaging mind-messages may keep us from developing our God-given gifts in adulthood, like in my experience.

Daddy made a low-average income, but Mom sewed well. For my dresses, she used mostly 100-pound flour sacks designed with lively gingham plaids or colorful floral prints. Sometimes, I got to choose the color-design before Daddy bought the flour. When Mom made me a dress, I usually wore it first to church. After I dressed, since she wanted Daddy's approval, Mom would tell me to show him the dress. Since I wanted approval from both of them, I went to him saying, "See my new dress, Daddy?"

Most often he read the Sunday newspaper before church. Without looking up, he grunted something like, "Uh huh. Don't be prissy now. Don't be a show-off."

Asking Daddy to look at my new dress, I was really asking, "Do you like *me*? Do you think *I'm* pretty?" His inability to give praise or approval gave me double messages. They said he didn't feel good about me; therefore, I couldn't feel good about me. They said he didn't approve of me; therefore, I couldn't approve of me. Weak self-esteem constricted my personality and bound the cocoon strands tighter, tying up a butterfly so eager to fly. In complying with Mom's requests, I "set myself up" for more criticism and rejection—part of compliance.

When I reached adulthood, the old tapes played on. "If you stand before others as a speaker, you're showing off. You can't feel enthusiasm about anything, because that's expressing emotion. Rather than serving God, your motivation rests on bringing attention to yourself." They also said that complying and disregarding my desires or opinions would gain others' approval. These lies I believed, destroying self-esteem and hope needed in developing God-given gifts.

God Uses "His Word" for Believers

Nevertheless, there are "truths" that can destroy Satan's lies and give us hope. The fourth source "God and His Word . . . move [us] from low self-image to the power for a new Christian self-image . . . from the disease to its cure."[8] When our outer world creates only stressful responses and circumstances, the disease of weak self-image causes us much emotional stress. In contrast, using the cure—God and His Word—relieves stress.

Yet, many parents were unable to nurture their child's inner world with loving acceptance. As a result, damaging mind-messages were formed. The devil uses those lies against us through guilt motivation, trying to destroy our hope. Using God's truths helps us break those messages since He uses His word *for* believers. That motivates us with love and gives hope. Hope plays a significant role through healthy self-esteem to develop women of excellence.

In my childhood, my earthly father didn't understand how to nurture my self-esteem; whereas, my Heavenly Father does. He says, "I created you in My image with mind, soul, and emotions. Since I have worth, you have worth—more worth than all the most costly jewels." I heard that truth, though, for many years before connecting it to self-worth. A few years ago, my emotions finally understood what my mind had already understood. *God created me in His image and gave me His immeasurable worth.* In that moment, a feeling of awe covered both my conscious and subconscious. I felt a heavy burden lift from my shoulders, and thoughts erupted within me: *I have God's immeasurable worth; I'm not worthless. I'm not a nobody; I am somebody. I'm created in God's image; I am important to Him.* In uncontrolled weeping, I thought and felt those words over and over.

At that time, I accepted God's worth for my self-worth. For many weeks following, each time I remembered that God's worth is mine, I felt awe and shed tears of joy—praising the Lord. That "truth" began a *new tape* in my mind. Little by little it's destroying the damaging mind-messages recorded long ago as a young child.

Accepting God's immeasurable worth changed my "feelings" of inadequacy. I began experiencing new spiritual and emotional growth; new **hope** activated me. My decision making became less traumatic, and I began developing some dormant gifts. A healthy assertiveness began to replace the stored-up compliance behavior. Also, my inhibited personality began changing back to the uninhibited one of years ago, before losses damaged my inner woman. Although breaking "old tapes" and making new ones took long, painful months, I learned God's Holy Spirit uses His Word *for* believers, not *against* us. That breakthrough shredded many cocoon strands.

Satan still tries to use "old tapes" against me by making me think, *I can't do things like others; I'm a failure. My decisions are always wrong. People don't like me. I'm a nothing—a nobody.* Usually, I recognize these attacks; but when I don't, a hopeless depression covers me. It feels like I've slipped into a deep, black, slimy hole that I can't climb out of. During these times, the Holy Spirit's soft, quiet voice ministers to me His love and truths. He whispers things like, "Don't listen to those lies, listen to My truth. I love you and created you as a person of worth. And nothing—emotional damage or others' sin—nothing can change those truths." As I'm able to receive and believe my Heavenly Father's nurturing love, I begin crawling out slowly from that black, slimy pit.

Conclusion

Responsibility for learning and memorizing God's truths, turning them into new mind-messages, rests on each of us. With that responsibility comes the importance of "bringing into captivity every thought to the obedience of Christ" (2 Cor. 10:5, KJV). This helps us control Satan's attacks with old, damaging mind-tapes and balance the "head-heart gap battle."That's the battle where our head (mind) tries to get our heart (emotions) to accept God's promises. For instance, many of us labor under the heavy yoke of emotional damage, yet God promises: "Come unto me and I will give you rest—all of you who work so hard beneath a heavy yoke. Wear my yoke—and you shall find rest for your souls; for I give you only light burdens" (Matt. 11:28-30, TLB). God wants to heal our emotions so we can accept and cope with our past. Believing and trusting Him replaces our heavy yoke with His light burden.

Getting that balance will help us avoid depression and learn to distinguish between the devil's lies and God's truths. Those choices help us facilitate spiritual growth. As we feel spiritual growth and listen to new mind-tapes, self-esteem feelings are nurtured. That helps us feel the hope that doesn't disappoint (Rom. 5:5-6).

4 Self-reliance that Builds Confidence

She expresses confidence . . . "She senses that her gain is good; Her lamp does not go out at night" (Prov. 31:18).

*A*lthough confidence is another needed dynamic in developing a healthy self-esteem, its development proves difficult for most of us. Confidence calls for full belief in the trustworthiness or reliability of a person—a self-reliance. When we struggle with emotional losses, though, we find believing in ourselves or others hard to do. One way to help offset this limitation comes through experiencing Christ's reliable trustworthiness. He promises, "Draw near with confidence to the throne of grace" (Heb. 4:16). "I will never desert you, nor will I ever forsake you." (Heb. 13:5). "God shall supply all your needs according to His riches in glory in Christ Jesus" (Phil. 4:19).

While we cannot always depend on others' trustworthiness or reliability, we can depend on Christ. His power and guidance help us take care of responsibilities to accomplish our goals. For those of us with damaged self-esteem, our relationship with Christ will cause a personality change as we shred cocoon strands, develop self-reliance, and confidence. Many believers, though, misidentify confidence as self-praise. As a result, they pin confident Christians with labels like, "She's too smart for her own good. She thinks too highly of herself."

Comparing Ourselves with Others

Yet, the Proverbs 31 woman models feelings of confidence. "She senses that her gain is good; Her lamp does not go out at night" (v. 18). Self-reliance helped her pursue responsibilities with a preparedness that came from an inner strength. Inner strength and self-reliance teaming together develop confidence. On the other hand, if we misunderstand confidence for self-praise, that may result in comparing ourselves with others. This is a common problem with most of us and damages our self-esteem, since comparing implies one is less important than another. Many of us do feel like we are less than others; maybe that is one reason Paul says *don't compare.* "We dare not make ourselves of the number, or compare ourselves with some that commend themselves: but they measuring themselves by themselves, and comparing themselves among themselves, are not wise" (2 Cor. 10:12, KJV). Paul surely wanted us to understand we're all created as unique individuals in God's image. Even if we share similarities in gifts and responsibilities, our unique designed-by-God selves have individuality. Whether or not we suffer from emotional loss, we can develop a strong self-identity. "Confidence, which implies a . . . trust in our abilities and a sense of inner strength, . . . enables us to . . . tackle new challenges. . . . If we are aware of our worth, we are on the road to a strong inner sense of identity."[1] Regardless of our marital status, ethnic background, age, or gifts, God's specially designed blueprints include *all women.* We are more precious to Him than the finest jewels. That's a good reason for us to feel good about ourselves and with confidence picture a useful life.

Since each blueprint is significant and unique, there's no reason to compare ourselves. Neither do we have time to waste in comparing, because there's too much to do for our Creator. Furthermore, all our gifts and personalities are needed. For example, with women and men living longer, people are needed desperately for ministering to senior citizens. And who can better understand seniors' despair, frustration or loneliness than other seniors? Even if a senior feels limited physical power, with her "mind power" she can *pray.* Praying for others remains a vital and needed ministry. If a woman is in mid-life, her spectrum of service broadens; she can sharpen abilities and gifts to concentrate on certain areas. For a younger woman, God's blueprint needs careful study; only lack of faith or imagination can hold her back. At any age, living out God's blueprint helps us picture useful lives and influence others for God, regardless of our situation.

Furthermore, God "blueprints" us to be ourselves—not to be someone else. Sosya, a great teacher who lived about seven hundred years ago, lay dying. His students asked him if he felt afraid to die. He answered, "Yes." In astonishment they asked why he feared death when he had lived an exemplary life like King Solomon and Moses. He answered, "When I meet my Maker, He will not ask, 'Have you been Moses or Solomon?' He will ask, 'Have you been Sosya?' "[2] We, also, must live out God's unique design. Being ourselves honors the Lord; whereas, comparing or measuring ourselves dishonors Him. It's saying in essence, "Hey, God, you made a big mistake when you blueprinted me. It's evident something went wrong on your drawing board." So instead of questioning God, we can take Paul's advice about not comparing ourselves to others. Why imitate another, when you can be **your** unique self?

Some of us feel emotional deformities, flaws, and handicaps. These losses developed from others' sins; some are noticeable, some are not. Identifying and revealing wounds that others cannot see can feel painful and risky. For once they're made known, many people judge or criticize from ignorance, while others don't know what to say and withdraw friendship. Nevertheless, God will use us in ministering to others when we turn our limitations over to Him.

After telling others about growing up in a troubled household, I've had opportunity to talk with and encourage other women who also struggle with emotional losses. Regardless of whether or not we suffer from limitations, God sees us "equal in value to" others. Since we're equal, we need not waste time and energy comparing or measuring ourselves. We can compete, but we have only one acceptable competition choice—competing with our unique selves by schooling God-given gifts and then using them. Competing with ourselves instead of others "improves our serve" for Christ and helps us build self-reliance. Both push us beyond comparing to self-acceptance.

Learning to Accept Ourselves

Accepting ourselves proves difficult for most of us, including Myrna. She's an attractive woman with a shapely 5-foot-7-inch body frame enhanced by beautiful, long, dark brunette hair. For many years this 44-year-old mother of 3 daughters has ministered to thousands through her powerful soprano voice. Besides performing through concerts each year, Myrna has recorded several cassettes. She enjoys performances, yet, that remains a constant struggle for her. The devastating losses she suffered from sexual molestation in childhood cover her like an ugly cocoon. Myrna sees herself as a person of worth and has stripped away much of her emotional ugliness. But, she still struggles with the work and pain of self-acceptance.

Self-acceptance involves being ourselves. Yet "being ourselves" proves most painful for those of us who live with damaged emotions. When we look at our reality, it's hard to believe that we have worth. If we don't see both our bad and good, we cannot acknowledge problems. When we don't acknowledge problems, we cannot grow spiritually or accept ourselves. Walter Trobisch writes,

> It is an established fact that nobody is born with the ability to love himself. . . . Self-love is either acquired or it is non-existent. . . . the foundation for this ability to accept oneself is laid in early childhood. . . . Because this affirmation is often withheld—especially in Christian circles—a type of Christian is created who loves out of duty and who in this way tortures not only others, but also himself.[3]

Consequently, the inability to give or receive love comes from not *feeling* loved, and that causes us to feel emotional torture.

Adding more in regard to "feeling" love, my husband Dick explains, "Many Christians believe the words '[if I] do not have love, it profits me nothing' in 1 Corinthians 13:3 mean we're to work to *have* love. But if we've never *had* love (acceptance and approval), we *can't* love. We can love only when we've first been loved." According to Scripture, love came first from God the Father and God the Son, who are love. They loved through creating humanity in Their image. Then, when humanity turned from God to sin, They extended Their love through Christ's death on the cross. God gave His Son; Christ gave His life. We have no greater model for giving and receiving love.

Their love, mentioned at least ten times in 1 John 4, runs like a crimson thread throughout the entire Bible. Yet, every time the Bible says "love your neighbor," it also says "love yourself." Loving ourselves, then, comes before loving others for "Self-love is necessary before we can be freed from ourselves. . . . Self-acceptance excludes self-centeredness. . . . it enables me to turn my attention outwards. . . . For love 'does not demand its own way'. . . . Self-acceptance and selflessness are interrelated."[4]

Many times in Scripture, Christ models self-acceptance and selflessness. John 13 gives one example. Jesus, at the Passover Feast, took a towel and a basin of water and washed His disciples' feet. He was trying to teach them an important lesson. Assuming the position of a servant, He modeled how to nurture others' self-esteem through serving them. Since only servants performed such acts, the disciples voiced amazement and confusion. Christ explained to them, "A servant is not greater than his master. Nor is the messenger more important than the one who sends him. You know these things— now do them! That is the path of blessing" (v. 16, TLB). Christ's self-acceptance freed Him to a selflessness which helped Him give of Himself in serving others. His modeling even includes us who suffer from others' transgressions.

Paul gives us another example of Christ's selflessness and self-acceptance. "Don't just think about your own affairs but be interested in others, too. . . . Jesus Christ, . . . laid aside his mighty power and glory, taking the disguise of a slave and becoming like men. . . . He humbled himself even further, going so far as actually to die a criminal's death on a cross" (Phil. 2:4-5,7-8, TLB). Although Christ suffered from other's transgressions, His strong self-identity enabled Him to model for us self-acceptance and selflessness. So, even while we're going through the process of stripping away emotional ugliness, we, too, can reach out and show compassion to others.

Though Christ knew He was born on earth for a criminal's death, He felt secure. Furthermore, because He felt love from His Father (John 10:17), He accepted His identity (purpose) freely. That choice strengthened His selflessness. Thus, His love for all humanity says we're copartners in self-esteem, and His modeling shows us how to confirm others through nurturing their self-worth.

"Feeling" love and self-worth comes before nurturing others. As mentioned already, we cannot give away what we don't have. Although Daddy accepted God's salvation through spiritual rebirth, he didn't know about the concept of God's worth. Thus, he did not feel a strong sense of self-identity and did not love himself. Since he did not love himself, he couldn't love others. In working for love and self-worth, he wore many church hats like Sunday School superintendent, teacher, deacon, and faithful tither. Yet, he remained the type of Christian that Trobisch describes. Daddy loved out of duty, which resulted in emotional torture many times for himself and his family.

Duty love causes a vicious cycle. This vicious cycle hampers spiritual growth and damages relationships. "We are unable to love others because we have not learned to love ourselves. We cannot learn to love ourselves because we are not loved by others or are unable to accept their love. We are not loved by others because we are unable to love them or we love them only 'out of duty.' We are unable to love them because we have not learned to love ourselves."[5] But God has good news for us. His love can break a duty-love cycle!

Although we are accepted in the Beloved, God loves too much to leave us where we are. Responding to His love means more than mere acceptance; His love means work, responsibility, and growth. It's work—reading the Bible and praying. It's responsibility—applying God's truths to our lives. It's growth—being conformed into Christ's image. All three belong to the process of spiritual growth, our reasonable service (See Rom. 12:1). And it rests on self-acceptance, what's actual and true, and God's acceptance of our reality—even if it means spiritual pruning.

God's pruning is painful at times. Pruning unneeded branches, though, seems to be His way of helping us turn loose those things we no longer need (John 15:1-7). Those "security blankets," which add spiritual or emotional deadweight, keep us from building trust in Him. One unneeded branch is a damaged past. Letting go helps bring emotional healing and spiritual growth, encouraging self-acceptance. Keeping a small notebook helps in this pruning process. In the notebook, record Bible study thoughts and Scripture verses through which God speaks to you. Also, record some of your conversations with Him, since it's so easy to forget the details of enriching times with God. A few times each year, read over some of the information and *look* for perspective or insight gleaned from God's Word.

Next, in noticing areas of spiritual growth, *allow* feelings of excitement to ripple over you. After that, *identify* areas of growing confidence and self-esteem; then, *thank God* for pruning unneeded branches. Although that process may hurt, it strengthens our feelings of confidence. Many in the Christian community misunderstand these confident feelings, calling them false pride. "Unfortunately, the Church is full of people who believe it is sinful to feel good about yourself. But what is wrong with acknowledging a spiritual reality? What's wrong with recognizing . . . strengths, feeling good about them . . . using them to serve God?"[6] The Proverbs 31 woman surely saw nothing wrong with such feelings. She sensed that her gain was good; her lamp did not go out at night (v. 18). Thus, she modeled for us the importance of confident feelings and self-acceptance.

From her behavior, the Proverbs 31 woman must have agreed with this concept. "If God can accept me . . . knowing what he knows, then I can accept me. If God can love me . . . knowing what he knows, then I can love me. If God esteems me as he esteems his son, Jesus, then I can give myself . . . esteem."[7] This shows the truism that we treat others the same way we feel about ourselves.

Actually, the following guidelines equal loving and accepting others like ourselves. "Do for others what you want them to do for you, and love your neighbor as yourself" (Matt. 7:12; 19:19, TLB, also see 22:39; Mark 12:31; Luke 10:27; Rom. 13:9; Gal. 5:14; Jas. 2:8). From those verses we see that loving and accepting ourselves obeys Scripture. This helps us squiggle through the process of shedding emotional ugliness, accepting both the bad and good about ourselves. That brings feelings of confidence, changes an ugly "caterpillar-like" self-picture, and equips us emotionally to accept others.

Learning to Accept Others

Accepting others is often difficult, especially if they have a controlling, judgmental, and hostile personality. Janice is a twenty-nine-year-old with long, golden-red hair. Since she grew up in a troubled household, accepting others is also difficult for her. She never knew her father. When Janice was about three, her mother began unleashing a vicious anger on her body. The beatings took her close to death many times. Along with the physical intrusions came verbal violations. Added to that, during her teen years, Janice also suffered sexual molestation. These violent intrusions built unhealthy thinking patterns regarding her self-identity and behavior towards others. Each nook and cranny of her emotions was damaged, almost beyond repair; her ability to relate to others with trust or risk remains crippled.

When Janice feels others' acceptance, she can respond to their friendliness. When she feels others' nonacceptance and rejection, her inner woman reverts to that damaged inner child. She's once again trying to defend and protect herself—trying to get back into a safe situation. Since we live in such a sinful and messed-up society, it's almost impossible to find an emotionally safe atmosphere. Yet, we're always facing change; especially in trying to accept others. It's normal for our damaged emotions to develop a "fear" of change.

Because change carries the **unknown**, it puts new stress on top of old stress, compounding the acceptance problem.

> There is no fixed, true and real person inside of you or me precisely because being a person necessarily implies becoming a person, being in . . . the process of change. . . . . Approach me, then, with a sense of wonder, study my face and hands and voice for the signs of change; for it is certain that I have changed. . . . . [For this reason] I am afraid to tell you who I am, because, if I tell you who I am, you may not like who I am, and it's all that I have.[8]

Many of us find accepting others difficult at times and fear telling them about ourselves. We fear others will reject us because *who* we are (our reality), not *what* we own, is all we have. That's why our acceptance of others' reality remains vital to nurturing their self-esteem. Accepting others includes recognizing that they continually change, but accepting others doesn't necessarily mean we approve of or like them. In a sense, accepting others means emotional hardships for us. One hardship involved in accepting others is the change process. Only Christ knows constant stability; He's "the same yesterday, today, and forever" (Heb. 13:8, TLB). Only Christ's stable "inner sense of self-identity" spoken of earlier gives us stability. Our self-identity stabilizes as we recognize we are God's created beings—we didn't just "explode" into existence. However, we must learn to live with the process of continual change.

Change is one of the biggest problems between partners. They hardly ever arrive at the same place at the same time in the change process. One may desire children; the other doesn't. One may want to move to another town; the other won't. One may be ready for retirement; the other isn't. Change also places great pressure on our friendships. While we become better acquainted, we're getting to know each others' change spots. Some friends develop a good self-image, while others lag behind. Some friends go through "burnout" and "mid-life crisis" before others get there. One friend received a big job promotion just as another was fired. Such change differences compound the acceptance problem and increase emotional hardships.

Another emotional hardship often involved in accepting others includes **telling others who we are**. That's hard because it involves risk. We can mask, trying to fool others; we can role play, imitating others; and we can play mental games, influencing others to like us. And if we succeed, we've only accomplished deception. People cannot love masks or role playing or games—just the individuals behind them. We can't offer others anymore than our reality. Yet, if we risk telling others who we are—our reality—it's possible they won't accept us. And when others don't give us acceptance, it's most difficult in return to give them acceptance since we *feel* their rejection.

As painful as rejection is though, when we cannot risk letting others see our reality, we haven't accepted ourselves. And when we don't (or can't) accept ourselves, we can't accept others. Many of us exist, rather than live; we don't feel motivated enough to "risk" being ourselves. Someone's sin has caused us to "feel" like an ugly caterpillar. Sometimes, other's sin keeps us from getting beyond the infancy emotional stage—where we feel the need for everything to revolve around us. However, we need to reach the adult emotional stage—where we can love ourselves and love others. This is living out God's instruction to "Love yourself and your neighbor as yourself." This is also the change process that makes it so difficult for us to accept others.

Still, another emotional hardship involved in accepting others rests on **coping with difficult people**. These difficult people at times cause emotional, pain-filled traumas for us to accept and cope with. "They are emotionally blind—they can't see your talents, skills, or successes. . . . They are emotionally deaf—they don't really hear what you're saying. . . . They have damaged vocal cords—they say the wrong thing at the wrong time."[9] Many of us agree with that description of difficult people and find it hard to accept them.

At times we feel, "I don't like to bother with difficult people! I want to just cross them of my social list; that will help me avoid some emotional discomfort." Nevertheless, Christ loves difficult people and tells us to love and accept them like ourselves. Self-acceptance includes both bad and good news. The bad news is we sometimes act difficult. We're sometimes emotionally blind and emotionally deaf, with damaged vocal cords. The good news is we don't need to act difficult. Even if we feel weary at times from stripping away emotional ugliness, we can still love others and relate to them as persons of worth. Understanding that concept helps us cope with the emotional hardships in accepting others.

Almost too late, Florence learned that truth. From early childhood into adulthood, she worked for her mother's approval. She got good grades and did well in everything she tackled. Later she became a loving wife and mother, and also a well-known author and speaker, not only in America, but in other countries as well. Still, Florence's mother couldn't give acceptance or acknowledge her daughters gifts. Then one day Florence's husband asked, "When are you going to grow up and . . . function without your mother's approval?" His pointed question shocked her. In working for her mother's approval, she hadn't seen herself irritating others—being difficult. His question helped Florence understand that getting along with others means accepting them like they are and not wanting something in return. In other words, we must accept others like we want them to accept us.

A few months before her eighty-five-year-old mother died, Florence did that. She realized her mother couldn't give approval so she stopped seeking praise from her. Instead, she began thinking of her aged mother's needs and how to nurture her self-esteem.[10] Accepting others like we want them to accept us builds strength and maturity into our inner woman. Accepting others, though, doesn't mean they will accept us automatically in return. Nor does it mean a friendship will always develop. We can control only our behavior; we are not guaranteed others will respond to a loving acceptance. But we are guaranteed this: "Thy Father which seeth in secret himself shall reward thee openly" (Matt. 6:4, KJV). God knows our motives. And when we reach out to others through acceptance, He will reward us with peace.

Conclusion

Along with accepting others, we stop trying to change them, learn to not compare or measure ourselves, and quit trying to force them to accept us. In so doing, their self-esteem and ours are nurtured. That's what Christ meant, "Love your neighbor as much as you love yourself. . . . Do for others what you want them to do for you" (Matt. 7:12; 22:39, TLB). Easy? Not for me! I've known a woman for a long time who relates to me mostly like Florence Littauer describes. When I feel her rejection, it's most difficult to relate in acceptance and kindness. Three things have helped me with this relationship: Learning I can't spend much time with her; reminding myself I can't change her; and remembering I'm also sometimes difficult.

Those choices also help me live out Romans 12:18. "If possible, so far as it depends on you, be at peace with all [women]." That challenge motivates us to try harder in accepting others rather than competing or comparing. Accepting others gives self-reliance that builds confidence and develops a special female self.

5 Perseverance that Builds Character

She experiences character . . . "Strength and dignity are her clothing" (Prov. 31:25).

*T*he overriding "I-want-it-now" mentality has provided for an abundance of fast-food restaurants, quickie divorces, and plastic-card money. This "provision" has succeeded in weakening the perseverance that built our society. In order to build character—another dynamic for developing a strong self-image—we need perseverance. Character is a distinguishing mark or feature or reputation. Christ has a distinguished reputation; the foundation for that character, established by His parents' teaching, began very early. At age twelve, He went to the Feast of the Passover with His parents and astonished the teachers with His understanding and answers. Later, Christ amazed His parents by telling them "I must be about my Father's business." From perseverance, He continued to "increase in wisdom and stature and in favour with God and man" (Luke 2:41-52, KJV).

Christ persevered through each phase of life, strengthening His character to prepare Him for death on the cross. That act gives salvation (cleansing from sin and entrance into heaven) to all of us who accept it. Salvation through Christ enhances our self-identity and helps build our character. The Proverbs 31 woman also models character, "strength and dignity are her clothing" (v. 25). Those distinguishing marks labeled her reputation from the way she related to others and carried out responsibilities. Like Christ, her character developed from perseverance.

Living with a Weak, Wounded Self-image

We, too, must learn to persevere. "Blessed is the [woman] who perseveres under trial, because when [she] has stood the test, [she] will receive the crown of life that God has promised to those who love him" (James 1:12, NIV). Perseverance calls for dealing with and working through guilt, anger, or lack of trust—plus much more—which resulted from past trauma. This "work" causes conflict. Sir Winston Churchill talked about that conflict. "I do not intend to take that cowardly course, but, on the contrary, to stand to my post and persevere in accordance with my duty." History records the difference made for freedom because he didn't run away but rather persevered in duty. Learning to stand and work through emotional struggles is equally important for us.

Giving up and quitting develops a weak self-identity, but perseverance develops proven character. "We also exult in our tribulations, knowing that tribulation brings about perseverance; and perseverance, proven character . . . because the love of God has been poured out within our hearts through the Holy Spirit who was given to us" (Rom. 5:3-5). That's the opposite of a weak self-image which causes us to feel we're being "dumped" on. Often, under attack from circumstances, I've asked questions like, "Why me, God? After all I'm still tunneling through the last trauma, and my neighbor has not had problems in months. Why do you always pick on me?" In the meantime, I've learned that coping with problems builds character.

Besides destroying my emotional privacy, Daddy's violence destroyed my physical privacy. No place felt safe, private, or secure. Mom was 16 and Daddy was 18 when they married. Mom's 5-feet and 5-inches carried a shapely 130 pounds with long, curly dark-brown hair and a pretty oval face. Daddy's 6-feet and 1-inch carried a gangly 150 pounds with short, straight black hair and a thin handsome face. Their bodies, though, like their marriage, with passing years became burdened with extra weight. Daddy's jealous and suspicious mind caused him to make Mom stop playing the organ at church. First he accused her of playing the organ only to get guys' attention, then he said she couldn't even attend church. In 1914 the mode of travel wasn't luxurious 350-horsepower Cadillacs, Oldsmobiles, or Fords. They traveled in bumpy, horse-drawn buggies or wagons. If husbands didn't want wives going somewhere, they didn't go.

Besides a violent anger, Daddy, at times, got drunk and gambled most of his small paycheck. Over the years, like a pendulum, his personality swung back and forth. At times he gave Mom respect and kindness, at other times he gave disrespect and meanness. When I was eleven years old, my eighteen-year-old brother died from carbon monoxide poisoning. He drove a friend's car that had its exhaust pipe broken under the driver's seat. The odorless fumes drifted up into the car, silently smothering my brother and his friend. Since Mom and Daddy could not share their grief, their relationship went from bad to worse.

For many months, Mom suffered deep depression and spent much time in bed. Daddy, on the other hand, tried to show his "spirituality" through refusing to feel grief. In his small grocery store, he talked and laughed loudly with the customers as though his son hadn't died. Months later, because of denying his grief, an intense anger built up within him. The physical violence started again, but all the other children had left home. Consequently, feelings of helplessness and hopelessness covered me, because I couldn't control his behavior.

By my mid teens, an intense hatred for Daddy boiled within me; it "boiled over" each time he came near. We had few conversations and most of them ended in word battles. Daddy's pendulum personality continued swinging, choosing times I wasn't around to vent his rage on Mom. While I felt responsible for Mom's safety, my strength couldn't physically protect her. So I tried protecting Mom with my morals, becoming a compliant teenager. As a child and a teenager, I could not separate my self-identity from Daddy's abusive attitudes, responses, and actions. Thus, growing up within an abusive atmosphere rather than a loving one made me *feel* very different from other teens.

Besides feeling inferior, I identified with Mom internalizing her feelings of disgrace, degradation, and disrespect from Daddy's violent intrusions. Inferiority, compliance, and shame became my constant companions. Although none of the kids I grew up with knew about our troubled household, I "believed" everyone knew. My inner child felt great pain and I suffered from a weak, caterpillar-like self-image. Diana Russell's research shows that one out of every seven American women is abused by her own husband but feels too ashamed to say anything about it. These figures for battered wives include the Christian community. The attitude that believers don't have problems causes many to feel shame and embarrassment; like Mom, they refuse to tell.

Since rape remains one of the most underreported crimes, exact statistics aren't available. At age twelve, Nancy suffered emotional destruction and turmoil from her stepfather's rape. In her mid twenties, because bad memories weren't dealt with, she developed a physical illness, and had to return from the mission field. Conversion hysteria, the doctor's diagnosis, means something is going on in the mind which has been converted into physical symptoms.

For thirteen years Nancy had forced the rape out of her mind, forgetting a horrible secret. After being hospitalized, she telephoned her stepfather, who had remarried after her mother's death. He said with laughter, "So you're in the hospital. What are you doing, having a baby?" His remark triggered an explosion in Nancy's mind, causing her to remember the rape. Old scenes started replaying in her mind; she couldn't stop the thoughts. After awhile, her thoughts turned into words that came tumbling out, revealing the nightmare experience to her nurse friend. That began a tedious, tortuous, physical, and emotional healing for Nancy. While weeks turned into months, some accepted and nurtured her; others didn't and judged her.

God guided her to a Christian psychologist who provided insightful and patient counseling, helping Nancy to release "poison, hate, and venom" caused by the violation.[1] I've known Nancy for ten years and have observed a balanced life which shows her love for the Lord. Now, as a licensed psychologist, Nancy ministers to others from her experience. A few states have finally declared spousal rape—even more difficult to prove—to be a crime. Mom suffered this crime many times. She'd been taught wives' submission included sexual relations; regardless, she didn't have a choice.

Even in the Christian community incest reports have increased. In her teens, Susan Forward, now a psychologist, lived for many months with her father's "seductive sexualized fondling." Although that relationship did not include penetration, her emotions suffered severe damage, and she felt like a "bad girl." Dr. Forward has worked with hundreds of victims, trying to help their emotions heal from sexual abuse. She defines incest as, "any overtly sexual contact between people who are either closely related or perceive themselves to be . . . (including stepparents, stepsiblings, halfsiblings, and even live-in lovers if they have assumed a parental role.) If . . . trust that exists between a child and a parent-figure or sibling is violated by a sexual act, [it] becomes incestuous."[2]

A nine-year federal Bureau of Justice Statistics' study says we average 450,000 acts of family violence yearly. The report also says many family violence instances aren't reported.[3] What's more, it isn't possible to gather accurate figures for battered children. Pretty and petite, Betty, a 35-year-old mother of 2, was a battered child. Her father died suddenly when she was 6, leaving her mother, Ruth, to rear three little girls. Ruth worked hard to provide for them, but the pressure was too great. The heavy burden of providing for them brought out the same violence in Ruth that had been in her background. She began repeating her father's abuse pattern. At times, Betty stayed out of school for a week, while bruises healed.

After graduating from high school, she ran away and married. They had two beautiful girls, but Betty lived in constant fear that she would repeat the abuse pattern. She found accepting her husband's affection most difficult and finally left. She loves her girls and hopes to have custody of them someday.

Because Diane did not *feel* valued and loved by her parents, she developed a rebellious spirit. Her parents did not know that beneath this behavior lived a sensitive, loving child—longing for loving acceptance. An invisible mountain separated them, and by the mid-teens alcohol became Diane's means of coping. This addiction caused many self-destructive choices like abortion and an arrest for driving under the influence. In her early twenties, Diane started attending Overcomers, a Christian organization for those struggling with substance abuse. She also received insightful counseling, which helped her become more efficient and settled in the workplace. Living the roles of wife, mother, and employee, Diane perseveres with Christ's loving power to keep her in "recovery" rather than under the influence.

Yes, many of us live with a weak, wounded self-image stemming from others' transgressions. Society has become so *mobile*, though, that most neighbors don't feel accountable toward each other. Many feel uncomfortable talking about violence and its damage; they are ignorant to its presence in the Christian community and believe it will "just disappear." We who struggle with addictions, damaged emotions, or rebellious behavior know that problems do not disappear by just hoping. God says, "My people are destroyed for lack of knowledge" (Hos. 4:6). "Come now, and let us reason together" (Isa. 1:18). Denying the self-destructive behavior or abuse from others isn't "reasoning" together. Christians must accept reality and give emotional support rather than stick their heads into the sand of denial. Denial keeps thousands from receiving nurture, care, and acceptance, because some have not said with clarity, "We want to know. We want to help."

All believers need spiritual food for building strong character to avoid hurting others. Yet, some of us think because all our life problems haven't been worked through we can't encourage or help others. Listening to hurting others tell how God has provided insight into some life area excites me. Although they still stagger under heavy emotional burdens, I can hear and see their excitement about God's love, which nurtures their damaged self-esteem feelings. Nurturing is caring; caring is accepting; and accepting is action. We who hurt emotionally need something substantial to give us hope that our pain will end. That *hope* comes from Christ through caring others. Others' nurturing and acceptance motivates us to let the past go and allow Christ to process a new future within us where the butterfly flies from its cocoon, stripping away a wounded "caterpillar" self-image.

Becoming Conformed to Christ's Image

Processing a new future involves turning loose of our distorted self-image and being conformed to Christ's image. *Conforming* means to make of the same form of character or likeness. But before we can make ourselves of the same form as Christ's character, we must learn what He's like and how He thinks. (1 Cor. 2:16). We do this through reading and studying the Book written about Him. As we assimilate the information into our minds, it begins to affect our thinking. While change is slow, it results in taking on the mind of Christ and stripping away layers of emotional ugliness. As layers fall off, we see a special female self emerging.

Taking on Christ's mind helps us picture life from a different perspective. We can see that our minds have developed blurred pictures of God's character, that we confused God's behavior with the behavior of those who sinned against us. We even said accusingly, "God let that happen." But now we see that God is love and is motivated by love—not hate, jealousy, or viciousness. We understand that our pain did not come from God; it came from people's choices, choices over which we had no control. God gives us courage to face problems rather than denying or running. His love helps us avoid the tendency during tribulation to doubt our self-worth. That's part of conforming to Christ's image as we become women of excellence.

Christ tells us, "In the world you have tribulation, but take courage; I have overcome the world" (John 16:33). He knows what hard times are, He doesn't expect us to suffer alone. Rather, He feels with us. In fact, Hebrews tells us that Christ suffered temptation like we do, yet He did not sin. Therefore, in confidence we approach Him for mercy (4:15,16). That specialness gives us courage. Thus, His love and courage working together help us persevere. We can also learn to see hard times as character builders rather than God's punishment. Years ago, I often felt hard times reflected God's punishment, like heavy-testing times rested only on me. Difficulties made me feel like the young teen—still getting punished for trying to save her mother's life. Many times I told God, "You don't love me as much as You love others. I don't feel special to You."

When we don't feel special, it's often because of many stressful experiences while growing up. For instance, my senior year in high school the football team chose me as their football queen. When the night came to crown me, no family members could share that special time. All my brothers and sisters had already moved away from home, and Mom and Daddy couldn't share special times. Since one of the princesses needed a place to dress, I suggested she use our small four-room apartment a few blocks from the football field.

I dressed in a baby-blue waltz-length gown of taffeta and netting, which I had worn the previous year to my junior prom. Wearing my strapless gown, white floral necklace and earrings, and white three-inch pumps, I walked with Lanora to the football field. Since the evening air felt warm and humid, we did not need sweaters. She talked laughingly about her nervous feelings, so I did the same. I didn't feel nervous. Actually, I felt rejected. I was seventeen years old, a senior in high school, and the crowned football queen, but no "significant others" were sharing the excitement with me. Yet, I didn't want anyone to know about my pain. So pretending with smiles and laughter made others think I had a wonderful time. In writing about it now, I feel the same stinging rejection I felt then.

Since I didn't feel special to my earthly parents, I did not feel special to my heavenly Father. Their lack of sensitivity to my emotional needs developed a strong critical "parent" within me. That critical "parent" never encourages me; it just talks about my weaknesses. Consequently, I've worked long and hard trying to rid my mind of this debilitating, emotional handicap some refer to as self-talk. This is our pattern of thought or belief system that forms either external speech (words) or private speech (thoughts). It begins developing in us at birth—maybe before. "Our emotions and behavior are not dependent on what is going on around us in our environment . . . . There is something else at work that determines emotional and behavioral responses to life situations . . . Self Talk."[4]

Self-talk becomes our mind's ongoing inner chatter. According to Dr. David Stoop, we talk "words" at the rate of 150 to 200 words per minute. Yet, we think at the rate of approximately 1,300 words per minute. That's a lot of inner chatter, which either works for or against us. For inner chatter to work for us, we must regenerate our mind (filled with old tapes of accusations and failures) with Christ's mind. In other words, with the Holy Spirit's help, we recreate, reconstitute, or make over our minds in a better form or condition. That process may take months or even years. The following are four basic principles that give a foundation to Self-talk.

• Our thoughts create our emotions. If we think, "Hey, you're a failure and a nobody," we also feel like a failure. Scripture tells us, "For as [we] think within [ourselves], so [we are]" (Prov. 23:7). In other words, the way we "picture" ourselves determines the way we "feel" about ourselves. If we picture ourselves as inferior, we feel inferior. *Thoughts do create our emotions.*

• Our thoughts and perceived center of control affect our behavior. At times, our accusing memories flash reruns of someone's degrading behavior, hurtful words, or abusiveness. The old mind messages whisper, *You can't do things like others. You're not special.* When we believe the lies, we live the lies. That means our behavior is determined by what or who we think is in control of situations. Using God's control, we have His help to forgive those who've sinned against us and to change negative thought patterns. We can picture ourselves as, "Accepted in the beloved" (Eph. 1:6, KJV); reborn spiritually (John 3:3); "a new creature" in Christ Jesus (2 Cor. 5:17); and having "the mind of Christ" (1 Cor. 2:16). *Thoughts do affect our behavior—that's the new perceived center of control.*

• We think irrationally. Often, we listen to Satan's self-talk, and his accusations splatter us on the wall in bright red. If inner chatter creates only critical feelings, we can never feel good about ourselves. We learn to let our critical inner-parent control us with accusations and criticism. Therefore, we never give ourselves complimentary encouragement like, "Hey, you worked hard this week. Reward yourself with lunch at your favorite salad place." Instead of respecting ourselves, we allow old mind messages to chew us up mentally. *That's thinking irrationally.*

• We create change in our lives by gaining control of our thoughts. In re-creating the mind, "right" self-talk is needed in taking on Christ's mind to control our thoughts.[5] That includes the Holy Spirit's self-talk. "Whatever is true, . . . honorable, . . . right, . . . pure, . . . lovely, . . . good repute . . . let your mind dwell on these things . . . and the God of peace shall be with you" (Phil. 4:8-9). That's using self-talk in a practical way to control a critical inner parent. Then, we gain control of our minds by thinking in accordance with God's Word. Both reading and memorizing Scripture fill our minds and help us conform to Christ's image rather than to the world's image. *That's creating life-changes through gaining control over our thoughts.*

In applying these principles, we need to remember that memories include feelings, concepts, patterns, attitudes, and tendencies toward actions. These things accompany the pictures on the screen of our mind. That's why our memories hold both experiences and feelings—not simply brain-stored pictures of the past. Because our thoughts influence the way we think and feel about ourselves, we need to "be transformed [become new] by the renewing of [our] mind" to take on Christ's mind (Rom. 12:2).

Taking on Christ's mind has influenced my emotions. Since I feel better about me, I feel better about others. I've forgiven my parents' lack of sensitivity and seldom compare myself with others. Now I know that difficult testing times are not God's punishment; rather, they are intended for our character building. During the development of these changes, this truth motivated me to accept His new future. "God who began the good work in you will keep right on helping you grow in his grace until his task within you is finally finished on that day when Jesus Christ returns" (Phil. 1:6, TLB). These new mind messages encourage us to transform our inner chatter so we can picture ourselves like God sees us—special and "equal in value to" others. Through taking on the mind of Christ and conforming to His image, we can overcome emotional losses.

Developing a Healthy, Strong Self-image

The opposite of conforming to Christ's image is developing feelings of low self-esteem.

> Low self-esteem is Satan's deadliest psychological weapon, and it can keep [us] marching around in vicious circles of fear and uselessness. . . . The person with low self-esteem is always trying to prove himself . . . constantly looking at himself . . . becomes extremely self-centered. This doesn't necessarily mean he is selfish. . . . But he is self-centered in that he is always looking at himself and wondering about himself.[6]

Self-centeredness can develop fuzzy mental pictures about what God has "already" done for us.

Adults usually respond to God's love through the same behavior response learned toward their parents. If our parents punished indiscreetly, we usually feel that God will treat us the same way. That's why Esther feared acknowledging sin. She believed God would respond in cruel unfairness like her earthly father had done. We make such associations in adulthood when damaging concepts from our childhood stay alive. But we can learn to identify and change harmful concepts in our "inner child" as we see the difference God makes in our lives as we learn to trust Him.

Similarly, **clear, concise pictures** about God's track record show us tremendous love for humanity. For some of us, that love is great contrast from the violence and other word battles that programmed us with a weak, damaged self-image. But now, we can rely on God's help to take charge of our life and change it. Paul Tournier tells us we can do this through reprogramming. "The main difference between the computer and the . . . living being is . . . the living machine manufactures itself and gives itself its programme, whereas a computer can never be anything more than . . . the programme of its operator."[7] We're not limited or locked in like a computer; rather, with the Holy Spirit's power we can reprogram our inner pictures and tapes. "Reprogramming" means developing new self-pictures which will free us from a pain-filled past, and involves three choices.

A willingness to change (to alter or make different) costs us something. Often, we're willing to spend money on everything except that which facilitates our inner healing. Just like we consult **medical** doctors for broken bodies, we need to consult **counseling** doctors for broken emotions. Christ, the "Wonderful Counselor" (Isa. 9:6), designed counseling for us. "With good counselors there is safety" (Prov. 11:14, TLB). "With those who receive counsel is wisdom" (13:10). "Listen to counsel, . . . That you may be wise the rest of your days" (19:20). Listening to counsel that identifies problems in our inner woman means we will allow time for emotional healing. Identifying problems, facing them, and working on them take time and energy. This "willingness" helps strip away emotional ugliness.

Acknowledging that self-worth comes from God also costs us something. When God created humanity in His image, He removed from us the heavy burden of trying to *make* ourselves good enough. He placed onto His own shoulders the burden of proof for our worth, making us "good enough" for others. Until we acknowledge that truth, though, it can't become reality for us. Thus, we must give up working for self-worth and leave the work to God. "My power shows up best in weak people" (2 Cor. 12:9, TLB). And, "out of [my] glorious, unlimited resources [I] will give the mighty inner strengthening of [my] Holy Spirit" (Eph. 3:16, TLB).

Accepting a new self-image (developing new self-pictures) also carries a price tag. The price for some includes the need to stop pretending and *own* a pain-filled reality. Placing ownership on our pain will help us accept a new, healthy self-image. It's humbling to receive God's worth without working for it, but Genesis 1:26-27 says He created us in His image. It's humbling to receive Christ's salvation without working for it, but Ephesians 2:8-9 says that's the only way. These amazing truths write the price tag for accepting a new self-image filled with well-developed pictures. "You need to persevere so that when you have done the will of God, you will receive what he has promised" (Heb. 10:36, NIV). The Holy Spirit's power, working through our perseverance with the three choices, builds in us a strong self-image.

Conclusion

Self-worth, remember, does not come from kindness, good works, appearance, performance, or status. A strong, healthy self-identity comes from believing that God created us in His image. His free gift takes our ugly "caterpillar" self-image and turns it into a special female self. This special self becomes a woman of excellence with the emotional maturity needed to develop sensitive serving skills.

Section *2* *Developing Sensitive Serving Skills*

S erving others has almost become a lost art in our society. Strong, vocal feminist groups have yelled loud and long that we should live for ourselves. They insist on self-centeredness (not serving), regardless of the cost to ourselves or others.

There are many people who honestly believe that the family has out-lived its usefulness and should be buried. Others would twist and modify it to fit their humanistic value system. For more than 20 years, the institution of the family has been subjected to an endless array of bad ideas, including the sexual revolution, . . . open marriage, no-fault divorce laws, devastating taxes, hostility to children, abortion on demand, ridicule of homemakers, war between the sexes, the gay life-style, the plague of obscenity.[1]

Those choices of social measurements stifle our serving skills.

The serving skills I speak of describe submission. Submission has become a confusing term for most of us, and rightly so. Besides love, *submit* may be the most misunderstood, misguided, and misused word in society's vocabulary. And next to love, **submission** may be the most difficult to live out—single or married. Misidentifying compliance, subordinance, and subservience, or masking for submission has caused both males and females to feel much confusion. For many years, I thought submitting was easy. Then I began to recognize that those words mimic the submission serving skills. But, there's one time when I didn't confuse their mimicking behavior with submission.

In our sixth year of marriage, Dick started work at a Bible institute in the Midwest. He had graduated from the school before going on to college and seminary. So going back to serve as Dean of Students was very special to him and me. At the end of his seventh year Dick's immediate boss—Dean of Education—retired. They had shared a good working relationship. But, the new dean held many views regarding student policy that were opposite of the former dean and Dick. These differences were evidently building sparks within him. One year later, those sparks joined together, ignited, and blew up.

The igniting force came from the four women deans who reported to Dick. That was in the sixties, when some Christians fought many battles over "short skirts." The institute decided female students could not wear clothing any shorter than one inch above their knees. Finding clothes that fit into such a limited range proved difficult. The Dean of Education insisted that skirt lengths had to have continual monitoring. So instead of doing their usual counseling and other duties, the women deans found themselves measuring skirt lengths. After many confusing months of playing skirt detectives rather than "deans," they felt frustrated and angry. They asked for Dick's permission to present a letter of protest to the dean. Since Dick believed they needed to make their frustrations known, he said "yes."

The women deans' differing views threatened the dean's viewpoints. He held Dick responsible for their views and asked him to resign his position as Dean of Students—immediately. The explosion blew us out of Chicago into Los Angeles and blew us out of a new house we had lived in for only eleven months. We seeded the lawn, hung curtains, put a "For Sale" sign in the yard, and sent Dick's resume for another job. That's when the Lord said, "Go West young man, go West."

Although only two weeks remained before we had to leave, our house had not sold. I believed Dick should go ahead, while the children and I waited for our house to sell. Pastor Hamilton, though, had another idea and counseled me with such words. "I believe you and the children should go with Dick to his new work. You need to move as a family. He needs your support." Since Dick felt the same way, after much prayer, I chose to take the children and go when Dick did. The "new work" did not have the money to move us, so we sold or gave away most of our furniture. Our 1968 pea green Pontiac station wagon could haul only a 6- by 12-foot trailer. We stuffed it with mattresses, bedding, towels, dishes, cooking utensils, clothes, Dick's books, toys, and two chairs from Mom.

While Dick and the four children got settled in our station wagon, I took one last look. Walking into the living room, I replayed mental pictures of decoration plans. I looked in the formal dining room where we had planned to entertain students. The elegant, gold chandelier held four cut glass lobes under each bulb. It gave the room a warm and cheery feeling. Then I walked into the breakfast room. With tears washing my cheeks, I prayed something like this. "Lord, I don't understand why You've called us to California and yet not brought a buyer for our house. I ask You to take care of it for us. Thanks for the eleven months here; we leave it in Your hands." Then I locked all the doors and got into our station wagon, and we headed west.

That submission choice to serve the Lord and Dick by leaving an empty, unsold house proved difficult. We didn't know when the house would sell or if we would be able to buy another house. We didn't know anyone where we were going or what kinds of problems we would face on the trip. We knew only that one door closed while another opened, and we chose to walk through that door. My submission choice brought many unexpected things—both enjoyable and not so enjoyable. Leaving friends and the "work" both of us loved dearly pained our minds and emotions. I was beginning to understand that serving through submission calls for many different types of choices and consequences.

6 Serving: Submitting to Christ's Leadership

She submits to Christ . . . "But as the church is subject to Christ" (Eph. 5:24).

*T*housands of us cringe when we hear words like *submission, obey, subordinate, subject,* and *subservient.* One reason for that response rests on those words not belonging in the same family. Another reason comes from misunderstanding their real meanings and applications. A third reason is that many Christian leaders tie the words together in confusion. A fourth comes from our childhood when many of our parents, following their parents' teaching, taught us blind obedience. That "blind obedience" says, "You obey me just because I say so." This attitude caused us to feel devalued since our parents did not communicate with us. Consequently, we grew up "feeling" that ourselves and our opinions were not valued.

In like manner, some place "subject and submit" on the same level with enduring others' emotional wounds. This denies that the wounds happened. Also, others use Christ for a model to endure abusiveness. Several times, though, Christ removed Himself from those intending to inflict violence on Him (see Matt. 12:14-15; Mark 3:6-7; John 8:59). And, some use His words in Matthew 5 ("turning the other cheek") to prove we should in blind obedience endure others' oppressiveness. However, Christ is talking about opposites and comparisons. He does not OK blind obedience or violence. When Christ let the multitude take Him captive, He wasn't approving their oppressiveness. In fact, when Peter cut off a slave's ear, Christ picked it up and placed it back on his head—rebuking Peter's violence (see John 18:10-11).

Violence, regardless of the type, remains foreign to Christ's modeling and teaching. Misunderstanding the Canon's teaching regarding submission gives us blurred and fuzzy pictures of God. At least 80 times God the Father and God the Son are pictured with "compassion." At least 142 times they are pictured with "loving kindness." At least 100 times they are pictured as "love."

They model these attributes for believers so we in turn can know how to relate with compassion, loving kindness, and love. Therefore, we can believe emotional trauma does not come from them; neither does any type of violence get their approval. On that premise, then, we can feel assured that submission does not fit together with violence or oppression. Nor can they join together. Emotional trauma cannot claim submission for a partner.

Describing Believers' Submission

While obedient, compliant, subordinate, and subservient do not fit with them, submit and subject do belong together. And they are often interchanged in the Bible. Yet, many make the mistake of teaming obey with submit even though they don't share the same meaning. *Obey* (*hupakouo*) means to hearken, listen, or do as one is bid. Whereas, *submit* (*hupotassomenos*) is a military term. In fact, instead of using *hupakouo* (obey) when talking to all believers, Paul used *hupotassomenos* (submit). (See Eph. 5:21-24.) He also used *hupotassomenos* when talking to wives (Eph. 5:22; Col. 3:18; Titus 2:5; 1 Pet. 3:1,5). Broken into three parts it looks like this:

HUPO next, after, or under
TASSO to arrange or to place in a certain order
MENOS oneself or you, yourself (an ending for a present, middle, or passive participle)

In sentence form it reads like this: Arrange oneself under or next to as soldiers are arranged . . . file after file or place oneself under. With more clarity, that means an individual places himself or herself willingly under the leadership of another.[1] Submit carries the connotation of a choice. We may or may not choose to place ourselves willingly under the leadership of another. In all circumstances, submission remains a choice; no one else can choose for us. And in our choices, we learn there are consequences to experience. On the other hand, obey is more like a command: Listen to me and do as I say. Therefore, we must discern well between obey or submit and their proper application.

Different forms of the "obey family" are found 139 times in the Bible. The various forms appear 87 times in the Old Testament and 52 times in the New Testament. Different forms of the "submit family" are found 57 times in the Bible—10 times in the Old Testament and 47 times in the New Testament. It seems that *obey* is used more in parent-child relationships, while *submit* is used more in peer relationships. That could explain why *obey* appears more often in the Old Testament, since the Jews were God's children. Quite often they were disobedient children and did not listen to or obey His voice. A priest represented them before God, so they could not share a one-to-one relationship with Him.

Later on, Christ's death and resurrection rearranged the work of priests or angels. The veil separating people from the temple's inner room, where priests made sin sacrifices, split open. This gave believers **open access to God through the Holy Spirit** (Paraclete). Since that time, we share a one-to-one relationship with God and an heirship with Christ.

Several dozen verses describe Jesus as God's Son, and numerous verses describe all believers as God's sons or children. Paul says in Romans 8:14-17 that we are *heirs with God* and *joint heirs with Christ. Heirs* are those who inherit or are entitled to inherit. Because of our "heir status," we inherit eternal life (sins forgiven) from God, and He becomes our Heavenly Father. Since Christ is God's only begotten Son and believers are God's spiritual, adopted children, we share the same Heavenly Parent. In addition, *joint* means combined or united; as, a joint force or joint efforts. Through joint efforts, therefore, we combine or unite with Christ as "joint heirs." The Paraclete goes along beside us—guiding, helping, strengthening. This work helps us live out God's goal for believers to grow up in Christ, take on His mind, and become mature and complete spiritual adults (Eph. 4:15; 1 Cor. 2:16; Jas. 1:4).

The words obey and submit also describe the process of growth in family relationships. For example when Christ reached the age where male Jews were considered men, He became subject (*hupotassomenos*) to His earthly parents. They gave Him a choice so He could "be about [His] Father's business" (Luke 2:51). Their modeling shows parents how to make a gradual shift in parenting. By moving teenagers from obedience to submission, parents can enhance the emotional maturity of their children. That transition helps teens learn to make responsible choices and build a track record their parents can trust. Moving teenagers from obedience to submission prepares them for adulthood, when they will relate through submitting rather than obeying.

Moving from obedience to submission also involves serving. Serving performs duties for others and has a definite use or function. Parents serve children through encouraging their emotional growth and maturity in letting them make choices. Choices, with parental guidance, help them develop into responsible and reliable adults. Children serve parents through performing duties out of obedience to their commands. Later, they serve parents through functioning and performing duties through mutual choices (submission).

This type of parent-child relationship helps young adults understand how to submit in their relationship with Christ. And submitting to Christ's leadership develops sensitive serving skills. In submitting our will to Christ's leadership, we see He never takes advantage of us. We see that Christ wants the best for us. Also, experiencing Christ's "pure love" helps us discern between His purity and humanity's impurity. Through subjecting ourselves to Christ's guidance, trust can build; we can't submit to another if we don't trust Him. Without trust, our behavior just *mimics* submission.

Subordinance, compliance, subservience, or masking imitate submission. But they are not the same. Many from the Christian community continue to use *subordinate* in sermons, books, and lectures. They evidently fail to acknowledge that this word's original meaning has changed. Just like the word *gay* has lost its original meaning, so has *subordinate*. As a result, while *subordinate* could be used during the apostle Paul's time, its meaning now has become degrading. *Subordinate* (placed in or belonging to a lower order or rank; of inferior importance) damages self-esteem. Subordinate does not suggest choice but rather demand. Therefore, putting ourselves in a subordinate position goes against our better judgment.

Compliance (complying with a demand or an order) over a period of time builds in unhealthy anger. Compliance "gives in" to demands or orders a person doesn't agree with. Therefore, it's giving up an opinion or viewpoint grudgingly, and it harms self-identity. *Subservient* (useful as an instrument to promote a purpose; acting as a subordinate) places a person in an inferior position. Someone using another as an instrument to promote a selfish purpose destroys self-esteem feelings and also takes away choice, as in the case of rape, incest, other sexual molestation, physical or verbal abuse. *Masking* (covering, disguising, and concealing) harms relationships. Since masking disguises true feelings, we pretend to submit. Underneath the pretense, relationships have no solid foundation to rest on. So they crumble and fall.

Picturing submit and subject as a choice, we see the importance of understanding a clear view. *Submission* is an act of the will. No one can make a submission choice for another. Accepting submission as a choice helps us see why New Testament writers were guided to use *hupotassomenos* rather than *hupakouo* in dealing with peer relationships. *Submission lifts up a relationship.* Placing ourselves willingly under another's leadership serves, shows trust in, and gives respect to that person's gifts. Submitting to another's leadership also develops our serving skills.

Acknowledging Which Believers Should Submit

Many males and females have debated about "who" belongs under the discipline of submission since Eve and Adam's first sin. One reason for this debate is that some do not believe that God designed *both* male and female with a submission plan. In order for us to carry out that plan, all His body members must cooperate. Males or females in mutual willingness place themselves under each other's leadership—mutual submission. But rather than cooperate, many believers concentrate on selfish and childish self-centeredness. "I'm the leader. No! I'm the leader."

The obsession to demand that things go the way we want them to go is one of the greatest bondages in human society today. People . . . spend weeks, months, . . . years in a perpetual stew because some little thing did not go as they wished.

In the Discipline of submission we are released to drop the matter, to forget it. . . . . The biblical teaching on submission focuses primarily on the spirit with which we view other people. Scripture is not attempting to set forth a series of hierarchical relationships. . . . In submission we are at last free to value other people. . . . . We discover that it is far better to serve our neighbor than to have our own way. . . . Submission . . . is a posture obligatory upon *all* Christians: men as well as women, fathers as well as children. . . . We . . . live a life of submission because Jesus lived a life of submission, not because we are in a particular place or station in life.[2]

According to Scripture, Christ modeled submission for *all* believers. And Paul's instructions in Ephesians 5:21 are very clear. Beginning in verse 18, Paul tells believers to use the Holy Spirit's control rather than wine. He suggests using different kinds of songs in singing God's praises, and he instructs believers to learn the art of thanksgiving. Then in verse 21 he expostulates that all in the body are to subject themselves to each other out of reverence for Christ. That "all" includes male and female, young and old. It's interesting that many leave out this short sentence, containing such powerful instructions, whenever teaching the fifth chapter of Ephesians. Nevertheless, God gave us those instructions for an important reason.

In order to mix quality with diversity, God designed His body with at least twenty kinds of gifts. These gifts are "for the equipping of the saints for the work of service, to the building up of the body of Christ." For how long? "Until we all attain to the unity of the faith, and of the knowledge of the Son of God." Why? So we will "no longer be children, tossed here and there by waves, and carried about by every wind of doctrine" (Eph. 4:12-14). God gave these gifts to be used—not to be set on our mental shelves, collecting dust. The only way *both* males' and females' gifts are used is through "mutual submission." Both sexes place themselves willingly under each other's leadership, enhancing spiritual gifts usage.

When any body of believers refuses God's design for using spiritual gifts, the body is weakened. God gives gifts to men and women. Using His gifts in His service strengthens our self-esteem as we equip the saints for the work of service, to build up the body. Therefore, all members of the body, male and female, submit to Christ's leadership. But, married females have an added dimension in submission: submitting to their husband's leadership. That submission, though, cannot be coerced or commanded. It's a choice. Wives place themselves willingly under their husband's leadership. Christ's relationship to His bride, the church, gives us the model for husbands' relationships with their wives.

Out of reverence for Christ, males and females—even husbands and wives—submit to each other (v. 21). A husband protects his wife (v. 23), gives up himself for her (v. 25), and purifies her with the Word (v. 26). He preserves his wife through union with her exclusively (v. 27), loves his wife as himself (v. 28,33), and provides for her as Christ does for His bride (v. 29). A husband leaves his parents and cleaves to his wife in oneness (v. 31). Those Christ-directed guidelines prove difficult, even impossible, without the Paraclete's help. The wife's help, also, proves most important.

In addition, males who live out Christ's marriage guidelines *will not* in any way take advantage of females. Through mutual submission, then, males build a trustworthy track record by protecting, purifying, preserving, loving, providing, leaving, and cleaving. Trust built between males and females can enhance either mutual or marriage submission. Whenever or wherever these two life-styles flourish, we see both sexes using their spiritual gifts. Gift usage enhances mutual respect, mutual (*agape*) love, and mutual submission—even marriage submission. All four areas must live in submission to Christ's leadership.

Recognizing Christ's Leadership

Many of us find submission to Christ difficult at times, especially when we want to know "why." At the same time, though, we can believe that Christ's leadership never takes advantage of us. God does not direct anyone to take advantage of another. We must learn to distinguish between God's righteous standards and society's unrighteous standards. If parents ask their teenager to steal, the teen can refuse. If he followed their request, the teen would be subordinate rather than submissive. Parents must understand that when they take advantage of teens and children, whether verbally, physically, or sexually, they have acted out subordinate behavior which goes against Christ's standards.

When a boss asks an employee to alter the books, lie to customers about delivery dates, or perform any behavior beneath God's standards, the employee can refuse. We need to learn how to tell our employer discretely, but directly, that those choices are subordinate behaviors, violating our consciences, and that we cannot perform what he has asked. We will suffer consequences, but greater emotional suffering results if we do not submit to Christ's standards.

Another type of choice comes when a husband beats his wife. Each time the beatings occur, the woman feels less human and more like an object being destroyed. Although removing herself from the situation may carry as much emotional pain as staying, she can choose to get help. Violence and oppression go against Christ's teaching about the marriage relationship. **Submission is not the choice** when others' actions violate Christ's standards. Staying in abusiveness becomes subservient behavior that destroys feelings of self-esteem. Most out-of-control males want limits put on their behavior since they don't know how to do so themselves. And, most husbands feel more respect toward their wives when they protect their bodies and emotions from damage.

Another example of choice occurs when a young woman becomes pregnant. She's urged by a birth control center, the father, a friend, or a parent to abort the baby. Since killing the unborn goes against Christ's standards, she can refuse to comply, although living out the pregnancy could be difficult for her. She can choose to preserve a life that some couple can adopt and love for their own. Knowing this, she can live in peace rather than guilt, for submitting to Christ's standards nurtures her self-identity.

At this time, Satan is "the prince of the power of the air" (Eph. 2:2). Yet, many of us (in ignorance) blame his work on God. Subordinate and subservient acts work against feelings of worth and self-identity; whereas submission, a choice, adds to self-esteem since it's designed to enhance relationships. Examples of life experiences which go against God's standards and mimic submission are endless. In discerning between submission choices and imitation behavior, though, the following guidelines are helpful.

Submit to God. Submitting ourselves to God's plans isn't always easy. Some teach that God "zaps" us with emotional or physical wounds so that He can then share His love and provision. Since Scripture *does not support* such thought, we can believe God doesn't approve of suffering or violence. He takes our pain caused from others' mistakes or sin and gives us emotional healing. In that sense, He turns our "ashes into gold." Using His guidance helps us avoid holding onto hate and anger or making wrong choices. Submission is a healthy choice.

Submit to Scripture and the body of Christ. In submitting to Scripture, we need to make sure it's God's voice and not someone else's that we hear. Mom believed she had to endure Daddy's degrading abusiveness in order to be a good Christian. She believed the wrong voice. Although living out God's truth often proves difficult, His instructions don't belittle, take advantage of, or degrade. God does not approve of oppressiveness; so, we must discern between someone's harmful behavior and His instructions.

This includes using spiritual gifts. When asked to do a job that does not fit into our gift area, we need to refuse. Furthermore, we can refuse in gracious firmness if our time and energy are already committed. Many of us find saying "no" difficult since we mis-associate others' approval with our need for self-esteem nurture. In overloading, though, we sin against our body and Christ because we're abusing a "temple" of the Holy Spirit. On the other hand, if asked to carry out a task that fits into our time and energy and gifts— and the Paraclete gives us peace—we can say an enthusiastic "yes."

Submit to family members and others. Choosing to submit to family members and others may be difficult, and decisions must be made with careful, discerning prayer. These choices fall under mutual submission, giving us opportunity to follow Paul's advice, "Do not merely look out for your own personal interests, but also for the interests of others" (Phil. 2:4). This includes sharing time, space, things, love, and listening ears. Many times I've found that although I feel tired, I'm helped by reaching out to others with kind words, heart-felt smiles, or happy greetings. However, few of us feel motivated to submit our thoughts or hopes to controlling, self-centered church leaders or an angry, critical boss. This becomes particularly hard if these "difficult people" overpower us with their abusive attitudes. When the mind or body or emotions get trampled on, our submission choice is destroyed.

Conclusion

Using the guidelines above to discern between submission choices and imitation behavior can help us avoid emotional pain. Paula Caplan, associate professor of psychology at the Ontario Institute for Studies in Education, says Freud believed women find pleasure in pain or suffering.[3] His irrational idea causes much confusion for those who try to understand the differences between males and females. Women do not want or need to suffer. But for those of us who have suffered because of others' selfish choices, we can, with determination, turn the experiences into strengths. Once we've known an emotional loss, we can "feel" with another who feels loss. Submitting to God, the body of Christ, family members, or others—when appropriate—respects Christ's leadership and shows the world "a different and better way." That living "lifts up" one another, refuses to take advantage of the other, and develops sensitive serving skills.

7 Serving: Submitting to Others' Leadership

She submits to others . . . "And be subject to one another in the fear of Christ" (Eph. 5:21).

erving others through submitting to their leadership is a common occurrence for many of us. But few recognize the behavior as such. In sports, players must place themselves willingly under their coaches' leadership, or the team disintegrates. In medicine, we must submit to the training and information of physicians, surgeons, dentists, and osteopaths, or healing doesn't happen. In school, students must subject their minds to teachers' information, or they don't learn. In a car, we must submit quickly to road rules and patrolmen, or chaos results. In the work place, we must submit to employers, or production may not happen.

Such behavior has taken place since the time of Adam and Eve. But, it doesn't sound right to most of us when that behavior is labeled mutual submission. Submission portrays a poor quality picture for most of us. And mutual submission portrays a poor quality picture for most males. In contrast, God produced both concepts from a clear, well-developed picture. And yet, submission can "feel" very threatening since it rests on trust. If unhealthy relationships destroyed our ability to trust, we must rebuild trust before placing ourselves willingly under other's leadership.

Learning to Accept Others' Leadership

Rebuilding trust takes hard work, time, and modeling. Our best modeling comes from a one-to-one relationship with God the Father. Feeling His acceptance, love, and provision—plus His guidance—helps us begin to see that He isn't taking advantage of us. This helps us become vulnerable enough to trust another who has a trustworthy track record. Feeling trust once again helps us gain confidence and go beyond ourselves to serve others. Serving means performing duties for others; having a definite use or function. Carrying out many different duties and functions, the Proverbs 31 woman shows how submitting and leading work together. She served through using the art of work willingness, planning for the future, and providing for her appearance. She discerned wisely in decisions and investments. She developed her work ethics with wisdom, kindness, and organization. She used creativity and initiative to enrich contentment. She served through establishing a contentment foundation, overcoming emptiness with achievement, and feeling contentment with fulfillment.

However, the Proverbs 31 woman *was not* a perfect, unattainable, bionic, superwoman. She was ordinary and took a lifetime to develop her special female self. And besides using her uniqueness in leading others, she modeled well how to serve through learning to cope with others' leadership. The following choices may not seem, at first glance, to fit with submission and leadership. But, upon realizing how widespread sexual promiscuity and abuse have become within the Christian community, we see the need for making these choices in dealing with leadership.

Believe that past hurtful experiences do not take away our self-worth. We must understand, though, that continual verbal attacks, critical attitudes, and violence destroy our *feelings* of self-esteem. These attacks and attitudes build in old mind messages like, "I can't do things like others. I'm dumb, a failure, and a nobody." Or, "Face it. You're an obstinate, rebellious female. That's why your parent tried to beat you into obedience." Those lies keep us from making new mind messages and hinder us from accepting others' leadership. However, building in trust toward God the Father will lay a foundation of trust for all other relationships.

The Census Bureau says approximately 2.2 million single adults shared living space with a person of the opposite sex in 1986. That figure is *four times greater* than the number of unmarried couples living together in 1970. Also, more and more females are choosing to live alone. Recent figures show 12.9 females live alone, compared to 8.3 males. Individuals who can't trust and risk in relationships often choose "no marital commitment" or "living alone." Such choices may identify a female as feeling unsure about her worth and value. Fear of marital commitment might say a female does not believe she is a worthwhile person. "I'm not pretty enough," "I'm too heavy," or "I'm not sexy enough." Although such mind messages are hard to break, we can do so with the Paraclete's help.

We must remember that choosing beauty, sexuality, or personality values based on others' standards can bring disappointment. Also, desire for marriage—just to get married—usually proves disastrous. "Many more women than men end up living alone. . . . It is vital, therefore, that women of all ages, single and married, realize that living without a man does not automatically mean that their lives must be lusterless, that they must be lonely and miserable."[1] Penelope Russianoff also says 1979 government statistics showed 14.6 million women over sixty-five live alone compared with 10 million men over sixty-five. At the same time there were one million more women of marriageable age than men. Accepting this reality will help us see the need to change outdated means of helping hurting females.

Determine how you feel about femininity. That term includes our feelings, intelligence, gifts, abilities, and potential. It is the God-designed quality or nature that distinguishes female from male. He designed this difference to enhance the identity of both sexes, whether married or single. Accepting our femininity cuts through unhealthy competition with masculinity. And singles, in remembering that more females live "single" than "married," may find encouragement from Paul. He thinks that singles have fewer problems than marrieds and can give more attention to "things of the Lord." He also says that his words were meant to encourage singles—not discourage or restrain (1 Cor. 7:25-40). Thus, singles refusing "pressure" from others to marry, just to get married, will help develop their special female self.

Luci Swindoll, a single, says it this way. "We must achieve a balance if we desire to rise above a prosaic existence characterized by futility and apathy. Neither can we live . . . in the realm of lofty aspirations and perfection, marked by idealistic pursuits . . . [by that] I mean . . . negotiating toward a settlement . . . between the two worlds of the ideal and the real."[2] "Ideal and real" may cause some of us difficulty in developing a balanced attitude toward femininity. A society's whose motto became "If it feels good, do it," encourages us to give in to every sexual desire. But Solomon says, "Above all else, guard your affections. For they influence everything else in your life" (Prov. 4:23, TLB). We agree with Dr. Gary Collins's view that our greatest source of sexual stress comes from the mind, and we understand the importance of balancing sexual feelings.

An important issue involved with femininity is learning to distinguish between healthy agape (loving acceptance for a person) and eros (sexual feelings). Many fail to understand that when we obey Scripture to *agape* (love) others as ourselves, our emotions "feel" good feelings for another. We cannot shut off our emotions and yet *think* we can love others. We don't love others with our thoughts; we love them with our feelings. The difference is, when Scripture tells us to feel agape for others, it does not tell us to feel eros for them. We need to learn to distinguish between the two. If we are single, our eros feelings can be acknowledged—but not consummated. If we are married, we must share our eros feelings exclusively with our spouse. Some scoff and say that kind of femininity takes away free choice. Actually, learning self-control while we are single prepares us for the control often needed in marriage. Travel schedules, illnesses, or pregnancy each call for a mutual commitment to sexual control.

When couples or singles have not exercised appropriate sexual control, most have difficulty remaining faithful in body *and* mind during trying circumstances. Consequently, serious problems like adultery and fornication can develop. Bathsheba's affair with King David and several highly publicized affairs in our society give us adequate warning. Paul says that whether one marries or stays single, she has made a good choice (1 Cor. 7:38, TLB); in other words, we need sexual balance. When we do not develop balance, we must reckon with guilt. Guilt becomes a drain that weakens will power and self-control. Sexual sins—regardless of what we call them—become masters over our emotions and fall short of God's standards. They can become a substitute for building meaningful relationships with others.[3]

Discern between sexual wants and God's standards. Some statistics show that teens, at earlier and earlier ages, become sexually active. Joy Dryfoos and Richard Lincoln analyzed 29 million teenagers' sexual behavior. They say between ages sixteen and nineteen, only *one-fifth* of young men and *one-third* of young women *have not had* sexual intercourse. "Teenage sex has come out of the back seat and is rapidly becoming one of the most politically controversial . . . issues in the country. . . . Nearly one half of the nation's 543,000 illegitimate births are to teens."[4] Believing such information helps us understand the confusion many feel about themselves as a sex object. Because of promiscuity, many find sexual compatibility in marriage almost impossible.

Many records show the average age of incest occurs between nine and twelve, but often includes babies and toddlers. Incest has little to do with sex, and nothing to do with intimacy. That's why 75 to 80 percent of victims prefer holding or cuddling over sexual behavior. They want intimacy, not sex. Many victims, though, become sexually active in their teens since that's the only way they learned to relate to the opposite sex. They need to learn to discern between intimate friendship and sexual behavior. But regardless of the reasons singles choose to become sexually active (or marrieds choose adultery), they've chosen wrongly. God's standards for sexual behavior remain "a cut above" those of society.

Since God created and designed the body, we can believe He's aware of our sexual needs and provides a healthy release for those needs. Sexuality is the physical and behavioral differences that separate female from male. It's the way in which we respond to anything with sexual content. Because society overemphasizes sexual behavior, it's hard for many to discern between needs and wants. The lie so many choose to believe says, "Whatever one fantasizes, dreams, feels, wants, desires, just do it—self-ownership."

That "self-ownership" goes like this: "My body or my life belongs to me, and what I do with it, either by myself or with consenting others, is nobody's business but my own, provided I don't inflict direct and tangible injury on unwilling others."[5] We can see quickly that self-ownership argues the opposite of God's truths. And whether one does or does not hesitate to inflict on unwilling others isn't the issue. There's no excuse good enough to justify living by self-ownership. Along with designing humanity with sexual feelings, God also designed ways for us to live with those feelings in honor. "No temptation has taken hold of you but what is common to human nature. And God is to be trusted not to let you be tempted beyond your strength, but when temptation comes, to make a way out of it, so that you can bear up under it" (1 Cor. 10:13, Williams).

Screening closely what goes into our mind through our eyes and ears begins the process of learning control. We choose to ignore society's subtle suggestion, "You're not worthwhile if you can't make a man happy," or "God just wants to take away your fun." These attitudes mark a self-ownership that is contrary to God's standard and destroy the self-control needed to develop a special female self. Numerous choices, involving feelings about femininity and masculinity, make up our relationships. In order to have healthy relationships, we must love and accept ourselves so we can love and accept others. That calls for discerning between sexual wants, needs, and God's standards. Healthy relationships call for different levels of intimacy, according to the depth of friendship. And, they call for mutual submission, which enables males and females to serve each other with understanding.

Learning to Understand Others' Leadership

Besides requiring trust, discernment, and acceptance, submitting to others' leadership requires understanding. More and more women are managers at all corporate levels. The Proverbs 31 woman is a good model and motivator for us as we see how she managed her family, friendships, and business with understanding. She hired well-qualified workers to help with household and business responsibilities, as well as the training of her children. That gave her more time and energy to spend on fun times with her children and husband. Fewer of us would suffer from "burn-out" if we followed her example.

One important truism about leaders is that each lives with disappointments, limitations, and some type of damaged emotions. If a supervisor suffers from PMS (premenstrual syndrome), as I do, there will be days when communicating with patience will be a problem. When a director comes to work following an argument at home, she may be distracted. After a manager learns about her teenager's problem with substance abuse, she will need time and space to make decisions. Now, I am not saying that women cannot handle problems that come from both their private and work lives. What I am saying is that leaders, like all of us, have difficult circumstances to cope with. We can serve them through giving them consideration and understanding.

While leaders need empathy, many have difficulty receiving that from others. One way to help them during trying times is by communicating with respect rather than making angry demands. Another choice is volunteering to take on some of their responsibilities that are transferred easily. A third choice is offering to listen or give input that may relieve some of their burdens at home. Each of these examples presents us with viable mutual-submission choices.

If one accepts your offer of service, you've placed yourself willingly in a position of serving the Lord through serving others. Some will not accept your offer, yet you can rest assured they have felt accepted, valued, and understood.

Christ offered Martha, sister of Lazarus, an opportunity to take a break from planning and preparing dinner for her guests. She chose busyness instead of His kind offer but exhibited an attitude problem brought on by compliant anger. Rather than scheduling time for listening to Christ *and* preparing dinner, she went to the kitchen grudgingly. Martha chose physical subservience over mutual submission. Instead of receiving in order to lighten her load, she burdened herself with unprofitable busyness (Luke 10:38-42). Her example shows us that an inner peace—not hostility—needs to permeate our serving. Performing duties for status, self-esteem, or self-punishment eventually leads to unhappiness and a poor attitude. Serving for the wrong reason is not understanding, nor is it submission.

Learning to Follow Others' Leadership

While it is true that submission is an act of the will, it involves much more than our will. Submission involves our mind and our emotions. The author didn't use the word, but the description of the Proverbs 31 woman shows us a person who related to others through mutual submission. Skills for leading and following were enhanced by family members who confirmed her feelings of self-worth. The strong self-identity she developed helped her serve others—for the right reasons. In today's Christian community we've seen the destructive results of those who did not balance leading and following. Regardless of our role and responsibilities, learning how to follow enhances our leadership skills.

Amy Carmichael once said, "You can give without loving, but you cannot love without giving." Submitting to others' leadership is giving. It's loving others enough to trust them, respect them, and serve them; it's letting them use their gifts. "Don't be selfish; don't live to make a good impression on others. . . . Don't just think about your own affairs, but be interested in others, too, and in what they are doing" (Phil. 2:3-4, TLB). That behavior can prove most helpful and encourage "leaders." Here are some choices that help us follow others' leadership.

● Commit to following with respect. Trying to lead when others won't follow becomes confusing, frustrating, and stressful. In any group, there can only be one leader (at a time). A person leads because she has the gift to lead. We give value to a leader through submitting under her leadership skills. In each group, there will be those we won't "like" much. But becoming good friends isn't usually a group's purpose. We can show respect to members' gifts whether or not a strong friendship develops. In addition, listening and responding in a respectful manner give a good atmosphere to any group setting.

• Commit to faithful attendance and use of gifts. In order to accomplish purposes and goals, each group needs to meet together consistently. Arriving and getting started promptly becomes the lifeblood of any group. Time spent waiting for the leader or members to arrive is wasted time and energy. Consistently arriving late becomes a negative attention getter and shows disrespect for other members. In any group, many different "gifts" will gather. Feelings of inferiority, fear of cloning others, reacting to others' competitiveness, lack of confidence, and ignorance of our own gifts can keep us from using gifts. That's why we need to take necessary steps to discern and use our gifts. For **all** spiritual gifts are needed to help equip and build up the body of Christ.

• Commit to an uncritical attitude and confront in love. Giving constructive criticism, if done in openness and kindness, can be most helpful to any group or leader. Stating criticism and offering feasible options show listeners the speaker values them. All involved will be built up and helped by an this kind of attitude. An accepting attitude encourages discussion as well as discourages dissension and arguing in the group. However, times for confrontation will arise; that's why our attitudes toward confrontation are most important. Confronting effectively means offering maximum information with minimum threats or stress. That shows loving concern for those involved. Having facts straight before confronting gives interpersonal communications a grand color.

Learning and following leadership skills can "feel" threatening when we suffer from emotional limitations. If unhealthy relationships damaged our trust, "teaming" with others may present problems. Many of us have fuzzy, distorted self-pictures that drain away the courage or confidence needed to join groups. While we have many gifts, getting involved feels too risky and scary. If we've lived under others' abusive control, it's too risky to place ourselves under other's leadership for fear they too will take advantage of us. To cover up our feelings of inadequacy we use excuses like, "I'm too busy." Unfortunately, we don't recognize these excuses as problems. In contrast, some who team with others feel so insecure they have to control them. We can use hard work and time, though, in learning how to *risk submitting* to others' leadership.

Conclusion

When we carry around a caterpillar like self-image, we tend to go in one of two directions: overachieving or underachieving. Overachievers tend to complain that only a small percent of believers discern, develop, and use their gifts. Underachievers say that discerning, developing, and using spiritual gifts "feels" too scary. Each complaint is valid and needs consideration. Some overachievers suffer from "burnout," since the urge to be in control is so strong they cannot allow others to use their gifts. Overachievers sometimes forget that they can't earn God's approval through performance. In addition, they need to make room for and show appreciation to those who are just learning to use their gifts. That helps all to grow toward spiritual maturity.

Paul questioned the Galatian believers concerning their spiritual maturity. He asked them what had slowed them down in running the race of obedience to God (5:7). Then Paul reminded them, "For you were called to freedom, [sisters]; only do not turn your freedom into an opportunity for the flesh, but through love serve one another"(v. 13). Then he instructed them to walk by and be led by the Spirit (vv. 16, 18) and to produce fruits of the Spirit: Love, joy, peace, patience, kindness, goodness, faithfulness, gentleness, self-control (vv. 22-23). He warned them against becoming boastful, putting down each other, or envying one another (v. 26). That's a **new** self-ownership.

This new self-ownership helps us live out the "community" we talked about earlier. The body of Christ gets together (*ekklesia*) to share their lives (*koinonia*) out of concern for each other (*agape*). Dr. Paul Brand, a surgeon, gives insight into community, gift usage, and mutual submission.

> The Spirit does not approach me in the solitude of my own soul, for that would leave me alone and unreconciled to my neighbor. Rather, He calls me to join a Body that binds me in love with a community of diverse cells. . . . In the human body, cells cry out to their neighbors when injured—the chemistry of the wound attracts healing cells—and the body responds on a local level. . . .
>
> Physicians and nurses do not heal; we merely coax the body to heal itself. Without its help, our own efforts prove futile. . . . The same is true in the spiritual Body composed of diverse members representing different races and statuses and income levels and intelligences and cultures. When we allow the Spirit of God to move in, hovering in-between the differences and disproportions and varied hurts and needs, He can direct the process needed for healing and for growth.[6]

That allows God's Spirit to direct our emotional and spiritual growth. Submission to the Lord and His Truth helps us learn to accept, understand, follow, and submit to others' leadership.

8 Serving: Submitting to and Respecting Husband's Leadership

She submits to her husband and respects him . . . "Wives, be subject to your own husbands as to the Lord . . . Let the wife see to it that she respects her husband" (Eph. 5:22-33).

*M*any have asked, "How can I submit to his leadership when he doesn't lead?" That question is difficult to answer. More and more males (single or married) seem to be withdrawing healthy assertiveness from relationships. Dick[1] says within the couples he has counseled, he's found that more problems rest with passive-withdrawn males than with aggressive females. *Withdrawal* is a denial or protection against reality. Thus, people use withdrawal to help them deny reality so that they won't have to deal with it. *Passiveness* is when we fail to respond to something normally expected that provokes expressions of emotion or feeling. Traditionally, males are expected to take leadership roles within marriage, family, work, or friendships. When they fail to lead, relational problems develop.

Confusion about roles and behaviors frustrates both males and females. But blame for the confusion usually lands on women. However, that confusion may have begun some years ago—in the Garden. When Eve offered knowledge-tree fruit to Adam, he chose passivity. Instead of giving the response Eve expected, "God said we can't eat this," Adam accepted and ate the fruit. Some time later, God came along to visit with them and discovered they had crossed over His one command. As God asked for the details, Adam again took the passivity route. Rather than "owning his behavior" he blamed Eve. She in turn, blamed Satan (Gen. 3:1-13). Their "blaming" started the sexes' confusing behavior of mimicked submission.

Passivity, Subservience, and Subordinance Confuse Submission

Role confusion baffles many of us and frustrates our relationships. During our dating days, I felt valued when Dick opened doors for me. When walking down crowded New York City streets, he would often take my arm or hold my hand. That felt special to me. An today, I still appreciate him or other males opening doors for me. Some women, however, refuse to let men open doors or assist them in any way. They say that accepting respect or kindness from men weakens their womanhood and personal freedom. These two conflicting views confuse many males, and they no longer know what women expect of them. If a "small" issue like opening doors causes problems, it is little wonder that many males today *feel* confused in relationships. The underlying principle has to do with submission and passivity. There are at least four reasons males give for choosing passivity in relationships.

• Fear of rejection. Any prolonged emotional pain while growing up may build in a fear of rejection. This fear, conscious or unconscious, can immobilize our emotions. Then problems of protecting and caring for ourselves or others develops. Emotional damage takes away an inner motivation to work on problems, which keeps us from building meaningful relationships.

• Apathy. Having felt no parental love or acceptance makes it difficult for them to feel vulnerable enough to trust. Without the ability to trust, they don't feel motivated to work on meaningful relationships. While these males may have experienced some casual friendships, the attitude of "why try" develops. Since they don't know how or can't give themselves in friendship, feelings of defeat take over, and they lose hope.

• Aggressive females. When males do not feel a strong self-identity, it's too threatening to try and build friendships with females holding feminist attitudes. When females express the attitude that males aren't needed or wanted, they feel demasculated. As a result, some become passive, while others become aggressive. Those taking on passive behavior change their lifestyles; some even turn to homosexuality.

• Ignorance. If a male has never known meaningful relationships, he doesn't know any better. Perhaps his father chose passivity in order to cope with a controlling wife, or he sees other males modeling passivity. So, he takes on older male's passive behavior since he doesn't realize that's the wrong role model for relationships. Male passivity for him becomes a cultural norm. In order to offset this learned behavior, he needs understanding.

Appreciating and understanding what others "feel" is labeled empathy. Males and females need to appreciate what the other feels and feel with each other rather than battling through chauvinism or feminism. This old Indian prayer holds the key. "Grant that I may not criticize my neighbor until I have walked a mile in his moccasins." Empathy, then, enables us to walk through the maze of submission. Another look at submission, subordinate, and subservient helps us understand the differences.

• Submission. We place ourselves willingly under the leadership of another.

• Subordinate: We're placed in a lower order or rank; we feel like we're of inferior importance.

• Subservient: We're used as an instrument to promote a selfish purpose; we act as a subordinate.

The Bible *never shows* the female in a relationship with Christ that is subordinate or subservient. For example. Jesus' close friend, Lazarus, had two sisters, Mary and Martha. In refereeing a misunderstanding between them, Jesus applauded Mary's mutual submission. He assured Martha that Mary chose the good part. The good part included listening with willingness to Jesus teach His truths instead of preparing dinner in subordinate anger. Martha, too, could have listened; she could have scheduled time for both listening and cooking. But instead, she placed herself grudgingly in the kitchen. She chose subservience over mutual submission and traditional values over Christ's "new values" for women. As a result of this, others felt her hostility (Luke 10:38-42).

In contrast, another woman made the right choice. While Christ waited at Jacob's well for His disciples, He asked a Samaritan woman for water. Tradition said a Jew could not talk with Samaritans. So His talking with the woman elevated her importance to that of man. During their conversation, not once did Christ relate to her in a subordinate or subservient way. Rather, He related to her in acceptance and forgiveness. He dignified womanhood by offering her the choice to turn from **an unstable past** to a *stable future.* Regardless of the reasons for her unstable past, Christ gently and uncondemningly gave a choice. Although she struggled with damaged emotions, she accepted that choice. She placed herself willingly under His leadership in declaring Him "the Christ" (John 4:6-42). Her choice lifted her out of degrading subservience. She shared a new kind of love.

That "new love" is what helps us begin to distinguish between subservient, subordinate, and submissive. However, the English language often confines and frustrates us, when speaking about love. We use *love* to express all kinds of feelings. Everything from, "I love orange juice," to "I love to watch the Dodgers play baseball." Since we've forgotten how to use words like *enjoy* and *like*, *love* has become weak and almost powerless.

The Greeks' language, though, helped them identify and express "love" with more clarity than our English language does for us. Rather than using just one word, they identified love with these four words: *Stergos, phileo, agape,* and *eros.* When a Greek said something like, "Betty and Julene, I feel *stergos* for you," that meant she felt natural affection for them. Generosity, kindness, courtesy, self-sacrifice, forgiveness, and sympathy come from *stergos.* Shakespeare once called *stergos* the "milk of human kindness," and it's used in the New Testament three times. Betty and Julene know little about this love, since verbal and physical beatings spanned most of their growing up years.

This stripped them of healthy feelings needed to respect themselves. Although they've worked hard to get beyond those emotional wounds, they still can't feel kind and sympathetic toward themselves.

When a Greek said, "I feel much *phileo,* Susie, when thinking about you," that meant he felt pleasure for her. *Phileo* feelings express a fondness, an unimpassioned and friendly affection for pleasurable qualities in the person loved. In particular, when those qualities are like qualities in the one expressing that love. It can lead to selfishness, if not kept under control. Yet, it is proper in its place, and *phileo* is used forty-five times in the New Testament, in various forms.

It's difficult, though, for Susie to believe others like her just for herself. At birth, Susie's mother abandoned her. She learned later that her father was also her mother's father. An aunt and uncle took Susie into their family and reared her. But when she was nine years old, the uncle (who she knew as father) began molesting her. She also suffered a gang rape in her early teens. From these destructive intrusions, Susie lost all feelings of self-esteem. She needs continual approval and works hard to make others like her. This holds such control over her actions, she hardly recognizes the compulsive behavior to perform for approval. Susie is trying to believe that others do feel an unimpassioned and friendly affection for her.

If a Greek said something like, "Helen, I feel *agape* for you," that meant he felt a preciousness for her. We're told that our *agape* feelings express a love of esteem, evaluation, and approbation (approving). *Agape* is devoid of sensuousness. It gives the idea of prizing or recognizing worth in a loved person and is used in the New Testament 320 times. During Helen's growing-up years, she did not feel precious or esteemed. She felt her father was not present emotionally and that her mother remained too distant for a close relationship. As a result, she developed fuzzy self-pictures and could not believe she had valuable qualities. This distortion leads her into compulsive behaviors like buying clothes she does not need. While that helps her "feel" some control in her life, she struggles in trying to believe others see her as precious. The compulsive need for control makes submitting to and respecting her husband very difficult. At times she succeeds, but not always.

If a husband told his wife, "Myrna, honey, I feel very close to you and want to share my special *eros* feelings," that meant his sexual feelings were seeking satisfaction. *Eros* in itself is not a bad word. A most common definition has been "the attraction of one sex for the other."[2] But many misunderstand this attraction. Myrna suffered incest, beginning at age five, which devastated her emotionally for many years. Because of emotional wounds, she's had to learn to deal with the consequences of someone else's sin. After marriage, problems developed as she shared *eros* feelings with her husband. At times she could not respond to him since it brought back crippling memories. Myrna has worked hard to clear away emotional garbage in developing healthy feelings. She'd learning to distinguish between old memories and the reality of a healthy sexual relationship with her husband. That helps her develop a balanced view of mutual submission and a healthy marital relationship.

I've often wondered why *eros*, the Greek word for expressing romantic love, isn't used in the Bible. Here's a possibility. Since God created *eros*, He knew its strength and power could take control of our feeling and thinking. He also knew that *eros*, alone, cannot minister to or build us up like the other loves, since it has little to offer by itself. Thus, God gave us needed instruction regarding the other "three loves" in order to balance our attitude toward sexuality. Newspaper, magazine, and television stories of sexual violence show us the need for that *balance*. We've lost the four balanced loves once felt by Adam and Eve. While we can't change the whole world, we can change our world. Those of us who've suffered losses in these areas can choose to overcome those "losses."

We can examine the four loves and identify which areas in our lives need work. Then, we can *list our qualities* as God sees them. For instance, God sees me as precious; He esteems me; and He prizes me. I'm a person of worth; I have value; and I have gifts and abilities. Continue naming those qualities you recognize in yourself. (It's not important whether or not you "believe" others will agree with your list; rather, it's the way you see yourself.) Next, *read the list* every day. After a few weeks, ask yourself if you've started believing the list. Along with that, read Joel 1 and compare the four different locusts with the losses in your life. Claim God's promise of Joel 2:25 and believe you will begin to receive back those losses from long ago. Then, *thank God* for the qualities He's given you and let yourself "feel good" about those qualities.

Since parts of the Christian community have not developed an accepting, healthy view of sexual relations between marriage partners, feeling good about sexual feelings is hard for most females to do. Those of us who struggle with damaged emotions find it even harder to develop a healthy view of sex. We must understand that God's view for marital love, though, is waiting to be found in the Book of Solomon. Since God "feels good" about all He created, that means He approves of marital eros—His own creation. But in order for a wife to share herself freely, she must feel her husband loves, respects, and accepts her personhood.

Picture a pyramid divided horizontally from top to bottom into four sections. Eros sits at the top of the pyramid in the smallest space. Stergos occupies the second space from the top; phileo the third space. Agape covers the entire base of the pyramid. This is a Christian perspective on the proper balance of the four loves. Society would have us see the pyramid differently. Society bases all relationships on eros, and that is the main reason our divorce rate continues to soar. God designed agape as the basis for all relationships.

That's why couples need to learn how to live together in respect, balancing the four loves.

Gaining insight and perspective about my upbringing has helped me understand the love areas most damaged. Talking about my love limitations helps Dick and our children to understand me better. Their acceptance helps me feel prized and esteemed (*agape*). They, plus a few friends and relatives, share with me a friendly affection (*phileo*). Those feelings joined with the kindness and self-sacrifice I felt from Mom (*stergos*) are helping me develop more of a love balance. These "three loves" working together help us place ourselves willingly under the leadership of another, whether we're single or married. Yet, when both male and female live out a love balance, submitting finds few problems. Finding a balance isn't always easy, since we struggle with many limitations. But, living out a "love balance" will give us clearer discerning between submission, subservient, or subordinate choices.

Wives Can Choose Assertive Submission

The role of submission confuses both married and single. The contrasted differences between *phileo* and *agape* from Dr. Kenneth Wuest give us better discernment in this area.

Phileo: a love of pleasure	*Agape:* a love of preciousness
a love of delight	a love of esteem
a love of liking	a love of prizing
takes pleasure in a love	ascribes value to a
called out of the heart	love called out of the
by the apprehension of	heart by the apprehension
pleasurable qualities	of valuable qualities
in the [person] loved	in the [person] loved[3]

This contrast shows us that *phileo* does more taking, whereas *agape* does more giving. Thus, the more a wife can give approval *(agape)* to her husband, the more she can place herself willingly under his leadership. That's what the New Testament means when it says to revere him. But submitting is difficult to do at times, whether he's unloving or lovable. While learning to revere husbands, however, wives must let them know they *cannot accept* disrespect, abusiveness, or violence. This behavior goes against Christ's instructions to husbands. We're told that most out-of-control husbands want help; they just don't know how to ask for it. One way to show an abusive husband we care is to tell him, "While I love you, I'm losing respect for you. I'll be glad to go for counseling with you so our relationship can improve." That's one form of reverencing him—accepting his self-worth.

Wives, therefore, use the same "love" in submitting to their husbands' leadership as they use in submitting to Christ's leadership (Eph. 5:22). Just like misunderstanding what submission means can cause conflicts, the terms "assertive and aggressive" also confuse us. Assertiveness is a healthy behavior, having to do with affirming or exercising rights and responsibilities. We act with assertiveness when we affirm in confidence and act positively in opinion or judgment. On the other hand, aggressiveness is unhealthy behavior, having to do with hostility and transgressing on other's rights and responsibilities. We act with aggression when we take the initiative forward boldly—**not caring whose rights we trample on**. Because assertiveness and aggression are often confused, it's difficult for many males to accept a healthy assertiveness in females.

In looking at the Canon's pictures, we see that the Proverbs 31 woman lived out assertiveness. She created and accomplished much; yet, she affirmed much. She didn't trample on others. Her opinions and judgments of others were positive. A healthy assertiveness helped the woman *serve* her employees, customers, husband, and children. Also, she carried out her responsibilities well. Yet in her assertiveness, we see "pictures" of subjection to her husband's leadership. The woman's life complemented him, and he blessed and praised her (vv. 23,28). Her subjection, though, did not come from passive helplessness, but rather from strength of proven character. And wives today can live out an assertive submission through strength of proven character learned from living life.

Paul says character develops like this: "We also exult in our tribulations, knowing that tribulation brings about perseverance; and perseverance, proven character; and proven character, hope; and hope does not disappoint, because the love of God has been poured out within our hearts through the Holy Spirit" (Rom. 5:3-5). In talking about tribulations, Paul says we have opportunity to learn from and overcome life's difficult experiences through the Holy Spirit's power. Paul's insight gives us hope and motivation to turn from either aggression or quiet withdrawal to healthy assertiveness. In assertiveness, we can work on overcoming tribulations.

Some of us have "blocked" traumas and don't remember them. In contrast, some of us "cannot block" our memories; we remember everything. But either way, certain destructive behavior patterns developed. We learned to relate to the opposite sex in flirtatious ways, or we live only to drink, eat, shop, or use drugs. We carry around a caterpillar-like self-image rather than see ourselves as women of excellence. Many of us have worked hard trying to understand why we can't break these destructive behavior chains. We wonder why rage at times, for no obvious reason, surges up and spills over from our insides where we've stored bad memories.

In some instances, no one knew of our traumas, since we felt too ashamed and frightened to tell. For others, family members knew, but they felt too helpless and weak to help us. In some cases, others just didn't care. In trying to cope with our losses, many of us turned to the self-destructiveness of food, alcohol, drugs, or sex. Some use them all. But rather than destroy ourselves, we can learn healthy ways to help us turn from self-destructive behavior. **One choice** is to change distorted self-pictures and mind messages. Going through that process will build in the proven character Paul speaks of and help us see ourselves as persons of worth.

Character helps us feel good about ourselves so that we can discern assertively between submissive, subservient, and subordinate choices. Stored up anger and damaged love areas make submission difficult for us. In confusion, we sometimes choose to place ourselves in subservient or subordinate positions. But these only mimic submission and damage our self-esteem. Learning to prize and esteem ourselves with God's worth and value helps us learn to also prize and esteem others. That's repairing the damaged love area of *agape*. And, **another choice** that helps us go beyond damaged love areas to submission comes from releasing anger.

> Anger is not a primary emotion, but it is typically experienced as an almost automatic inner response to hurt, frustration, or fear. . . . Anger is physiological arousal. . . . Anger is the coiling of the spring in you, an intricately designed internal process which gives you the capacity to manage the difficult and threatening parts of your life. . . . How we use our anger is learned. . . . When we are angry, all the power of our person is available to us. We become equipped to act decisively in the interests of resolution and healing. Instead of creating trouble for ourselves, we can use anger to cope with the pain sources we encounter.[4]

Many believe that feelings of anger are sinful. Yet, feeling anger isn't wrong; rather, it's what we do with anger that can become destructive. Instead of repressing anger or exploding with it, we must learn how to express anger in healthy ways.

Dr. Neil Warren says he's found four different patterns which people use to express anger. Can you identify your pattern?

● Exploders. Those who pound desks, slap faces, cuss loudly, and give bitter put-downs. Usually without warning, they explode. What triggers the explosion isn't always the underlying cause of the anger.

● Somatizers. Those who have ulcers, high blood pressure, headaches, and pain of undetermined cause. Overeating and overweight problems, plus others, can be added to the list. They use their bodies (soma) for anger expression instead of other people or things.

● Self-punishers. Those who never "get" angry, but they're chronically depressed. They shred themselves to pieces for the smallest mistake, suffocating their spirit. They require much approval from others because it's so difficult for them to approve of themselves.

● Underhandlers. Those who use the "silent" treatment on others. When asked what's wrong, they usually say "nothing" and then shoot angry daggers through the air at their victims. This can be done through pouting and becoming bad losers or poor-me'ers. They find this method of anger expression safer than stating their anger and its cause.[5]

Identifying our anger patterns can help us discern between submission and compliance, the anger builder. Regardless of our anger expression patterns, we must learn to place anger where it belongs. If our anger comes from past unresolved emotional wounds, it belongs *on* those who violated our space, even if they no longer live. As contrary as it may sound, placing our anger where it belongs enables us to work through the forgiveness choices to forgive our offenders. After a few weeks, check your anger level to see if it's going down. As your anger fuse grows longer, you will feel more control in stressful situations. Using the brain-power forgiveness process helps us learn to discern between anger or compromise, another troublesome area causing problems for most of us.

Wife's Submission Respects Husband's Leadership

Compromise used to be a bad word for me. I confused Mom's compliant suffering when Daddy inflicted abusiveness on her with compromise. Added to that, I often heard preachers say "do not compromise with the devil." So the two drew me a confused, scrambled picture of compromise. Since then, I've learned that compromise has several meanings. The one I use says, "A settlement of differences by mutual concession." That's the *compromise* we need to use when working on relationships. Wounds we carry may have taken from us mind, emotion, or body privacy. Our losses were not of mutual consent, and they may have built in certain victimization behavior patterns. Therefore, it's important we learn to identify those patterns.

Looking carefully at our behavior shows us where we chose assertiveness over aggression or submission over compliance. Learning to negotiate concessions helps us choose between healthy anger and self-destructiveness. Healthy compromise also helps us choose submission over giving in to pressure, which encourages compliance. Listing our damaged emotions and choosing helpful compromises benefits us. Talking about those times when we made wrong choices will motivate us to think and pray before continuing in unhealthy behavior patterns. And while we persevere through these painful choices, a *proven character* develops. This character strength helps us submit assertively, whether it's mutual submission or marriage submission.

Character strength also helps wives respect their husbands. God designed some extensive, precise, and burdensome responsibilities for husbands. He does not explain why, but husbands are to care for their wives like Christ cares for His bride, the church. That seems to balance the burdensome responsibility of wives submitting to and respecting their husbands (Eph. 5:22,33). In that "balance," many things come under wives' responsibility.

• Accept your husband's gifts and abilities. That's difficult for some, particularly if his abilities appear inferior to someone else's. In our materialistic-minded society, it's easy to think green-eyed envious thoughts toward others, especially if salaries are larger or jobs carry more status. Envy even makes a showing in the church when someone else's husband appears more involved and concerned with "church work." Gifts like teaching or administrating seem to carry more glamor than the helping gifts or than maintaining church property. Controlling wives fail to see an equality in the marriage relationship when they don't honor their husbands' decisions. In not treating them as equals, they demasculinize them. Also, envying other husbands is wasted energy and hinders the acceptance of our husbands' gifts.

• Accept his personality. Society, including the church, places great importance on winsome, outgoing, macho males. If we judge by society's standards, God made some boo-boos, because He didn't blueprint all males with outgoing, effervescent personalities. If an outgoing, active, controlling female, therefore, marries a quiet, reserved, unambitious male, she acquires work—the work of accepting and approving his personality. The same principle holds true for a quiet, sweet, unassuming female who marries an outgoing, ambitious, winsome male. Many mothers do everything for sons instead of teaching them responsibilities as they do with their daughters. Many sons are not taught to clean their rooms, wash clothes, or cook; and they grow up dependent. Some wives complain about the helpless males, while others try to keep them dependent. But either way, unless a wife accepts her husband's personality, the marriage relationship suffers.

• Accept his limitations. Regardless of great abilities or personalities, husbands have limitations. Some see God's statement in Genesis 3:16 "he shall rule over you" as a prediction instead of an announcement. Since a husband has limitations, in that sense, he rules over his wife. Some men's stifling emotional losses come from verbal putdowns, a lack of loving approval, and other intrusions in childhood. Many men feel vocational limitations because they do not have enough education. Others compete with their wives rather than appreciate them. Through insecurities or jealousies, some stifle their wives instead of encouraging them to develop their gifts. At times, these limitations have to be lived with; at other times, wives' acceptance helps bring about change. While equal peers means equal responsibility, the limitations often lose their hold when wives give sincere praise, encouragement, and acceptance. We will discuss these principles in more depth in section 3.

Failure to give acceptance goes along with messages of strong vocal feminists. "Marriage has existed for the benefit of men and has been a legally sanctioned method of control over women. . . . The end of the institution of marriage is a necessary condition for the liberation of women. Therefore, it is important for us to encourage women to leave their husbands and not to live individually with men."[6] Matthew talked about such messages and the type of people who teach them. "Beware of false teachers who come disguised as harmless sheep, but are wolves and will tear you apart. You can detect them by the way they act, just as you can identify a tree by its fruit. Yes, the way to identify a tree or a person is by the kind of fruit produced" (7:15-16,20, TLB). Feminists' fruit destroys a husband-wife respect.

When a wife errs in listening to the wrong messages, her marriage relationship becomes stifled. It stops up; it cannot breathe or grow. Yet, it's easy for those of us who grew up in dysfunctional families to hear the wrong messages at times. Many of us had a poor family model; many did not have a foundation of trust built into our formative years. Some of us take our marriage model from society, while others have never worked through their wounds from emotional damage. As a result, we don't feel good about ourselves or our husbands. Attending seminars for inner growth, reading books on emotional healing,[7] and receiving professional counseling on how to go beyond our damaged emotions will help us.

We can look for groups or help start a group where women with damaged emotions are learning and growing. Helping ourselves learn, grow, and heal shows respect to our husbands as well. Because caring enough to work on the healing process shows we listen to the right messengers, love ourselves, love others, and love our husbands. When we learn to see ourselves with worth and value, we can then become more realistic with expectations. To get there, we need encouragement from new mind messages like, "You gave your husband a nice compliment. Thinking of him, remembering to pray for him, was giving of yourself. Accepting his explanations without question reveals you're beginning to trust. Taking care of your appearance shows you're feeling better about yourself." Such messages are not self-pride; they're needed self-esteem nurturing.

Conclusion

Please remember: Satan never stops trying to defeat us. Peter says the adversary "prowls around like a roaring lion looking for someone to devour" (1 Pet. 5:8, NIV). Satan's ravenous appetite never gets completely satisfied. That's why we must learn to distinguish between his attacks and God's standards.

Discerning between subservient, subordinate, and submissive gives us emotional stability. Using assertive submission instead of giving into pressure avoids compliance, the anger builder. Identifying anger patterns helps us begin to place anger where it belongs and work through forgiveness. That helps us work out helpful compromises with mutual concession. Healthy compromises help us work on relationships and choose assertiveness over aggression.

Those choices continue shredding cocoon strands in freeing the butterfly that wants to fly. This change reveals a special female self and helps wives place themselves willingly under their husbands' leadership—respecting and complementing them.

9 Serving: Complementing Husband's Life

Her life complements husband's life . . . "Her husband is known in the gates, When he sits among the elders of the land" (Prov. 31:23).

*W*omen are emotional, spiritual, and intellectual beings created in God's image. Females and males alike are persons of worth with open and equal access to God. "Then Jesus shouted out again, dismissed his spirit, and died. And look! The curtain secluding the Holiest Place in the Temple was split apart from top to bottom" (Matt. 27:50-51, TLB). Christ's death and resurrection and the ministry of the Holy Spirit have given **all** believers relationship with God the Father. It's taken a long time for many males to discern between Jewish traditions and God's design in this area. Yet, accepting females as equals—spiritual or intellectual—is difficult for some male egos. However, as men feel our loving *agape* rather than competitive attitudes, they feel accepted and valued by us. As they observe differences the Holy Spirit's power has made in us and our relationships with them, men are coming to see women in a different light.

Getting Beyond Ourselves

While we frequently use the word *intimacy*, we often don't understand what it means. To some, *intimacy* is no more than their latest sexual fantasy. Yet intimacy does not refer exclusively to sexual behavior and is missing from most marriages. We can participate in sexual behavior without feeling intimate. But we cannot "feel" intimacy without the vulnerability of trust. Nonetheless, those of us who suffer from emotional loss find that getting ourselves to *trust* is difficult. If our intrusions came from males, we think, *Since a male took advantage of me, I see all males as the same.* Inability to trust keeps us from trusting and risking in associations, friendships, and marriage. Some estimates place the divorce rate at 80 percent in marriages where one spouse suffered sexual violations in childhood. Until we work through it, emotional damage may keep us from submitting to and complementing our husband.

Paul shows us that relationships are important to God. That's why He developed such clear pictures in the Bible about dwelling together in peace and harmony. Since God designed sexuality, He's the "authority" believers should listen to—not society. But Janelle didn't listen. She had become so accustomed to saying "yes" at wrong times, she forgot to say "no" at right times. Years earlier she had said yes to wifing and and birthing children. While she liked those roles, there just wasn't enough money for family needs. The pastor needed a secretary, so Janelle decided she could help her church and family at the same time. She enjoyed helping and encouraging others. Since the pastor was experiencing much stress, he needed encouraging. But little by little, they confused their phileo feelings for eros and developed an unhealthy relationship. The *intimacy* they looked for did not develop.

Marsha tried to listen to God, but she hadn't felt much love from her parents. Now, her husband didn't seem quite as loving and understanding as she thought he would be. They argued constantly. She started attending counseling sessions with a recommended counselor who proved helpful and understanding with his insight and suggestions. After a number of weeks, he began to greet her with a hug. His hugs felt warm and comforting at first. Before she realized her trust had turned to gullability, it was too late. Their healthy agape feelings became overpowered with strong eros feelings, and an irreversible choice caused even greater emotional damage for Marsha.

In contrast, Laura did listen to and obey God. She's a tall, trim, attractive, strawberry blonde in her late twenties. Her husband works nights, leaving her alone with their two-year-old. One of her husband's friends always found time to compliment her appearance. One night when her husband was working, Bill, loaded with alcohol, knocked on the front door. Seeing him through a window, she refused to open the door. He left but later came back, yelling and pounding on the door. Again she ignored his obnoxious behavior, and soon he left. Frightened and crying, she telephoned her husband. He told Bill's parents, who talked to Bill about his behavior. He respects Laura because she chose a healthy behavior that showed she valued their marriage.

Of the three women, Laura complemented her husband's life and modeled the difference talked about in 2 Peter 1:1-9. Peter says that God gave believers everything pertaining to life and godliness through the knowledge of Christ. For balancing our behavior, we should add these seven qualities to our faith: moral excellence, knowledge, self-control, perseverance, godliness, brotherly kindness, and Christian love.

Moral excellence, virtue, is a change brought about by God's helper, the Paraclete. That change continues as we gain *knowledge* of Christ through Bible study. Using that knowledge helps us begin living out God's instructions.

Living what we learn helps us develop *self-control*. In living with self-control, *perseverance* is built into our lives. As we use perseverance in testings and trials, *godliness* becomes a way of living. From godly living we learn how to share a *brotherly kindness* (phileo). And through sharing brotherly kindness, we learn to feel *Christian love* (agape). Cultivating these seven qualities helps us avoid destructive choices that confuse phileo or agape love with eros feelings. They help us get beyond ourselves and are a good basis for developing intimacy.

Getting Beyond Phoniness

Phony means something fake or counterfeit; one who is not genuine. If you are married, how do you relate to your husband when he asks for your input and opinions? Do you keep up with what's going on in the world in order to carry on intelligent conversations, or have you delegated that to others? Without realizing it, maybe you've developed the "ring" of a phony. The author doesn't tell how, but the Proverbs 31 woman moved beyond any temptations she might have felt to relate from phoniness. She modeled how to live a trustworthy and faithful life, exercised self control, and extended acts of good will. She felt self-worth; she put God in proper perspective; she felt hope, expressed confidence, and developed character.

Her life produced a clear, precise picture that identified a life-style which influenced other people's opinions about her and complemented her husband's life. "Her husband is known in the gates, when he sits among the elders of the land" (v. 23). His identity impressed others at City Hall Elder Gate where he worked. Since he helped carry on the city's business, they surely attended social functions where others observed her behavior. Thus, she influenced her society through business dealings, social functions, and family affairs. She served with her personality, mind, will, emotions, and body—throughout a lifetime. Her service was genuine, not counterfeit. The Proverbs 31 woman was no phony. Some say God designed a "chain of command" where husbands rule by making all the decisions. Donald and Robbie Joy say they discovered that high price in learning to distinguish between mutual submission and a chain of command.

> Unilateral passivity will guarantee . . . the chain of command will work in any situation and for any cause. . . . Unilateral submission and its partner, unilateral use of power, present a quiet tragedy. In the early stages, the passive victim often retreats inward with some hostility or pouting. Eventually, as the intellectual energy atrophies from lack of use, a distinct price is paid in moral and mental rigor. . . . Many women have been reduced to a "childhood mentality" by the chain of command—[it] comes at a very high price.[1]

Mutual submission opens up serving; whereas, a chain of command "chains" serving. The wife who performs duties just to keep a husband happy or because society expects it doesn't complement him. Genuine serving needs to come from willingness. But we must discern well within our gifts, time, energy, and budgets. Only wives whose husbands see them with spiritual and intellectual equality, though, have the "space" for complementary lives.

Ruth Graham fits into that category. For over forty years Ruth has served through praying, caring for her children, speaking to women's groups, counseling with women, helping in various ways during crusades, and writing several books. From a distance I've watched her perform these functions. One night over thirty years ago Joan Winmill Brown told me of Ruth's influence in her life. During the crusade in London she counseled with Joan. Besides the clear scriptural truths, Ruth's winsome personality helped Joan choose Christ. When my four children were young, I thought often of Ruth and her five. The heavy responsibility of caring for them with Billy gone so much encouraged me to keep going.

Patricia Gundry fits into that category. Many know Pat as a mother, author, and lecturer. With the publication of *Woman Be Free* in 1977, she became a household name. Those who agreed with Pat's views loved her; those who disagreed were not so kind. Yet through loving care, Pat balanced the time and energy spent in writing and speaking with fulfilling commitments to her husband and children. Her husband, Stan, encourages the use of her gifts and abilities. Pat gives us a balanced view of serving God by serving others.

Beverly LaHaye also fits into that category. For many years she served through parenting her four children, speaking to women's groups, counseling women, and helping Dr. LaHaye during many years in the pastorate. She has authored several books. And in 1979, she and other women founded Concerned Women for America (CWA). This conservative group gives a choice to women who do not agree with the National Organization for Women (NOW) and other radical feminist groups. I've watched Beverly challenge believers to fight together against abortion, child abuse, divorce, pornography, and many other issues. She models well how to serve.

Phyllis Schlafly, too, fits into the category. She worked her way through college and graduate school, birthed and reared six children, and wrote nine books. She's a member of the bar and ran for Congress twice. She's been a syndicated columnist and television commentator. Phyllis started Eagle Forum, a conservative women's group lobbying for pro-family issues. In working to end abortion and pornography, Eagle Forum also battles for textbook content quality. Phyllis started "STOP ERA" in 1972, which played a large part in keeping ERA from passing in Illinois. But, commitment to her six children and lawyer-husband, John, remained top priority. During the last fourteen years, watching Phyllis use her gifts and energy, I've been challenged to use mine. She models a balanced serving.

These women don't represent serving phonies. They aren't fake or counterfeit; they're genuine. They use their God-given gifts and abilities to help others. And in so doing, their lives complement their husbands' lives. When males and females come to understand the biblical model of submission, they are freed from society's stereotypes. We submit to Christ's lordship and submit mutually to each other. Females are freed to develop their special female selves; males are freed from society's burdensome expectations of the "macho" male. In addition, when husbands give wives understanding acceptance, wives are freed to serve.

Developing a Serving Philosophy

Philosophy holds many meanings. But the definition that fits with serving says, "It's a system of principles for guidance in practical affairs and a wise composure in dealing with problems." God designed a system of principles (1 Cor. 12) which gives wise counsel in dealing with the problems of serving. In this chapter, Paul deals with spiritual gifts and their use. He gives us two distinctions regarding the importance of gifts and ministry.

Paul says, "There are varieties of gifts, ministries, and effects but the same God is over all—making them into one Body. God has placed in the Body these varieties just as He desired, and none can say 'I have no need of you' " (v. 4, author). We, like our gifts, share equally in importance; even though we are unique in difference. That difference rests on our physical power, body builds, personalities, body functions, interests, and emotions; not, as some suggest, on spiritual or intellectual power. Similarly, spiritual gifts, such as administration, apostleship, compassion, discernment, evangelism, exhortation, faith, giving, aid to others, healing, helps, miracles, prophecy, teaching, tongues, tongues interpretation, serving, shepherding, word of knowledge, and word of wisdom for doing His work.

God gave those gifts to individuals in the church for a purpose. "God's people will be equipped to do better work for him, building up the church, the body of Christ, to a position of strength and maturity; until finally we all believe alike about our salvation and about our Savior, God's Son, and all become full-grown in the Lord—yes, to the point of being filled full with Christ" (Eph. 4:12-13, TLB). Dr. James Dobson, founder/president of Focus on the Family, conducted a study that shows weak self-esteem remains females' number one problem. The proof of that study comes from most of us having a "caterpillar-like" self-image. We don't believe that our gifts are needed, like others', for serving.

The church may contribute to the way we feel about our gifts. Since our gifts are sometimes overlooked and unused, we feel "devalued" by those who mean so much to us. Christ has called each of us to discover and use our gifts. In serving others we fell better about ourselves. When we follow the Holy

Spirit's guidance in finding ways to serve, we learn the importance of our spiritual gifts.

Paul second distinction has often been overlooked. As a result, many of us do not receive the support and encouragement we need. "And if one member suffers, all the members suffer with it; if one member is honored, all the members rejoice with it" (1 Cor. 12:26). The church seems to do well with *honoring* others, a macho football player or other type of celebrity. But, many church members fail to *suffer* emotionally with the hurting and wounded; they don't want to identify with them. Or what about those of us who feel "loss" from an imbalance in mutual submission. We need believers who will come alongside of us and help us bear our burdens (Gal. 6:2).

There are males, however, who have (through mutual submission) learned from suffering and suffering with others. Charles Swindoll writes,

> I have found great help from two truths God gave me . . . when I was bombarded with a series of unexpected and unfair blows (from my perspective). . . . **Nothing touches me that has not passed through the hands of my heavenly Father. . . . Everything I endure is designed to prepare me for serving others more effectively. . . .** Things may not be logical and fair, but when God is directing the events of our lives, they are right. Even when we suffer the painful consequences of serving others.[2]

Paul's statement about suffering reveals a need for the church to play "catch-up." Believers must give members who suffer and hurt a place *equal to* honoring the celebrities.

> On the contrary, it is much truer that members of the body which seem to be weaker are necessary; and those members of the body, which we deem less honorable, on these we bestow more abundant honor. . . . But God has so composed the body, giving more abundant honor to that member which lacked, that there should be no division in the body, but that the members should have the same care for one another (1 Cor. 12:22-25).

For centuries believers have associated this distinction with our gift usage only. We must broaden this application to include the weaker (hurting) body members.

Hurting body members seem weaker and less honorable to those who've either denied their wounds or have never suffered pain. They don't understand why the wounded can't "just pray and leave everything with God." They've never felt a pain from cutting, name-calling. They've never felt flesh bruised or broken from beating. They don't know the heavy burden of depression. They've not faced personal tragedy--the grief of losing a loved one, the pain of rebellious children. They don't see life as "hopeless" like berated, helpless, battered seniors.

Yes, they have problems understanding others' excruciating and hard-to-manage emotional pain. And yet, "understanding" isn't the key to suffering with hurting body members. *Believing* they hurt and *reaching out* to them in useful, meaningful ways is the key. Loving, caring leaders in the body of Christ need to "bestow more abundant honor" on the "weaker" and see them as important. For we are weaker in the sense of burdensome secrets we carry with us and need healing strength. We are weaker in the sense that we need nurturing *stergos*, *phileo*, and *agape* love. When "caring" nonhurting members begin to treat hurting and wounded members the same as celebrities, healing will happen. **Healed members can, in turn, serve others.**

God seems to have created females with more of His sensitivity than males. This doesn't mean that males are insensitive. But since God placed on males the heavy burden of protecting, purifying, preserving, and providing for females (Eph. 5:23-29), He knew society would need balance with sensitive nurture. Now that barriers to females in the work place are coming down, more women are serving in strategic positions. The church also needs our uniqueness and balance, since both sexes were created as equal, intelligent beings of worth. Wives freed to serve honor and complement their husbands. Serving brings joy, gives grace, and shares love. "Joy is the enjoyment of being enjoyed. Grace is the acceptance of being accepted. Love is seeing another as precious, just as you know yourself to be precious."[3] That serving philosophy frees wives to complement their husbands' lives and produce a serving phenomena.

Using the Serving Phenomena

"To measure your own worth or to feel yourself a person of worth only when the respect is coming in, is giving others far too much power. . . . To learn is to change. To learn is integrative, not addictive, so all real learning involves a change of one's core self. . . . Change is possible."[4] Constructive change in attitudes toward weaker body members will come through the phenomena, an exceedingly remarkable thing or personage, of serving. Here are three ways to "bestow more abundant honor" through serving the weaker, hurting body members.

Become more creative in ministry and outreach. At Whittier Area Baptist Fellowship, many groups give honor to the hurting. Together Learning to Control Cancer reaches out to those diagnosed with cancer. Overcomers helps those with alcohol or drug dependencies, as well as family members. New Hope works with children of alcohol-dependent patients. Grief Recovery helps those who have lost loved ones. Free to be Thin works with those trying to lose weight by eating in a better way. S.M.I.L.E.S. helps those who've suffered sexual abuse. New Beginnings helps those turning from homosexuality. Inner development helps those with eating disorders. S-Anon works with sexual addiction. Insight helps those with eye loss. Single Focus encourages those over thirty. Unwed mothers, latchkey children, meals for seniors, and mentally and physical handicapped persons are only a few of the endless opportunities for "serving." Explore your ministry opportunities through your church or other local agencies which rely on the work of volunteers.

Don't label one family life-style as superior to others. The nuclear family (father—salary maker, mother—homemaker, children—live-in dependents) makes up only 13 percent of today's society. Singles, with or without children, make up 37 percent. Couples, no children, make up 23 percent. Dual salary-maker families and all else make up 27 percent. Those figures show that the "nuclear family" known before the sixties no longer exists.[5] Today's church can continue in "denial" or she can accept "reality" to create constructive change.

Caring, constructive change from *agape* love heals the hurting. *Healing* the "nuclear family" will help it emerge again—healthier, stronger, happier—to live out God's design for families. However, almost one-half (45.2 percent) of women are single, with a large percent being single parents, and they need help. "For the worker is worthy of his [her] keep" (Matt. 10:10, NIV). Since our intelligence and abilities equal that of males', we need the same "keep" for the same work. Christian fathers need to remember God's fathering model in John 5 and Paul's instructions. "But if anyone does not provide for his own, especially for those of his household, he has denied the faith, and is worse than an unbeliever" (1 Tim. 5:8).

Those who have more discretionary money than time can give to benevolent funds for the needs of families in crisis. Many churches already have such funds established. In other cases, community organizations offer avenues to help others. A long list of ways to help others assist themselves awaits creative use. Retired men or women can use time, energy, and ingenuity in caring for children and training teens. Retirees with the skill can help others fix broken appliances, leaking pipes, or minor car problems. In God's family, there are no unimportant people; there's no room for totem-pole importance. We may be young or old; attractive or unattractive; or rich, poor, or in-between. We may be male or female and married or single. But all believers are "equal in value to."

Encourage and make use of gifts.[6] Mutual submission for believers is God's design that helps both sexes respect and accept each other. "And be subject to one another in the fear of Christ" (Eph. 5:21). That opens the door for gift-usage or appreciation between the sexes.

Women who discern well in their gifts, time, energy, and budgets can give much to Christ's body. In carrying out their responsibilities, they develop wise serving skills that others may lack. Paul says older women should train younger women for living life; they should urge young men to behave carefully and live seriously (Titus 2:4-6). Their teaching gifts, however, aren't used in many churches, quite the opposite. Most mature women (many think "over thirty" is old) are quietly but quickly shuffled aside. Some can stuff envelopes or lick stamps for pastor's letters. A few may be asked to make coffee at church socials, but not to *train* young women or *teach* young men who are over eighteen.

Women teach men in universities, trade schools, colleges, high schools, industries, corporations, hospitals, law schools, medical schools, and politics. However, in some churches women aren't allowed to teach men. Wise instruction, whether from males or females, is vital to the growth of believers.

Various books are available in church libraries or bookstores teaching how to discern our gifts. Reading such material helps us identify gifts that God wants used. Each believer has one or more of these gifts, which multiplies to thousands and thousands. If females don't use their gifts, about half of those are lost or remain undeveloped.

The Lord used several people and their input to guide me through the difficult maze of discerning and developing gifts. Dr. Dan Baumann's insight regarding this process gave me explicit help. He suggests using five E's based on 1 Corinthians 12 and Ephesians 4. **Explore** the possibilities. Talk with others and read books regarding interests. **Experiment** with many possibilities. Work with as many different interests as possible. **Examine** feelings regarding success or lack of success. Enjoyment in working with gifts should increase. **Evaluate** effectiveness in working with gifts. Determine if helpful results are taking place. **Expect** confirmation from the body. Ask for others' opinions regarding results from using particular gifts.[7] Although this process takes many, many months, these five E's will help those who persevere.

Understand more clearly the mutual submission between husbands and wives. Our first choice is submitting ourselves to Christ's leadership. That choice affects all our decisions. Submitting ourselves to Christ helps us submit to others' leadership, regardless of sexual difference, especially, if we see submission as serving. A serving attitude nurtures others' self-esteem, just like it nurtures ours. Many men, though, don't understand the role of mutual submission and believe it negates their headship.

A husband living out mutual submission enhances and strengthens his marriage relationship. He frees his wife to serve under her discretion. Instead of *head* signifying power or authority, as chain of command advocates suggest, it means *responsibility*—giving up self; being protector, purifier, preserver, lover, and provider; leaving parents; and cleaving to wife. Dr. Donald Joy likens the head to a periscope that locates trouble, scouts terrain, and cares for the person's safety. He gives us five descriptions of the "head" and its choices.

● The head is an "identity point" for the total person. Along with that identity goes the responsibility for every area of life.

- The head is an "entry point" for nourishment. That's where responsibility for proper nourishment decisions rest—which kinds of food, kinds of drinks, and types of medication.
- The head "articulates." Responsibility for communicating wants, hopes, desire, needs, and wishes rests on the head. It must find ways to carry out those assignments.
- The head is "vulnerable." Responsibility for building trust, friendships, relationships, commitments, faithfulness, loyalty, and kindness falls on the head. Carrying them out is hard work.
- The head is "naked." Here, responsibility is very heavy. Openness and transparency are difficult for most males. Instead of sharing in openness they seem to "cover up" automatically. Healthy openness develops only from hard work.[8]

From those five descriptions, we see that *head* signifies responsibility—not authority or power, but great responsibility. And in order for that responsibility to be accomplished, the head needs help. A head needs help from its "body." A head can't walk, run, jump, leap, dance, ride a horse, drive a car, or throw a football. It can't put arms around another, wipe away tears, or wash its hair or face. It can't feed its mouth, drink fluid, take medication, blow its nose, or comb its hair. Both head and body must "team together" to accomplish responsibilities given the head. Cooperation, interdependence, mutual submission, and equality in need and importance are necessary. A head needs a body, and a body needs a head; God designed them to complement each other.

Similarly, God designed husbands and wives to complement each other; at the same time, they share unique differences. Another way to say that is,

> The marriage we long for is one in which together we can be sure of the best decisions, the fullest set of options, the most balanced perspective, the best-resourced effort. Such a marriage means absolute trust, honesty, integrity, and mutual respect. It means that neither of us alone is always right, always strong, always the leader, or always the follower. But together we can face anything.[9]

That kind of serving gives principles for guidance in practical affairs and a wise composure in dealing with problems. It helps wives avoid the phoniness of pretense so they can develop their gifts. It removes from husbands the burden of macho performance and frees wives to serve in ways that complement their husbands. Those principles will move couples or singles toward a serving philosophy and will free them to live out God's design for mutual submission. Seeing submission from God's perspective gives us **serving power** to develop reliable relational skills.

3 *Developing Sensible Relational Skills*

*F*ive sisters and four brothers preceded me. One of the girls, Mom and Daddy's third child, died from diphtheria at age five. So I grew up with the distinct position of the ninth and youngest child. Growing up in a large family, I learned much about relationships—both bad and good. Much of the "fun" my older brothers and sisters experienced, I missed. When I was only two my oldest brother married. Three years later, he and another brother found themselves in the middle of World War II. Saying "good-bye" through tears, I wondered if I would ever see them again.

That year Oklahoma passed a new school law. It declared that children becoming six before a spring semester could begin school the previous fall. Since we didn't have kindergarten, I began first grade at age five. For transportation from the farm to school, we rode in a large, yellow Ford school bus. I had never ridden in a bus. Outside, cool September air blew against the bus windows. Inside, warm breath from talking children blew against the windows. Soon, a misty fog covered all the windows, hiding trees and fence posts alongside the dirt road. Even though my older brothers and sisters rode with me, I felt closed in with a bus full of strangers because I couldn't see out the windows. I felt frightened and bewildered that first morning.

When we arrived at school, one sister took me to my room and said, "Your teacher's name is Mrs. Smith." Then she went to her class, leaving me with a roomful of first-graders and my teacher—all strangers. I felt all alone.

A tear rolled down my cheek opening a floodgate of uncontrollable loud sobs. Mrs. Smith stood me on her desk and told me to stop crying or she would spank me. The possibility of a spanking frightened me, and I cried even harder. I supposed she decided her threat didn't work because she told me to sit at my desk. Sitting on my desk seat felt much safer than standing on top of her desk. She began talking with the class and soon turned her back to me. I slipped quietly from my desk and walked quickly down a hallway to find my sister's classroom. After finding her, she told me I should go back to my class. But I said, "No! I'm going to stay with you. I don't like that teacher." Soon, though, her teacher saw me and took me back to my classroom and Mrs. Smith.

After a few weeks, my feelings toward Mrs. Smith changed; I began to like her. In fact, I remember her as one of my favorite teachers. It's just that "change" and "new experiences" have never come easy for me. Therefore, emotional trauma played a large part in my growing-up years. Struggling with feelings of ugly "caterpillar" self-esteem, guilt, and depression made relating to others difficult at times. Relationships with many levels of closeness levels made up my life. Relational skills at their best, worst, and in between have played a significant role in those relationships.

10 Being Trustworthy and Living Faithfully

She is trustworthy and lives faithfully . . . "The heart of her husband trusts in her, And he will have no lack of gain. . . . She does him good and not evil All the days of her life" (Prov. 31:11-12).

We usually think of living faithfully as something marriage partners are supposed to do. That's God's standard. However, we also need faithfulness in all our relationships. We can recognize faithfulness in others' strict performance of duty, unswerving devotion, and loyalty to promises. Performance of duty and loyalty to promises have kept many not-so-qualified employees on their jobs, because most employers want "faithful" employees. We also need trustworthy friends who are faithful, reliable, and worthy of confidence and trust. "How sweet it is" dealing with individuals whose life patterns show they are worthy of trust or confidence. On the other hand, "How sour it is" dealing with individuals whom we cannot trust. Their unreliability causes us emotional headaches.

An old adage says, "Your actions speak louder than your words." That may mean we say one thing, yet do another. Such behavior, though, didn't describe the Proverbs 31 woman. Verses 11 and 12 show that she related in a trustworthy manner and lived faithfully. "The heart of her husband trusts in her. . . . She does him good and not evil All the days of her life." Her husband and others could trust her to keep promises, perform duties, and live reliably.

The author doesn't say how she developed these qualities. But a sensitive conscience could have been the starting place. George Washington is once supposed to have said, "Labour to keep alive in your breast that little spark of celestial fire, called conscience." The Bible warns about searing (making callous or insensitive) our conscience. When we sear our conscience, we're limiting the Holy Spirit's power. As a result, we become insensitive to His voice. Then we and others suffer because of resulting sin.

Peter said our lives are enhanced by "keep[ing] a clear conscience, so that those who speak maliciously against [our] good behavior in Christ may be ashamed of their slander. It is better, if it is God's will, to suffer for doing good than for doing evil" (1 Pet. 3:16-17, NIV). Often, people misunderstand and question our motives. Such times prove discouraging and frustrating. Nonetheless, it's better to suffer from living out God's truths than limit the Holy Spirit's power. While failing to live out God's truths can result in wrong decisions and rotten attitudes, living out His truths results in trustworthiness and faithfulness. Hard work, commitment, and perseverance are required to develop these qualities, which are all connected to good listening skills.

Learning How to Listen

Learning good listening skills may prove difficult for us who did not experience others listening to us during our formative years. While listening and hearing are often interchanged, they play different roles. Listening means more than hearing. Listening is giving close attention in order to hear or to give ear. At times, it's helpful to look at the speaker's lips; other times, at the speaker's eyes. Concentrating on both help us give better and closer attention to the speaker's words.

Hearing is different from listening. It has to do with the act of perceiving sound, the faculty or sense through which sound gets perceived. The ear receives auditory impressions and transmits them to our brain. Dr. Paul Swets describes the process like this. "The outer ear, sculptured like a sound trumpet, catches sound waves and guides them into the auditory canal. . . . Waves vibrate the eardrum sending vibrations across three bones of the middle ear moving the innermost bone in and out. Then a fluid translates sound waves into nerve impulses and stimulates nerves to send messages to the hearing center in the brain."[1] Our ears are fantastic, God-designed mechanisms.

When we listen to someone, we chose between perceptive and passive listening. Perceptive listening involves identifying and understanding feelings, attitudes, or meanings behind others' sounds, words, and messages. Passive listening involves only the sounds, words, and messages without trying to identify or understand others' feelings, attitudes, and meanings. Passive listening can miss the real meaning behind spoken words, and cause misunderstandings. The following suggestions can help us become active listeners:

(1) Listen for ideas and feelings behind spoken words, but don't make assumptions. Most of us hide our true feelings, fearing others will laugh at us or reject us. The listener, then, needs to listen carefully and with confidentiality. Feeling trust in relationships frees us to share our thoughts and feelings. Also, an atmosphere of loving acceptance must cover the conversations. *Acceptance* does not necessarily mean approving someone's behavior. It means the listener sees and relates to others as individuals of worth.

(2) Display a desire to hear what the speaker is saying. Eye contact during conversation helps the speaker feel listened to, cared for, and important. Often listeners look at others, pick their nails, or stare at the floor rather than the speaker. This can embarrass and frustrate the one talking. So while you look at a person, listen for attitudes, feelings, or meanings behind the spoken words. That will help you understand more clearly what the speaker is trying to communicate.

(3) Repeat, clarify, or feed back some details. Clarifying or repeating helps avoid making quick judgments and assures the speaker someone is listening. Use *door openers* like, "Here's what I hear you saying," or "That's interesting, tell me more," or "It sounds like you're angry with me." Nonjudgmental feedback can help us avoid assuming or criticizing. It gives opportunity for a person to explain her viewpoint and give clear information to the listener. This increases mutual understanding between speaker and listener.[2]

Developing perceptive listening is important for all relationships, even friends. "The staying power of a friend's listening ear can help restore perspective to what may be little more than mass confusion."[3] I've experienced a friend's listening ear during mass confusion. Dick left on a business trip, and my daughter, Faith, moved to Washington, D. C., for a semester. My daughter, Lynn, moved into an apartment; my son, Richard, moved away to college; and, my son, James, went into high school. All these events happened within a few days of each other, leaving my emotions open and raw.

After Dick left, Lynn and I had an argument. When Richard agreed with her, I felt great rejection. Since I felt so much rejection from my father in my teens, it's hard for me to cope with rejection. I slipped into a depression and wouldn't leave my bedroom or talk with my children. The next day, I called my friend Suzanne and asked her to come talk with me. She spent two hours mostly listening to me. I don't remember much of what we talked about, but I remember her *perceptive* listening. She identified with and understood my feelings of rejection. Her understanding and care nurtured my self-esteem.

When Suzanne left, I felt strong enough to talk with my children about the argument. We talked through the misunderstanding and restored our relationship. That took away my feelings of rejection, and the depression disappeared. Through looking for feelings, attitudes, and meanings behind spoken words, my friend accepted me. Because she listened to me rather than giving advice or criticism, I felt cared for and loved.

Paul, in Galatians, gives us a dual role for relationships. "Share each other's troubles and problems, and so obey our Lord's command. If anyone thinks [she] is too great to stoop to this, [she] is fooling [herself]. . . . [In addition] Each of us must bear some faults and burdens of [our] own. For none of us is perfect!" (6:2-3,5, TLB). Through perceptive listening, we nurture others' self-esteem, and they nurture our self-esteem.

Learning When to Talk

Although we often interchange the words *communicating* and *talking*, they differ in meaning. *Communication* is the imparting or interchange of information, thoughts, or opinions by speech, writing, or signs. Whereas, *talking* means uttering words in exchanging or expressing thoughts. Each of us has probably talked, at least one time, and wished later that we had listened instead. But just like we can learn *how* to listen, we can also learn *when* to talk.

One frustration involved with talking comes from this.

> Instead of creating understanding and closeness, our words sometimes produce the very opposite effect. . . . We hurt another's feelings, provoke anger, create psychological distance even when . . . we . . . desire . . . understanding, intimacy, and companionship. . . . Gradually even the quantity of conversation becomes . . . the agony of cold silence.[4]

We don't always say what we mean or mean what we say; therefore, our words sometimes produce the opposite effect from what we intended. We learned poor communication skills from significant others. Thus, we often fail to communicate understanding in our conversations. That's why poor communication skills harm interpersonal relationships.

Yet, we aren't computers capable of doing only what others programmed us to do. Paul reminds, "We can do all things through Christ who strengthens us" (Phil. 4:13, author). We can reprogram poor communication skills through identifying their causes. The following are three bad-root causes. Weeding them out and planting good roots will help us learn when to talk.

Lack of Sensitivity. For many of us, this learned behavior developed from others' unwanted intrusions. Those losses built fears of rejection, losing emotional control, and criticism. Many of us deny these fears rather than own them; therefore, we limit our communications and harm our relationships. Growing up not feeling others were sensitive to our needs limits our sensitivity to others' needs. Identifying this bad root motivates us to go through the "weeding out" process. Learning to "see" ourselves as persons of worth helps us move beyond unhealthy fears or insensitivity.

Tapes of Criticism. Receiving harsh criticism during childhood creates negative mind-messages. During childhood, most of us heard, "Sticks and stones may break my bones but names can never hurt me." Yet, name-calling and criticism can damage our self-identity; these messages play back often in our thoughts and words. We can reprogram those distortions with new messages that say, "God loves and cares for me. I'm not stupid or lazy or inferior; I'm a person of worth. I can get beyond emotional struggles." Believing those messages builds a healthy self-identity. They help free us from anger and inferiority and help us relate to others without criticism.

Reading Others' Minds. When parents second-guess children's motives rather than ask for reasons, children build judgmental attitudes toward themselves and others. False accusations damage a child's sense of self-esteem. Faye experienced that damage. She told me, "Often, when I was growing up, others accused me rather than let me express my feelings and opinions. This made me feel very inadequate, and I lost the courage to express my ideas or opinions." Now, she struggles to make decisions and express her opinions.

To help Faye and each of us feel confidence, Dr. Paul Swets has designed four essential elements for **talk**. We can use them to develop interesting conversation topics and avoid killing our conversations.

> Think before talking; consider what will interest the other person.
> Assert yourself; share your deeper thoughts or feelings.
> Listen intently; pick up on clues to deeper meaning for warmth, significance, or humor.
> Know what to talk about; look for knowledge to expand your vision of the world and others.[5]

Using these elements will help us "weed out" poor communication skills. They will teach us both how to listen and when to talk. In chapter 15, we'll discuss how to control the tongue.

Learning to Identify Obstacles That Hinder Relationships

Developing our inner woman requires insight, commitment, and hard work. Although we can't get away from the work, we must remember that "hard work" does not gain for us feelings of self-worth. Hard work, however, nurtures our feelings of self-esteem. When we feel good about ourselves, our relationships with others are enhanced. This process becomes more labored when significant others did not follow God's standards. When parents, teachers, religious leaders, or others fail to relate in trustworthiness to children under their care, they hinder the development of those little ones. Thus, adults who do not live trustworthy lives disappoint and confuse children and teens who are trying to develop stable relational skills.

The Canon produces a clear picture about the consequences of adults' sins: "The Lord . . . [punishes] the children for the sin of the fathers to the third and fourth generation" (Ex. 20:5, NIV). Children usually take on their parents' behavior—both the good and the bad. Therefore, even young children observe whether adults are worthy of trust.

We usually aren't aware of mimicking our parents' patterns until someone brings this to our attention. For example, Mom and Daddy did not give us affectionate hugs or kisses. They did not give us praise. As each of my children reached the toddler age, I automatically stopped giving them hugs and kisses. I did not notice this until I saw that my sister-in-law still hugged and kissed her children, even though they were teenagers. Her healthy behavior said to me, "Hey, Jane, you can change that habit of neglect and rebuild a pattern of showing healthy affection to your children."

We aren't told how she managed, but the Proverbs 31 woman moved beyond any obstacles that might have stopped her from developing healthy relationships. "She does him good and not evil all the days of her life" (v. 12). Employees, business associates, friends, and family members found her to be a reliable, trustworthy person. These qualities do not describe everyone; there are many obstacles that keep us from developing healthy relationships.

Breaking trust, *one obstacle*, does what it says—breaks trust or confidence in something or someone. The "inner child" (our seat of feelings) feels inquisitiveness, spontaneity, curiosity, adventuresomeness, and trust. If these feelings are damaged, they travel with us into adulthood and stay until we gain enough insight and perspective to go beyond them. Until we can see ourselves as *that person of worth God created*, the damaged "inner child" has trouble trusting others and coping with problems.

Betty, physically traumatized by her mother, still finds it difficult to establish trust in relationships. That's why she left her husband and little girls. Helen, who suffered verbal intrusions, acted out behavior like bulimia (gorging with food then vomiting to avoid weight gain) and stealing clothes. Although she's gained insight into those behavior patterns, Helen still finds it difficult to give devotion to others. Janelle grew up with a father who could not give her acceptance, healthy affection, or honest praise. Her husband of ten years relates to her in the same way. So, after an excellent teaching record spanning twenty years, Janelle began losing control of herself and her classroom. She turned to alcohol to cope with stress; she gained sixty pounds and started ignoring her appearance and hygiene. These stories show us how emotional loss can hinder us in developing healthy relational skills.

Telling lies, *another obstacle* hindering relationships, is intentional untruthfulness. The "inner parent" (our storehouse) stores in our mind everything learned or experienced, including the intrusion of being lied to. When significant others lie to children, they're saying, "You're not worthy of trust." Being great imitators, they take on their parents' destructive behavior without realizing the devastating consequences. They also tend to blame themselves for their parents' lying. "Mom and Dad never do what they say. I must not be good enough for them to respect; I'm pretty awful." To cover up their guilt feelings, many develop the lying habit. It seems like coping with life becomes easier when creating reality through lying.

Therefore, lying about popularity, accomplishments, and possessions seems OK. In addition, pressure for peer acceptance becomes very real for most teens. Teens, especially those with weak self-identity, look to others for acceptance and approval. What their peers think of them means more than what their parents think. Teens want to hear peers say, "You're OK." They often conform to peer pressure although the behavior may differ from their own or their parents' standards. That places self-identity on a false basis, not on reality. For awhile, lies may give feelings of importance or worth and seem to ease reality's painful feelings, at least until the "lying habit" catches up with them.

Jackie lied so much it became difficult for her to distinguish reality from fantasy. Her "inner parent" was damaged in her formative years. Soon after becoming a Christian, she discovered the "lying habit" still controlled her. She realized this behavior needed reprogramming. Days later, she told another lie. Jackie prayed for strength and courage to admit her lie to the offended person. That proved difficult and humbling, but the apology made her strong for the next time. Months of studying God's Word, apologizing, and receiving others' acceptance and forgiveness enabled her to reprogram the "lying habit."

Stealing, *a third obstacle* hindering trustworthiness, is taking away something dishonestly. Like lying, stealing is a learned behavior. The "inner adult" (a seat of choice) helps us learn to evaluate and test reality. In other words, the "inner adult" influences our decisions. When parents neglect to build meaningful interrelations with their children, they fail to build responsible choices into them. This neglect becomes emotional abuse and creates feelings of worthlessness in their children; the children, then, feel unimportant and unloved. In filling these deep emotional holes, they often turn to stealing. If they can't have their parent's *love*, they can get *things*—even if they have to steal them. In a sense, "things" represent the love they don't receive from their parents.

Neglected by her parents, Jamie never experienced a meaningful parent-child relationship. Consequently, her "inner adult" didn't learn responsible choice-making. She began stealing in the second grade. When she acted out negative behavior, the teacher made her stay indoors during recess. Her creative mind remembered the other children's lunch money. She went to each desk and took the money so she could buy "things" for herself. Since she didn't receive loving acceptance from her parents, the "inner adult" (a seat of choice) was damaged. Since she didn't feel her parents' approval, "things" represented approval to her; and having money to buy "things" made her feel important. While it proved a poor substitute for her love needs, stealing became a way of life.

Stealing goes on in every area of life—involving both Christians and non-Christians. Employers lose millions of dollars each year through employees taking office supplies without permission. Each year, thousands get their self-identity stolen when others lie about their character. Many believers steal from God through buying unneeded things instead of giving a tithe. Stealing, a learned behavior, influences every area of society. After becoming a believer, Jamie realized she needed to develop responsible "choices." She decided to reprogram her learned behavior of stealing. She memorized Scripture, reprogramming her mind to think like Christ. As a result, over a period of time she was able to change her behavior from stealing to making responsible choices. She became trustworthy and her changed behavior enhanced her relationships.

Through God's love and power we can change self-destructive behavior. When broken trust or habitual lying or uncontrolled stealing keep us from healthy relationships, like the Proverbs 31 woman, we can learn to live trustworthy and faithful lives.

Learning to Be Trustworthy and Live Faithfully

Living faithfully and being trustworthy are similar. Both require perseverance and commitment; they do not just happen. Faithful people are strict in performance of duty, unswervingly devoted, and loyal to promises. Trustworthy people are reliable. These two qualities are essential to all relationships. Are you sometimes unfaithful in responsibilities? Do you work or live with those who sometimes choose unfaithfulness? Those behaviors damage relationships. Many obstacles can hinder us from being trustworthy and living faithfully; we will only focus on three. Turning from them will help in developing good relational skills.

One obstacle results from using manipulation. *Manipulation* means to manage or influence by artful skill, often by unfair tactics. Since parents are stronger and more knowledgable, it's easy for them to manipulate children through unfair tactics. Dr. Cecil Osborne talks about the deceitfulness of manipulation. "Children who learn about love and tolerance on Sunday but live with the opposite six days a week are going to be influenced most by what they experience at home."[6] I experienced that situation, since my father's pendulum-swinging personality lived one way at church and another at home. What children *see* affects them more than what they're told. Because of that, they can feel manipulated when parents live by one set of standards, yet insist their children live by another.

Considering what Mom lived with for so long, I believe she performed her duties in devotion and lived a faithful life. Nevertheless, at the end of my sophomore year in high school I learned my parents, again, planned to separate. I had just ordered my senior class ring. It cost $16.00 and was made from yellow gold with a mother-of-pearl inset. However, $16.00 in 1952 represented a lot of money for our family.

The anxiety of providing for us controlled Mom. Although my ring was not scheduled to arrive until springtime, Mom urged me to tell Daddy I needed the money at that time to pay for it. I said, "I can't tell Daddy a lie." I feared him and was scared of telling a deliberate lie. She expressed anger with me for not getting the money, even under false pretenses. I felt like a disappointment and failure to Mom; consequently, I felt much guilt. Then, once again, Mom and Daddy decided to stay together. When the ring arrived months later, Daddy paid for the ring. Having the ring helped me feel "equal" with my classmates. Somehow, the emotional pain from living in an unstable household seemed a little more tolerable. The ring was one of the few things, while growing up, I could feel good about.

I now understand why Mom feared trying to support us without job skills. But, manipulation, regardless of the situation, isn't God's standard for relationships. Most people are blind to their manipulative behavior. Manipulation comes from fear and selfishness. Reprogramming this behavior calls for four choices. First, identify manipulation, and second, recognize when using it in relations to others. Third, apologize to the offended individual; also, ask for her and God's forgiveness. Fourth, examine the situation to identify why manipulation was used. Seeking God's timing, plus provision, help free us from fear and the compulsion of selfish manipulation with others.

"The righteous [woman] leads a blameless life" (Prov. 20:7, NIV). "Stop listening to instruction, my [daughter], and you will stray from the words of knowledge" (19:27, NIV). Listening, talking, and God's truths, not manipulation, are involved in living a trustworthy life.

Another obstacle hindering faithfulness and trustworthiness comes from a lack of parent supervised responsibility. *Responsibility* means that for which one is responsible. Parents should give children chores around the home. Picking up toys, drying dishes, dusting furniture, helping put away groceries, and a host of other tasks teach children the importance of following through on assignments. After explaining the task, parents need to "show" their child how to do the chore properly, then supervise the work to completion. This type of supervised training prepares children for responsibility in adulthood.

Lorreta's parents failed to provide for or supervise her responsibilities. As a result, she finds keeping promises, performing duties, and living devotedly most difficult. In fact, most often, she can't carry through with her commitments; therefore, it's hard for her to keep a job. Since her parents did not give respect or responsibilities in the home, she didn't feel like she belonged. She developed the behavior of laziness and a feeling of weak self-identity. She grew up feeling unloved. In adulthood, she's trying to reprogram a learned and destructive behavior. The following three suggestions will help free us from self-destructive behavior:

● Accept the fact that you have suffered unwanted emotional damage. Believe that with the Holy Spirit, you can take charge of your life (Phil. 4:13).

● Recognize your need to forgive those who hurt you. Remember, though, that change comes slowly. As it takes time for broken bodies to heal, it takes time for broken emotions to heal.

● Take inventory every few months; praise God for growth and change—

regardless of how small they may seem. Believe the truth that nothing can take away your self-worth since God established your identity when He created you in His image.

A third obstacle hindering faithfulness results from "overload." *Overload* means to put too large or heavy a load on; an excessive burden. Overloading comes when we can't say "no" without feeling guilty. In working for self-worth, we allow others to determine responsibilities, schedules, and emphases—instead of the Holy Spirit. Trying to please others through working for self-worth cannot remain life's focal point, because God has settled that issue. Believing we're persons of worth helps us say "no" to overload without feeling guilty; that also frees us to say "yes" at *right* times.

Here are some choices that can help us say no when we're overloaded. (1) Listen carefully to what's presented and analyze its content. (2) Ask yourself, "Are you already overcommitted? Does the task fit in with your gifts and interests? Does it make the best use of your time and energy?" (3) Pray in particular for God's guidance and peace. (4) Tell yourself, "Self-worth is an established fact; it does not rest on pleasing others." Don't apologize if you believe "no" is the best answer. God is our behavior judge, not others.

"When you expect another person to protect you from your own unwillingness to be in charge of what you can give, you are placing an impossible demand on that other person. . . . It is only through the acceptance and recognition that you are you, and not like anybody else, that you can become your own person and have your very own life."[7] Saying yes continually to responsibilities and commitments, before thinking or praying about them, is compliance. That causes anger buildup. But, learning to say "no" without feeling guilty **reduces** anger.

Conclusion

Paul says, "Faithful is He who calls you, and He will also bring it to pass" (1 Thess. 5:24). Living faithfully isn't an easy task, but Christ provides the power to live faithfully. Many of us have problems with relationships, and many have developed patterns of self-destructiveness like or similar to the ones mentioned above. Through hard work and perseverance we can enhance our relationships by learning how to listen and when to talk. Then we can identify the obstacles that hinder us when we try to be trustworthy and live faithfully. Like the Proverbs 31 woman, we too can learn to keep promises, perform duties, and live in devotion. These choices move us from an ugly "caterpillar" self-image into a woman of excellence.

11 Exercising Self-control

She exercises self-control . . . "She girds herself with strength,
And makes her arms strong" (Prov. 31:17).

*L*et it all hang out became a household phrase for our society in the
sixties. Since exercising control over actions or feelings seemed old-
fashioned and outmoded to so many, *self-control* became a "smirk"
word. But when we consider that self-control involves overcoming
self, the need to discern wisely in our behavior becomes clear. "I count [her]
braver," Aristotle once said, "who overcomes [her] desires than [she] who
conquers [her] enemies; for the hardest victory is the victory over self." Overcoming self is a hard victory to win, yet we have the Holy Spirit; His power
helps us overcome ourselves.

Gaining control over "self" influences the way we picture ourselves. If we
see ourselves created with God's worth, the need for ourselves is clear. If we
fail to picture ourselves created with God's worth, we deny the need for self-
control. Healthy relationships, though, rest on self-control and the supposi-
tion, "we don't know what can be done, until we try." The Proverbs 31 woman tried; because "she girds herself with strength, and makes her arms strong"
(v. 17). She didn't share the philosophy of "letting it all hang out." Rather, she
exercised self-control; she had learned that, among other ingredients, relationships need wise discernment in behavior.

Controlling Our Behavior Patterns

Discipline brings to a state of obedience and order by training and controlling our behavior. Since this is a lifetime process, discipline seems like a chore
to many. They don't feel motivated to choose discipline over hanging loose
and letting their lives just happen. Solomon, however, tells why discipline is
important. "God will bring every act to judgment, everything which is hidden, whether it is good or bad" (Eccl. 12:14).

Using that caution, the Proverbs 31 woman lived her life in wisdom. She related to family, employees, or customers with concern and respect. She lived a faithful and trustworthy life, extended acts of goodwill, and exercised self-control. She felt hope, self-worth, and confidence and put God in proper perspective. She worked willingly; planned and provided wisely; displayed kindness, wisdom, and organization. She created contentment, achieved fulfillment, and experienced character. But, she did not become this kind of person all at once, in the same day or week, or even in a year.

She became this kind of person **over a lifetime**. Any other way of growth would harm our mind, emotions, and spirit—overwhelming us with guilt. God doesn't motivate through guilt; He motivates through love. He shows His love through giving us self-worth and salvation. That love is the motivation for our behavior. In love—not guilt—we're assured, "For I can do everything God asks me to with the help of Christ who gives me the strength and power" (Phil. 4:13, TLB). This is the key to help us avoid legalism. We do everything *God* asks us to do, *not* everything others ask.

Exploring the difference between discipline and legalism makes those choices more distinct. Legalism lives by law; discipline lives by grace. Dick sees discipline as *discipling.* He says, "Discipling is helping others become disciplined to God's truth so they can grow into spiritual maturity. It's helping them in the process of discovering and obeying God's Word. But before we can help others, we first must become Christ's discipled ones." That is, we follow and adhere to Christ's "teaching, rebuking, correcting, and training in righteousness, so that the man [woman] of God may be thoroughly equipped for every good work" (2 Tim. 3:16,17, NIV). When being "equipped for every good work" becomes our motivation, disciplining our behavior takes on different meaning. Control, we see, serves the purpose of equipping us *for* action, rather than keeping us *from* action.

On the other hand, many of us grew up with "guilt" motivation, and we find it extremely difficult to relate to God's love. We fear He will treat us the same way others did; therefore, we respond automatically to guilt motivation. If an earthly parent *damaged* our *self-esteem* through breaking trust with us, we'll believe our Heavenly Father is untrustworthy. Consequently, it's difficult to "trust in" God. If earthly parents *destroyed* our *self-worth* with physical abuse, we'll believe our Heavenly Father will also fail to protect. It's hard, then, to "feel worthwhile" to God. If parents *shattered* our *self-identity*, we'll believe our Heavenly Parent will also shatter with criticism and putdown. "Feeling closeness" with God, therefore, is most difficult. If we will allow ourselves to experience God's gentleness and provision, these unhealthy fears toward Him will begin to disappear.

Another way we can learn about God's character is by looking at the ways Christ related to women. "Women are drawn to him because he understands them perfectly, loves them as individual persons and has demonstrated this love by giving his perfect life for their sins. In the Gospels, we never find him belittling or degrading women. . . . Christ had great concern, compassion and commendation for women in many different circumstances."[1] For example, the two sisters of Lazarus (Mary and Martha) enjoyed a close relationship with Christ. As His understanding and acceptance draws us to Him, we too can feel worth and closeness. Regardless of our past experiences, learning to trust Him will enable us to discipline our behavior. Our discipline will not be done out of legalism, which is salvation by good works rather than by grace.

We've established already that both salvation and self-worth are God's free gifts and we can't work for them. Controlling oneself for any reason, then, except to love the Lord and become fully equipped for service, gets into legalism. Legalism makes us rigid in working for approval, while healthy discipline sets us free to love and serve. Paul instructs us, "Whatever you do in word or deed, do all in the name of the Lord Jesus" (Col. 3:17). Working from legalism means we act in our name rather than in Christ's name. We can *not* say "yes" to every project or opportunity we're asked to consider, because we are human—not divine.

Since she had forgotten she's human, legalism work overtook Grace, dean of a Christian college. Because she "feels" guilty when saying "no," overload was crushing her. Besides administrative responsibilities, she teaches three subjects and takes care of household chores, her daughter, and her husband. She told me, "I yearn for some quiet place to escape to so that I can get away from everything." After awhile, Grace began to realize that, although it wouldn't be easy, she could picture herself important and loved. She could say "no" when necessary, relieving guilt, stress, and overload. That choice would also free her from anger and resentment toward herself and others.

Controlling emotions and actions by God's standards frees us to grow into spiritual maturity. Paul explains, "You used to walk in these ways, in the life you once lived. But now you must rid yourselves of all such things as these: anger, rage, malice, slander, and filthy language from your lips. Do not lie to each other, since you have taken off your old self with its practices and have put on the new self" (Col 3:7-10, NIV). Rather, we must teach our "new self" the discipline of spiritual fruit. Paul says, "But the fruit of the Spirit is love, joy, peace, patience, kindness, goodness, faithfulness, gentleness and self-control, against such things there is no law" (Gal. 5:22-23, NIV). God's ways show us that discipline in becoming fully equipped for service sharpens our relational skills.

Asking these questions will help us avoid legalism and distinguish between the Holy Spirit or others' voices in making choices. "Am I motivated to become equipped in serving others through self-discipline? Am I using my time, energy, and gifts according to the Holy Spirit's guidance?" Truthful answers to those questions will influence the disciplining of our behavior patterns.

Getting Along with Difficult People

Earlier, we discussed three characteristics of difficult people. They're emotionally blind (can't see others' talents, skills, or successes), emotionally deaf (can't hear what others say), have damaged vocal cords (say wrong things at wrong times). The Proverbs 31 woman must have dealt with difficult people. Perhaps she acted difficult at times and was hard to understand or deal with. Actually, when we picture ourselves without worth, our relational skills suffer; we react like difficult people. So, since all of us live that behavior at times, we can see the importance of trying to understand and cope with, not avoid, difficult people. There are numerous causes for acting difficult, but we will only focus on two reasons.

Premenstrual Syndrome (PMS). One PMS counselor says, "Premenstrual syndrome is a hormonal deficiency disease that is characterized by a clustering of symptoms in the premenstrual phase and an absence of symptoms in the postmenstrual phase.[2] PMS presents both physical and emotional symptoms one to ten days before the onset of menses. When menses begins, symptoms disappear until the next premenstrual period, bimonthly period, or occasionally. Physical symptoms include headaches, bloating, swelling, dizziness, craving for sweets and chocolate, blood sugar level difficulties, asthmatic attacks, increased allergies, fatigue, and significant weight gain. Emotional symptoms include depression, anger or rage, lethargy, irritability, anxiety, confusion, insecurity, and suspiciousness.

Dr. Carol Francis, Christian psychologist, believes at least 80 percent of women suffer to some degree from PMS. Studies vary in percentage, but she says 40 to 60 percent have mild- to moderate-severe symptoms while 5 to 20 percent feel severe effects. Statistics show about 60 percent of violent crimes committed by women occur during the one to ten days before menses. Some female athletes perform more poorly during the premenstrual period and significantly better immediately following menses onset. Also correlated with PMS are family arguments, child abuse, spousal fights, and breakups.[3]

"For centuries women have been going through emotional ups and downs brought about by the hormonal changes going on in their bodies. And for centuries we've been misunderstood, misinformed, and mistreated."[4] Since males don't experience anything similar to PMS, most can't understand its severe attacks on our relational skills.

Sometimes, **half of a battle is won through identifying the cause.** Women need to choose a doctor who's knowledgeable about PMS and who understands its effects. Many women have found help through natural progesterone liquid, suppositories, or tablets; B-complex (vitamin B-6), magnesium and calcium; diet change; exercise; and counseling. Vitamins, minerals, and herbs can help control the anger, aggression, depression, anxiety, nervousness, and fears associated with PMS. While using them may eliminate the need for prescription medications, make sure you consult your physician before taking them.

Recording emotional feelings and levels of physical energy one to ten days before menses begin can help identify PMS symptoms. This information can prove most helpful to a doctor in identifying the source and solution. About ten years ago I began experiencing anger or rage about every three months. At first I didn't recognize the symptoms because the anger came so irregularly. The rage or strong anger wasn't toward anything said or done by someone. It's a result of body chemistry change that goes on each month. Through reading competent material and talking with a doctor, I began to identify a pattern of PMS. At first, my doctor helped me with medication. I later learned about vitamins, minerals, and herbs. Taking them enabled me to go off the medicine. I also take amino acids, avoid most caffeine, and try to get sufficient rest during those days. I've asked the Lord to help me *do* what I can do and *trust* Him for what I can't do. Thus, I'm learning to cope with PMS stress.

In addition, a good attitude toward ourselves and PMS helps us during those days each month. Giving in to an ugly "caterpillar" self-identity, uncontrolled anger, or unhealthy fears may deepen a depression prior to menses. Looking for reliable intervention helps us fight PMS attacks and improves relational skills.

> It takes a tremendous amount of energy to maintain a home and raise a family. Add to that the stresses of an outside job plus symptoms of PMS, and you have the elements of a time bomb. Many women today are in high-stress jobs, and their home usually isn't any less stressful. . . . Stress can have a detrimental effect on both hormone balance and emotions.[5]

That's why those of us who suffer from PMS need to find and follow competent medical advice in helping our relationships.

Because it requires so much supervision, PMS is an ongoing war. Many female doctors, psychologists, counselors, psychiatrists, and dieticians have written about PMS and also about menopause. Through research and experience, they've discovered valuable information which helps with these menaces to relationships.

> Aside from the so-called liberated women who claim that acknowledging PMS would cause even more discrimination for women, we have other doubters in the ranks. Many women who have never experienced PMS tend to discount it and are unsympathetic to those who do. Often women who have PMS deny it, thinking a good wife and mother, a real Christian, would never act or think like a PMS woman.[6]

Women who do not accept or understand this problem adds to the PMS

menace. Females experiencing PMS and menopause need helpful information. Talking about PMS with friends, spouse, family, or doctor can help relieve some of the emotional tension that builds up each month. Various books
on both areas are in most libraries or Christian bookstores. Living out helpful
information can enhance our relational skills in getting along with difficult
people—even ourselves.

Totem-Pole Importance. Some people seem to picture others from their
totem pole. Depending on where they sit, they see others more important or
less important than themselves. They don't understand God's principles of
self-worth. They don't see themselves as created with God's worth. They're
either working for self-worth or feel they've already obtained it all by themselves. It's hard to get along with both those types of difficult people. But it
can be done. We can learn to picture others from God's perspective, as "equal
in value to."

"All humans have a fundamental need to beloved and admired, to be special. The infant longs for its parents' total, undivided love. That deep need,
which later lies buried and largely forgotten in the 'inner child of the past,'
never dies completely. It reveals itself in the adult longing for recognition,
honors, popularity—any form of positive attention."[7] Maybe you've felt this
love and acceptance need. Recognizing this basic human need helps us understand more clearly that totem-pole importance should be wiped out. Society
pictures some important, while others are pictured unimportant. But that's
not God's view.

Totem-pole importance says we either feel inferior or superior to others.
That's why some of us "name drop"; we hope to feel important and accepted
by identifying with certain people. That brings us back to the acceptance issue. How can we accept both the good and bad about ourselves and others?
How can we picture others created with God's worth and relate to them like
they have worth? In talking about human worth, Dick often uses a "ladder of
progression."

Seven steps make up the ladder. When we feel others have **worth**, we will
talk with them. Believing others have worth, we will treat them with respect.
Relating to others in respect, we **listen** to them. Listening to others takes time.
Our time is important. Thus, taking the time to listen shows others they are
important. While listening to others, we begin to **hear** them. Hearing others,
reveals things or information about them. As they explain their thoughts, decisions, and actions, we start to **know** them. The more others tell us about
themselves, the more we get to know them.

By getting to know others, then, we begin to **understand** them. Digesting
their information, we begin to understand why they think, choose, or act in
certain ways. Learning about others helps us understand that, like us, they too
have limitations. Understanding leads to **acceptance**. Mentally, we put our-

selves into their shoes in order to accept rather than criticize. Accepting others leads into deeper relationships. We then can go beyond casual weather conversations to talking about our feelings, hopes, and opinions.

Through acceptance, we gain the courage to become vulnerable and transparent. That openness helps us **share** our reality with others. Sharing shows we trust them. Trust shows them they have worth and are "equal in value to." Such openness can free others to give up their totem-pole picture of importance. Those choices help our inner relations with difficult people.

Developing a Kindred Spirit

Relationships that are congenial and allied by the same tastes or beliefs result in a kindred spirit or attitude. Developing a kindred spirit requires candor, closeness, and cooperation. These behaviors become a part of our self-control as we develop good relational skills.

Candor, being open or straightforward, produces the opposite of masking. *Masking* is an art of hiding the inner self, rather than being open. Most of us began masking early in life or whenever we suffered repeated unwanted intrusions. That painful lack of acceptance built in this nonverbal decision, "It's too painful to continue with such rejection." This began our pattern of relating from behind a mask. We found that communicating behind an invisible mask felt safer and carried less emotional pain. Such constriction of my personality began at about age nine and continued for many years. I related through either a mask or openness, depending on whether I felt others' approval or disapproval.

Candor leads us toward similar tastes or beliefs, while masking leads in the opposite direction. For instance, we either feel embarrassment or assertiveness, fear or confidence, and shyness or a relaxed inner spirit. We may feel verbal inhibition or hear our thoughts flow with words. Masking leads to a weak self-identity which weighs heavily on our emotions. Sometimes our shoulders droop because we feel inferior—like an ugly caterpillar. Looking into others' eyes, giving specifics about ourselves (nothing sounds good enough to tell), or asserting ourselves to seek leadership roles seem too difficult.

Our weak self-identity makes us "feel" inferior to others; it can lead to envy of their gifts and skills. Inferiority makes us feel resentment toward those who don't accept us. Developing a kindred spirit is difficult when envy and resentment control us. Also, miscommunication can keep us from allying tastes or beliefs in congeniality. That's why relationships call for transparency in feelings, speech, and behavior. Kathy and Alice see openness like this. "It seems God planned for us to do our spiritual and emotional maturing in relationships . . . Christian friendships are designed to promote . . . maturity by helping us see God and ourselves. They can also help meet our deep emotional needs as we accept, care for, encourage, forgive . . . one another. As we do this . . . we reflect the Lord to one another."[8] Friends spend time together because of common concerns and interests. They share their lives with one another.

Paul gives some how-tos. "Speaking the truth in love. . . . Speak truthfully to [your] neighbor. Do not let any unwholesome talk come out of your mouths, but only what is helpful for building others up. Be kind and compassionate to one another, forgiving each other" (Eph. 4:15,25,29,32, NIV). Earlier, we talked about how Suzanne ministered to me through perceptive listening. However, we're very different in personalities. I'm more compliant; she's less compliant. She's more controlling; I'm less controlling. She likes more one-to-one interaction; I like more group interaction. I like speaking; she likes teaching. We share some likenesses; still, we seem incompatible for friendship.

For instance, a few years ago I became uncomfortable with Suzanne's need to be in control. To let her know how I felt, I had to speak the truth. Even though I thought I spoke in love, she felt offended and rejected. We talked and wrote several times before our rocky time passed, but we talked for the purpose of building up each other. Speaking the truth in love didn't feel good. Yet, using kindness and compassion, we worked out a personality difference. We forgave each other and continue in candor (openness) toward a kindred spirit.

Closeness, the state of being near, intimate, or confidential, gives another ingredient to kindred spirit. Although the New Testament mentions *agape* love many times, most believers fear this closeness. One reason is because some people misassociate *eros* (sensual feelings) with feelings of *agape*—loving another just for herself. Consequently, we fear our "good feelings" for each other. Also, we cannot trust others because of our emotional damage and the fear of "getting hurt again." At times, we begin feeling comfortable with others' similar beliefs, tastes, or attitudes. But when we recognize the congenial feeling of "I like you," fear takes over.

We fear ourselves, not just others. Thus, we can't trust ourselves or others to live out what God says several times. "Love your neighbor as yourself." Since our good feelings are, sometimes misassociated with inappropriate feelings, we withdraw from the friendship. Or we believe others have wrong motives and, therefore, can't trust them. Either way, our needs for *agape* aren't met, since we cannot trust ourselves to have a "good feeling" of closeness. Yet Paul says, "Love does no harm to its neighbor. Therefore love is the fulfillment of the law" (Rom. 13:10, NIV). To love others, we must crawl through the maze of becoming vulnerable again. Christ's example shows us that healthy agape brings good feelings of closeness.

Closeness involves OK hugs, pats on the arm to lift low spirits, a kiss on the cheek to cheer someone who's feeling down, or smiles that say, "Hello, I value you. I'll share my good feelings with you." These are needed to live out God's instructions for healthy friendships. They do not go beyond God's boundaries or bring emotional harm to ourselves or others. From Suzanne's hugs, many in our Sunday School class became aware that they needed hugs, too. But some felt such fear of themselves that they couldn't build closeness by responding with a loving hug.

Cooperation is a third ingredient of kindred spirit. We may learn many theories about candor and closeness; but unless we learn to work or act together, a kindred spirit cannot develop. However, cooperation doesn't mean giving up or changing opinions or views because someone disagrees. Neither does it mean wearing a pretense mask nor trying to please everyone. While working together isn't always easy, it's our attitude about ourselves and others that adds steadfastness in cooperating. Learning to cooperate requires the hard work of trust. Since both of us suffered unwanted intrusions into our childhood space, trusting is hard work for Suzanne and me.

Although Suzanne and I shared similar beliefs, tastes, and attitudes, we had not chosen a congenial cooperation. We needed to forgive each other, restoring candor and closeness for a kindred spirit. Of course, developing good relational skills involves an ongoing reassessment process. "Real understanding always brings with it a going beyond one's self. People so very different by nature are nevertheless made to complement each other, [so] . . . they may discover . . . much of what they've not known or sensed before."[9] Going beyond ourselves helps us learn the value of cooperation.

On the other hand, some of us fear working with others because of a fuzzy self-concept. J. B. Phillips explains why our emotional underdevelopment affects our relations with God and others. "The early conception of God is almost invariably founded upon the child's idea of [her] father . . . If the child is afraid of [her] own father, the chances are that [her] Father in Heaven will appear to [her] a fearful Being."[10] I understand this cooperation fear. Trying to develop feelings of worth *to God*, trust *in God*, or closeness *with Him* have proven most difficult. Some years ago, I realized why.

Growing up in a dysfunctional family where Daddy hurt Mom made me fear him. Daddy's verbal criticism and putdown destroyed my feelings of worth. Added to that, when I asked for permission to do something or go somewhere, he always said "no." That communicated to me that he didn't care about my needs. After becoming a Christian, consequently, I didn't feel cared for by God my Heavenly Parent. In praying to God, the same desperate feelings surfaced that I had felt toward Daddy. "He will only say 'no' to my requests, so why should I bother asking?"

To help me go beyond those damaged emotions, a friend suggested I study what God is like, so I made a character list—holiness, purity, love, kindness, mighty, compassion, strong, comforting, merciful, truthful, gracious, and for-giving. When reading Scripture that described God with those adjectives, I placed the references on my list to reread often.

Also, I began to pray, "Father, God, help me learn to trust You so I can cooperate with You." At that time, I always put the two titles of Father and God together; it felt safer than just calling Him "Father." Some months later, feelings of trust began to build and I felt comfortable when saying, "Father, I love you." I noticed that He answers "yes" to my requests, not just "no." This changed my prayer life, and I began enjoying that time. His answers built in feelings of worth; I felt important and loved. While I don't always understand His answers, whether He says "yes, no, or wait awhile," I can believe it's best for me. His track record of caring gives encouragement, helping me work together with Him and others.

Conclusion

Remembering our behavior motivation—equipped for every good work—gives value to self-discipline. Christ in us—the crimson thread running through our behavior patterns—helps us get along with difficult people and develop a kindred spirit. As a result, we will feel good about and accept ourselves; we will feel good about and accept others. This discipline enhances our relational skills and helps us extend acts of goodwill to others.

12 Extending Acts of Goodwill

She extends acts of goodwill . . . "She extends her hand to the poor; And she stretches out her hands to the needy" (Prov. 31:20).

*O*ne typical attitude says, "I'm too busy to care for my neighbor; she can fend for herself. So what if she suffers from an illness, lives on a fixed salary, or lives alone." Some reports say almost half (45.2 percent) of all females are single, which includes single parents. More women with small children work out of their residences than ever before. The 1980 Census of Population recorded these statistics for females.

Married: Except separated	54.8 percent
Singles: Divorced and separated	9.8 percent
Singles: Never married	23.0 percent
Singles: Widowed	12.4 percent[1]

With such a drastic diversity in society's makeup, it's no wonder we hear so much about "women in burnout." Many tried to become the twentieth-century Wonder Woman, forgetting about emotional, physical, mental, or spiritual health. So it's understandable they took on Cain's attitude, "Am I my [sister's] keeper?" (Gen. 4:9). The Proverbs 31 woman, in contrast, displays a different attitude. While she spends time caring for herself and her other commitments, she also takes time and "stretches out her hands to the needy." She achieved an apparent balance in doing for others and taking care of responsibilities, plus herself. She became her sister's keeper, by giving caring concern. "She extends her hand to the poor" (v. 20).

Those acts don't just happen; they have to be planned. Extending goodwill to the less fortunate requires commitment, work, and time. Needy people need emotional, mental, and spiritual nurture—not just financial help. Regardless of the type, acts of goodwill should originate from love rather than compulsive behavior.

Understanding Our Motives

To understand our motives, we must first clarify a definition of *goodwill*. The definition I use says "readiness or zeal; benevolence and favor." Taking care of our responsibilities yet feeling a zeal or readiness to care for others is tiring. Feeling benevolent or charitable attitudes toward others when we are already overloaded produces pressure. Doing favors or kind acts for others after they've criticized or rejected us again feels stressful, especially when we suffer from an ugly "caterpillar" self-esteem.

It's easy to confuse low self-esteem and self-centeredness, since feelings about ourselves control our behavior. Similarly, our self-picture develops from either a healthy, strong image or an unhealthy, weak image. "As children, when we did wrong, we learned that some form of punishment would usually follow . . . from a parental frown to total rejection . . . even the withdrawal of love, the rejection which the child fears more than any form of physical punishment. . . . Because our childhood concepts are still partly alive, we tend to project onto God the feelings we had toward our parents."[2] Until I understood that God motivates through love rather than guilt, I projected onto Him my feelings of fear, hate, and mistrust I felt toward Daddy.

And yet, self-identity cannot rest on "works." It rests on the established fact that God created both sexes in His image, giving us His worth. Allowing this truth to permeate our behavior frees us to extend acts of kindness. We give because we love and love because we're loved. Receiving love from God and from others helps us give freely without wanting in return, which is God's model of giving in freedom. As we accept His free gifts—**worth** and **salvation**—we learn to give freely.

Settling the self-esteem issue from God's perspective helps us extend goodwill like Paul suggests. "Don't just think about your own affairs, but be interested in others, too, and in what they are doing" (Phil. 2:4, TLB). Showing interest in others rather than living in self-centeredness helps establish good relational skills. It also ministers to others' needs. But what about the times we know others hurt, yet we also hurt and feel overloaded? Reevaluating commitments and involvements may help with that dilemma, which involves saying "no" at wrong times and "yes" at right times.

Some believe fear of rejection is one of our hardest problems to cope with.

> Fear . . . shows up in an incredible variety of situations as the underlying force behind what we do or experience. . . . The root of our fear is that we are not acceptable and that exposure of who we really are will bring rejection. . . . Although our ultimate fear has to do with rejection by God, we learn to attach the fear to someone more tangibly present . . . [like] parent . . . friend . . . spouse, children, employer, pastor, and society.[3]

This fear of rejection becomes the main culprit causing commitment **over-**

load—commitments that we don't want or enjoy doing.

Paul understood this fear and overcame it. He said he had become all things to all people; he understood that *all* are "equal in value." He didn't exhibit totem-pole importance where some are important and some are not. He believed God cares for all of us regardless of age, race, status, performance, or appearance. He took God for his spiritual judge, not others. That freed Paul to make choices based on his best judgment rather than others' false guilt.

Coming to that place was most difficult for me. When I was growing up, compliance became my way of relating to authority. So in adulthood, I feared believers would think me "unspiritual" if I said "no" to church responsibilities. Even when I felt overloaded or when the responsibility didn't make the best use of time, gifts, or abilities, I couldn't refuse. Little by little, though, I began to understand that God is my spiritual judge, not others. Each time I answered "yes" or "no" based on my best judgment, it strengthened me for the next decision time. People's opinions meant less and less; God's opinions meant more and more.

Taking charge of our lives through the Holy Spirit's guidance frees us to give from a sincere goodwill rather than out of a false guilt or pretense. Discerning between the Holy Spirit's voice and others' voices helps us determine how to answer. If we're asked to help serve in some way, yet feel overloaded, we can make this known with kindness and discretion. In understanding our motives, we can also accept human limitations and ask God to use them. Accepting those limitations frees us to evaluate serving opportunities under the Holy Spirit's guidance. But unless our serving motives remain clear of emotional tangles (like fear of rejection or working for self-worth), we are only pretending to serve.

We cannot live out the Holy Spirit's role. He ministers to *all*; we can minister to only a few. If *yes* abounds where *no* needs to, we can through prayer eliminate wrong responses. This strengthens us for future decisions, when we need to eliminate commitment overload with "right" answers. This clears our serving motives to encourage others.

Encouraging Others

Extending goodwill inspires others with courage, confidence, and hope. To encourage, we relate through love, rather than judging, condemning, or wanting in return. Encouragement calls for giving our time from a generous spirit. "A generous [woman] will prosper; [she] who refreshes others will [herself] be refreshed" (Prov. 11:25, NIV). The Proverbs 31 woman refreshed others through ministering to their emotional, physical, and mental needs. Matthew gives a good foundation in how to encourage, refresh, and help others. "Do for others what you want them to do for you" (7:12, TLB). This does not mean that when a person extends goodwill others respond automatically in like manner. "Difficult people" may never be able to show gratitude or appreciation for others' kindness. Thus, in trying to encourage others, we must keep going back to Christ's model. He gave without condemning, judging, or wanting in return.

While writing this book, a number of people encouraged me. Uncovering many of my damaged emotions has proven most painful and difficult. I've sought the Lord's confirmation often so that sharing these and others' experiences would help hurting women. At one point, I felt depressed and feared too much had been revealed. I feared "Jane" was getting promoted instead of Christ. The next Sunday morning, in tears, I told my pastor of my fears. He listened, asked a few questions, prayed with me, and encouraged me to "keep writing." Later that day, I talked with Suzanne about my fears. She listened, asked some questions, and reminded me of her emotional support and hope that I would "continue writing." That evening, I explained my fears to Dick. Then he asked questions, reminded me of some positives in my life, and said to "keep going."

None of them said I should stop feeling what my emotions felt or suggested I wasn't living close to the Lord. None said, "Just trust the Lord more." Rather, they inspired me toward courage, refreshed my emotions, and helped me beyond a scary time. They responded without condemning, judging, or wanting in return. That's the essential emotional need of encouragement. Yet, we must be careful not to sabotage our lives with unrealistic goals. At times, to reach a goal, we must find someone with whom to become accountable. Cathy has done that through joining Weight Watchers.

She's an attractive thirty-three-year-old brunette, who suffered unwanted sexual intrusions when she was a young girl. One result of that damage is compulsive eating. Cathy works hard to keep her weight under control. At times, though, she caves in, especially when she has to be near the one responsible for her emotional damage. When that happens, she has to regroup her thinking, planning, and doing to get her eating under control. Weight Watchers helps her reach the attainable self-picture she's created.

There are numerous helpful groups where "others" may receive needed encouragement. After choosing an area where we want to give time, energy, and perhaps money, we can help others through that particular group. Aside from groups, there are other ways to give encouragement. We've heard much about the wrongs of abortion, but little has been said about helping someone through an unwanted pregnancy. Married women, as well as single women, find themselves in that predicament.

In the first four years of my marriage, I gave birth to three babies. Dick was a full-time student, so we lived on a non-existent budget. His parents had put us on their health insurance when we married, so that's the way my doctor and hospital bills were paid. When our first baby was born, some women from the church in Wheaton, Illinois—where Dick was ordained—gave me a baby shower. Dick's two older sisters also shared baby clothes with me. Of course, mothers then used cloth diapers. Twice we had a baby and a toddler in diapers at the same time. Since I owned only two dozen, they had to be washed, dried, and folded continuously.

At that time I lived with the compulsiveness of a workaholic. I could not allow myself time for friendships. When our second child was thirteen months old, I learned that our third baby had been conceived. For several weeks I suffered from depression. In a true victimization pattern, I felt inadequate and guilty for having conceived another baby so soon. Mom volunteered to come when the baby was born and take care of us. I cannot express how her coming encouraged and ministered to me. Knowing she was caring for my two little girls and Dick while I was in the hospital gave me peace. Her presence also gave me time and energy to get acquainted with my precious baby boy. I felt loved, cared for, and important. That's what happens when we give of ourselves to encourage others. There are many ways to extend goodwill, and they become the foundation that "reaching out to others" rests on.

Reaching Out to Others

The Proverbs 31 woman modeled reaching out to others. She extended her hands to those who she identified as poor and needy. Reaching out to others can take place in groups or on a one-to-one basis. We can serve through ministries of our church or find our own individual ministry. Either way, we need to keep our motives clear and reach out in Christ's name using Luke's suggestion. "Try to show as much compassion as your Father does. . . . Whatever measure you use to give—large or small—will be used to measure what is given back to you" (6: 36, 38, TLB). Compassion is "feeling" for hurting others even while we hurt.

Numerous avenues exist to extend a caring hand to others. Some reports show that 75 percent of teen runaways "run" because of incest. Many turn to prostitution so they can make a living. They reason, "I've already lost my innocence, so what difference does it make." Most don't have the courage to make the "secret sin" known. Although they're hurt and scared beyond measure, many refuse to tell because they fear that the one who violated their space will be hurt or get into trouble. They take the blame, since they haven't received "permission" to *place* the blame where it belongs. Others "act out" trying to destroy themselves with an intense anger, which was caused from the unwanted intrusions. Some turn the intense anger on themselves and become withdrawn and depressed.

They need loving assurance over and over that "blame" rests on the transgressor. Even then, believing it and turning loose of the destructive false guilt still remains hard to do. Nonvictims can help with this need. With patience and love, we can reach out through understanding acceptance in Christ's name. In reaching out, though, we're risking. We risk being misunderstood, unappreciated, or taken for granted. Nevertheless, we do not reach out to be understood or appreciated. We must keep coming back to Christ's giving model of not judging, condemning, or wanting in return. His *giving model* will motivate us to extend goodwill to other poor, needy, or hurting people through trust and risk.

Barni and Sherrie know about trust and risk. Because of unwanted intrusions in childhood, they reach out to other victims through S.M.I.L.E.S. (Sexually Molested Individuals Lending Earnest Support). They meet with others, helping them learn to cope with the reality of their losses. They help free them from shame and false guilt to live productive lives. They also show educational films to parents and children.

Pauline and Bob know about trust and risk. Bob, a recovered alcoholic, and Pauline, his wife, reach out to other alcoholics and their spouses, children, and parents. Through Overcomers Outreach, a national organization they started and direct, they're helping alcoholics learn to function without an alcohol or drug addiction. This long process begins when one can admit he or she is an alcoholic. They've trained groups in over seven hundred churches.

Denise Thomas, Christian psychologist, knows about trust and risk. Besides her counseling practice, she helps women with eating disorders. She works with women in small groups, helping them recognize and "own" personal problems that lead to uncontrolled, unhealthy eating habits. Krista and Phyllis, directors of Living Alternatives, know about trust and risk. They reach out to unmarried pregnant women, offering counsel and showing them an alternative to abortion. Based on Christ's loving forgiveness, they inform women of ways to either keep their baby or allow Christian parents to adopt the child. They and other volunteers minister to emotional hurts in the young women's lives, showing them loving care.

Childcare USA encourages individuals to reach out and become involved in working toward child abuse prevention. Laws related to child abuse for each state can be obtained through the local department of social services, city or county attorney's office, a law enforcement agency, or the state attorney general's office. Their national number is 1-800-4-A-CHILD. Their national headquarters telephone number in Woodland Hills, California, is (213) 347-7280. National Coalition Against Domestic Violence (NCADV) provides counsel, nurture, and shelter for battered wives and children through their eight hundred shelters. Their toll free number (1-800-HELP-4-ME) remains open 8:00 a.m. to 4:30 p.m., although an answering service takes calls at other times. Last year more than 91,000 desperate women with 131,000 children found safety and help from NCADV.

Another national organization, Homosexuals Anonymous (HA) begun in 1980 by two committed Christians, keeps expanding and reaching out to hurting people. HA supports individuals seeking freedom from homosexuality. It's nonsectarian and works interdenominationally and nondenominationally. Rather than encouraging the homosexual subculture, HA contributes to its decline. Contact can be made at HA Fellowship, P. O. Box 7881, Reading, Pennsylvania 19603.

Many Christian counselors have designed small groups to help hurting people. Regardless of the type, abuse hurts. Paul tells us to bear one another's burdens (Gal 6:2). Whether we reach out one-to-one or in groups, we're living out Christ's designed community. The body of Christ gets together (*ekklesia*) to share their lives (*koinonia*), because they're concerned for each other (*agape*). This community operates with two or many people.

> Once having had the priceless experience of mutual understanding, the desire for even better understanding grows. . . . [Understanding for] things of which we are ashamed, things in our past that we should like to blot out, things for which we feel ourselves responsible. . . . Every deliverance from loneliness, fear, suffering, or remorse is a result of the loving mercy of God.[4]

God shows His mercy through believers who help Him deliver others from loneliness, fear, remorse, or suffering. "Reaching out" must rest on the recognition that all are "equal in value." In keeping our motives clear and avoiding burnout, though, we need balance in caring for ourselves, responsibilities, and others. We can't minister to others while looking down our social noses at them—feeling superior—or picturing ourselves inferior. Maybe you want to reach out and nurture hurting others but don't understand what they have experienced. Some books give insight into the pain that others feel.[5]

While we cannot reach out to everyone we meet or right all the wrongs we see, we can encourage some people and right some wrongs. Heeding the Serenity Prayer will help us in developing that balance. "God grant me the serenity to accept the things I cannot change, the courage to change the things I can, and wisdom to know the difference." When we learn to feel good about ourselves, we can then feel good about others and show them the same compassion our Heavenly Father does. That's the Proverbs 31 woman's balance. While she extended her hand to the poor and stretched out her hands to the needy, she had time for work, family, and herself. That learned balance enhances relational skills, freeing the special female self God wants to mold into a woman of excellence.

Section 4 *Developing Reliable Work Ethic Skills*

G rowing up as the youngest child in a large family, I saw many different work models. With four older brothers and four older sisters,
plus Mom and Daddy, I had many people to answer to. In large
families, accountability seems to pass from one peer to another. So,
I learned much about work ethics, both good and bad.

Life on a farm presented numerous kinds of work opportunities. On the
other hand, work was never finished, and the pay was never very good. In
fact, during the early forties, most farmers and rural people still struggled to
go beyond "the Great Depression." They worked at whatever they could for
money to buy enough food and warm clothing for all family members, plus
pay for housing. Although Daddy worked a rural mail route, being a small-
time farmer made it difficult for him to provide for his large family.

With two sons in World War II, one daughter married, and one working in
the California shipyards, Mom and Daddy had only five children left at
home. Nevertheless, in August 1943, Daddy decided we were going "cotton
picking." He hired someone to feed and water the cows, hogs, horses, and
chickens. He also asked someone to watch the house. We loaded home-
canned food, cooking utensils, silverware, dishes, mattresses, bedding, towels, washing supplies, and clothing into his 1939 black Ford pickup. The seven
of us climbed into and onto the overloaded Ford and started a 300-mile trip to
Altus, Oklahoma. Pickups didn't travel as quickly in those days. Neither were

the highways as good as the ones today; many Oklahoma roads were dirt—not blacktop.

A day's travel took us to our home for two months: a small empty schoolhouse. Before we unloaded our pickup, Mom decided which rooms would function as a kitchen, an eating or sitting area, and the bedrooms. Like on our farm, we used outdoor toilets. Since everyone would start picking cotton the next day, we had to unpack everything and find a place for it before going to bed.

After unpacking, we found our working tools: heavy off-white canvas cotton-picking sacks. The sack sizes averaged about five feet long by two feet wide. A three-inch strap about thirty to thirty-six inches long was attached in two different places to the open end of the sack. Before an individual started picking cotton, she placed an arm through the strap slipping it over her head to rest on a shoulder (like a female's over-the-shoulder bag.) That left both hands free to pick cotton bolls and stuff them into the sack. The movie *Places in the Heart*, featuring Sally Fields, dramatically portrays the hardships of picking cotton.

While a picker walked down the rows, the sack was dragged behind her. When a sack was full or too heavy to drag, she pulled her sack of cotton to the weighing scales. Two men weighed each sack of cotton; then a field supervisor wrote down the number of pounds next to her name. Those men dumped the cotton into a large truck. The picker then returned to her picking spot and picked more cotton. At a day's end, pickers were paid according to the number of pounds picked. Sometimes an owner changed the original figures to reduce amount paid. Pickers had to either work for less or find another cotton field to pick in. Fortunately, that didn't happen to us.

I remember a delightful experience at the end of that cotton-picking season. It's one of my earliest work ethic lessons. My small, six-year-old body had worked hard, but a bag full of cotton proved too heavy for me to pull. Just then, my brothers and sisters decided it would be fun for me to take a full bag to the scales. They came over to my row and started pulling off cotton bolls putting them into the sack. When it was full, one of them pulled my sack to the weighing scales. They all cheered, while the men lifted my bag and weighed it. I felt loved and important. My brothers and sisters put aside their weary tiredness to help me accomplish something I couldn't do alone. They extended "acts of goodwill" to me. That loving lesson impacted my life; it affected "for good" my attitude toward helping others and work.

13 Willing Industrious Workers Who Live Responsibly

She's a willing . . . industrious worker who lives responsibly . . . "She looks for wool and flax, And works with her hands in delight . . . She is like merchant ships; She brings her food from afar . . . She rises also while it is still night, And gives food to her household, And portions to her maidens" (Prov. 31:13-15).

*L*ike *self-control*, *work* also became a "smirk" word for many in the sixties. These people either didn't know or had forgotten about God's attitude toward work. Each day during creation God looked at His work and saw that, "It was good." On the last day He saw that, "It was very good" (see Gen. 1:1-31). God felt good about work and modeled how to work for Christ, His Son, and all of humanity (John 5:17-20). One description of *work* says it's exertion directed to produce or accomplish something, to labor or toil. Adam and Eve learned to produce and accomplish because God gave them particular responsibilities. He told them to "Be fruitful and multiply, and fill the earth, and subdue it; rule over the fish of the sea and over the birds of the sky, and over every living thing that moves on the earth" (Gen. 1:28).

God created a beautiful and perfect work situation. He evidently wanted humans to enjoy their responsibilities, but after the Fall, things changed. When Adam and Eve chose to go against God's commandment, they had to leave their beautiful and perfect surroundings. No longer could they enjoy the trees laden with luscious fruit and the plants that bore an abundance of vegetables. Instead, God said to them, "Cursed is the ground because of you; in toil you shall eat of it all the days of your life. Both thorns and thistles it shall grow for you; and you shall eat the plants of the field; by the sweat of your face you shall eat bread" (Gen. 3:17-19). They learned quickly that they could get their food or other needs only through toiling. And humanity still toils for food or other needs through laboring to produce and accomplish something. God hasn't changed His mind regarding the work ethic.

While work for humanity is important to God, His priority with our work isn't a place, type, or title. It's our attitude toward producing and accomplishing. "And whatever you do in word or deed, do all in the name of the Lord Jesus. . . . do your work heartily, as for the Lord rather than for men. . . . It is the Lord Christ whom you serve" (Col. 3:17,23-24). The Proverbs 31 woman's work ethic shows she also held work high on her importance list. Since her time, society's work needs have changed many times. Work roles for females and males have broadened and multiplied time and time again—all within God's scope and vision for humanity.

The Art of Willingness

But we've produced different kinds of pictures in our work ethic skills. Many of us are workaholics, while others have lost all "carry-through" motivation or initiative. Some of us go from job to job, while others "fear" leaving unchallenging, low-paying jobs. Others lack job skills since money or confidence needed for training or schooling are missing. Still, many never receive rightful promotions or recognition, although they're intelligent, capable women. These work-related behavior patterns carry on in part because of emotional losses in childhood. Since God designed work, emotional damage cannot take away our gifts or abilities although we may feel inferior, intimidated, or inadequate.

On the flip side, we receive intelligence (mind), creative energy (emotion), and initiative (spirit) from being created in God's image. That's why we need to picture work from God's perspective: "[It's] good." It is also expected. Paul says, "If anyone will not work, neither let him [her] eat" (2 Thess. 3:10). That strong ultimatum rests on our unwillingness to work. Willingness has to do with the will, a faculty or power of conscious and deliberate action. God encourages cheerful deliberate action. "Each man [woman] should give what [she] has decided in [her] heart, not reluctantly or under compulsion, for God loves a cheerful giver" (2 Cor. 9:7, NIV).

The Proverbs 31 woman modeled the art of work willingness. "She looks for wool and flax, And works with her hands in delight" (v. 13). Her attitude shows that looking and planning for work makes up part of willingness. *Self-motivated* describes the willing worker. She looks for work rather than sitting and waiting for it to look for her. She enjoys her work more than a reluctant worker. That's the type of employee employers like to hire, and they usually receive the best raises or promotions. Mom was a willing worker; she modeled the work ethic of self-motivation, initiative, orderliness, and neatness. Mom married at sixteen and birthed ten babies. Although she worked long days caring for them, living most of her years on a low income, she didn't complain. She enjoyed working and helping others until her death. Her work ethic has influenced both me and my adult children.

Mom and my sisters swept floors with brooms—no vacuum cleaners. Usually the kitchen, dining room, and living room floors had inexpensive linoleum for coverings. The bedroom floors had bare boards (no soft, warm throw rugs for cold feet). During summer months, they filled dozens and dozens of canning jars with food—green sweet peas, yellow corn, red beets, green string beans, red peppers, green spinach, yellow kraut, red tomatoes, green sweet or sour pickles, yellow peaches, white pears, purple plums, blackberries. **No one's canned food tasted as good as her own.**

Mondays, for many years, meant using a galvanized two-gallon bucket to lift water from our well and carry it to a large black iron pot. Mom then built a fire to heat the water. Next, she cut up a large bar of Ivory soap and dropped it into the water. When the water heated to boiling, the soap melted and made a good cleaning solution for the clothes. Then my brothers carried the hot water and poured it into the gas-motored, wringer washing machine. If the motor didn't work or if there was no money for gas, they had to clean the clothes by rubbing them on a "rub board." That's bad news for the hands! Yet, Mom modeled an art of work willingness.

Most women today buy and prepare food, wash clothes, or clean house differently than in the past. Just before World War II ended, more females participated in the "work world" than ever in America's history. But when that war ended the female work force took a sharp drop. Thousands of men came home needing their old jobs back or seeking new ones. Added to that, the strength of the economy allowed many wives to stop working outside their home. That's when the Cinderella Syndrome invaded our society.

During the fifties and sixties many television series portrayed women as homemakers. They performed in nice dresses, hose, and heels, with hair "beautified." But those roles never showed them using brain power, creativity, or ingenuity. They overindulged children by keeping them from the real world of responsibility and work. Then, the women's movement became more prominent and vocal. Frustrated with the Cinderella Syndrome, many became involved with ERA, N.O.W., or other vocal feminist groups. Betty Friedan says her first written sentence for N.O.W. states, "Take action to bring women into full participation in the mainstream of American society now, exercising all the privileges and responsibilities thereof, in truly equal partnership with men."[1]

N.O.W. organizers evidently didn't know God **equalized male and female** many years ago when He created us in His image. But Connaught Marshner says equalizing female and male isn't what feminists vocalize. "Macho feminism has deceived women in that it convinced them that they would be happy only if they were treated like men, and that included treating themselves like men."[2] *Equalization* and *alikeness* are not the same thing. God created us differently so that we would complement each other—single or married. Refusing to accept His designed difference puts macho feminists in a competitive position rather than a complementary position with God. Accepting "God's designed difference" complements God just like accepting His *free gift* of self-worth complements Him.

God designed "work" for all able-bodied females and males. Joni Erickson Toda shows us that able-bodied even includes quadriplegics. Joni, an artist, speaker, author, and wife, does not sit and wait for work to look for her. Rather, she looks for work and holds a paintbrush in her mouth to paint beautiful greeting cards. Although she can't use her hands, she's authored several books. She's traveled all over the world to speak about God's love and grace and does all this from a wheelchair. In 1982 Joni took on the responsibilities and relationship of wife. In all these roles, she models the art of work willingness, which influences each area of her work.

The Art of Working

Work is a word with many different meanings. Solomon, a king wiser than all men, said of work, "Work brings profit" (Prov. 14:23, TLB). Christ said, ". . . My Father is working until now, and I Myself am working" (John 5:17). God saw that His work, "was very good" (Gen. 1:31). Paul said, "If anyone will not work, neither let him eat" (2 Thess. 3:10). Boaz said to Ruth, "May the Lord reward your work, and your wages be full" (Ruth 2:12). Ruth's work provided for herself and Naomi, her mother-in-law. Queen Esther's work saved the Jewish nation (see the Book of Esther). Mary and Martha's work (sisters of Lazarus) gave them the privilege of hosting Jesus in their home (John 11).

How we feel about our work is most important. We have varied work opportunities today, whether inside or outside our residence. That's why our responsibilities often "feel" stressful. If we feel embarrassed or held back by our work, we may need to look for another type of work either within our present company or another. We may need to relabel our work in determining if the feelings come from others rather than ourselves. The Proverbs 31 woman evidently felt good about her work because she modeled industrious working, both inside and outside her residence. "She is like merchant ships; She brings her food from afar" (v. 14).

Before her, though, God modeled for us an industrious work example. And Solomon said, "[She] who tills [her] land will have plenty of food" (Prov. 28:19). He was defining industrious work rather than saying all women will make their livelihood through farming. While I spent many years living on a farm, I'm not a farmer. Yet, my working hours are just as long and as versatile. Sitting at a computer to create a book is work—hard work. Giving birth to four babies, caring for them, teaching them, and training them for life is hard work. Likewise, teaching graduate and seminary students, directing a graduate school of psychology, and counseling others regarding life's problems is hard work. Yet, they have similarities—creativity, tiredness, perseverance, problems, initiative, disappointments, goals, rewards, accomplishments, and discouragements.

Whatever we do to "work," industriousness needs to control our behavior rather than complacency, laziness, or apathy. The following suggestions can help us work with industriousness: (1) If your work doesn't stimulate and challenge, relocate in a different job either within the present company or another. Using the Holy Spirit's power , we can accept frustrations as well as rewards. This helps us create an optimistic attitude which represents Jesus Christ honorably at our work place. (2) Apathy and boredom create emotional stress, so take care of boring tasks as early as possible. Then work on more enjoyable tasks. Find pleasant ways to relax; take a break with a cup of decaffeinated tea or coffee. During frustrating times, don't give up, keep trying; everyone makes mistakes and wrong decisions. (3) To protect your eyes, observe the work lighting; your office or work area needs uniform lighting that doesn't glare. (4) Wear clothes suitable for working conditions since tight-fitting clothes or shoes can cause work distraction. Make sure your chair, desk, or workbench is the right height to avoid discomfort and backaches. (5) For one month at a time (twice a year), record your physical and emotional highs and lows. If your estrogen level is too low, you may need vitamins or medication to increase your energy level. Since estrogen levels can affect monthly periods, watch for menstrual flow changes, check your breasts monthly, watch for menopausal signs, and have medical checkups yearly. These keep us informed and help maintain good health.[3]

These suggestions are applicable whether we work inside or outside the home or both. Remember, though, that wheresoever it is, work becomes enjoyable when we "work as unto the Lord." God designed work so we can use gifts and abilities to serve others and provide for our livelihood. While carrying out God's "blueprint" may not prove difficult for some, others do have difficulty. If we grow up hearing verbal criticism and putdown, we begin to believe the lies like, "You're no good, a failure, fat and ugly, or dumb and clumsy; you can't do anything right." The lies go on. Loretta grew up hearing those putdowns. She didn't hear compliments or encouragement, and neither parent taught her to work.

As an adult, she struggles with bad feelings about herself and finds keeping a job stressful. Since she felt putdowns instead of acceptance, she struggles with living out God's blueprint to serve others and provide for her livelihood. Whatever the work categories chosen, we need hope to cover us. God hasn't promised "ease" for our work, but He gives us this caution and promise. "Hard work brings prosperity; playing around brings poverty (Prov. 28:1,

TLB). "[So] work hard and cheerfully at all you do, . . . remembering that it is the Lord Christ who is going to pay you, giving you your full portion of all he owns. He is the one you are really working for" (Col. 3:23-24, TLB).

In viewing a wide picture of "the art of working," we must distinguish between hard work and the responsibility-obsession battle. Georgia fights that "balance battle." From a very early age, she suffered her mother's physical abuse and was locked in a closet for long hours at a time. By age ten she had been slapped so many times Georgia dodged automatically when a hand came near, even if her mother was just reaching into the cabinet for a dish. She worked fearfully to please an unreasonable, irrational parent. Yet, regardless of good behavior, the feared physical intrusions came—again and again for many years.

Working hard to please her mother and avoid undeserved punishment, Georgia became a perfectionist. She's known for punctuality on the job, good communication patterns, and an honest day's work. It's habitual for her to work an extra hour each day even though she isn't paid for overtime. Her compulsiveness comes from intrusions that destroyed self-worth feelings. Although she's worked through much anger, depression, and forgiveness, Georgia still suffers victimization patterns. Those patterns influence her relationships as she tries to gain self-identity through pleasing others, especially on her job. Hopefully, with passing of time, she can exchange "pleasing others" for a wholesome and balanced work ethic.

The Art of Responsibility

Responsibility seems to mean something different to each of us. Whether responsibility feels pleasing or annoying usually depends on how significant others, parents in particular, modeled that art. When parents model irresponsibility, their children usually develop irresponsible behavior. While some of us have problems finding enough inner resources to "carry out" responsibilities, others "overload." Evidently the Proverbs 31 woman found that balance. Besides work willingness, she modeled well the art of responsibility in work. "She rises also while it is still night, And gives food to her household, And portions to her maidens" (v. 15).

Responsibility can be described as that for which we are responsible; a trust, obligation, or duty. Accepting responsibility rests on the perseverance that builds character. Through an honest day's work we take care of duties, whether in or outside our residence. We carry out obligations with punctuality on the job, in appointments, and in commitments. We fulfill a trust by completing assignments and tasks within an expected time frame. Most supervisors or directors observe quickly whether an employee responds to responsibility with willingness or irritation. It's annoying to assign instructions for a job and find them either forgotten or ignored. In assuming tasks, taking notes during instruction time is one way to assure we won't forget or carry out wrong the assignment. Franklin D. Roosevelt once said, "It's common sense to take a method and try it. If it fails, admit it frankly and try another. But above all, try something." Accepting responsibility is trying something.

Developing a balance in our work responsibility can prove difficult when we have damaged emotions. They cause very capable, intelligent women to feel inadequate and lack confidence. Dr. Ted Engstrom tells why self-confidence is necessary before we can excel. He says, "Self-confidence is not unspiritual. Quite the contrary, it is an honest belief in the gifts and talents given to you by God. . . . Success leaves clues . . . achievers are not born. They are made."[4] Developing a work-responsibility balance is important in every area of life. It involves risk taking. Risk taking can hold us back, when we haven't recognized and worked through victimization patterns.

For example, if we grew up with criticism and putdown and then discover our boss is critical, it's hard to *feel motivated* in carrying out assignments. If a parent was manipulating and we now work for a manipulator, it's very hard to *feel trust* toward that person. If a controlling, angry person intruded into our space and we now work for or with an angry, controlling person, it's most difficult to *feel safe* in that situation. In same or similar situations, each of us will respond differently, according to our personality and built-in behavior patterns.

Suzanne, my friend mentioned before, was molested as a child. Very early she learned to please others through "working" for approval. She found that staying busy helped crowd out memories and guilt feelings; overloading helped her deny emotional pain. While rearing three children, Suzanne worked outside her residence as she earned her bachelor's and master's degrees in counseling. At the same time she took on church and social responsibilities.

Now, besides being a licensed M.F.C. counselor, she works as a public school counselor. Although Suzanne holds an excellent record as a responsible worker, she told me, "Overloading costs something special inside. It is unhealthy behavior which eats away *time* that's needed for the thinking and learning essential for our emotional healing. That's why we need someone to help us identify when we slip back into the unhealthy denial behavior of overloading. That identification helps destroy *denial* and moves us into healthy coping behavior like contemplative prayer time which enables us to cope and get through painful experiences."

Even though we suffer from damaged emotions, it's still our responsibility to work out unhealthy patterns so that we can develop healthy work habits. That means we choose the kind of work we do and where we do it. These personal preferences and life directions need to come from God's unique blueprint.

Whether working as entrepreneurs, working for others, or working as homemakers, women are involved in making their livelihood. Single women with or without dependent children take on obligations inside and outside the residence. (Of all women, their role may be the most complicated.) Married women with or without dependent children take on obligations both inside and outside their residence. Those obligations need to be in harmony with the spouse's obligations since they share and work toward common goals. Regardless of responsibility, titles, or positions, we must hold to sound financial accountability. Therefore, single or married, women carry a responsibility. That responsibility, Mary Shideler says, includes loving work. "We are known by our work, as God is known by His work. . . . They who love their work, and for love do it well, grow into the full measure of personhood."[5]

Conclusion

The Proverbs 31 woman was known for her financial accountability and an honest day's work. Others could trust her to take care of duties, keep appointments, and follow through on commitments. She modeled a well-balanced work ethic that influenced her obligations in business, marriage, birthing, and rearing children. Thus, we can conclude that her responsibility balance resulted because of love. But her "responsibility balance" also came from using others' assistance. Since her bright, clear picture comes from God's Canon, we can produce it with confidence. We can accept unchangeables and change the changeable in developing a special female self. Through carrying out our obligations or duties according to God's blueprint, we'll develop healthy behavior patters in our work ethics.

It's pleasant working with women who've learned the art of responsibility through recognizing and changing unhealthy work patterns.

> Are you settling for less than the best? . . . Or will you choose to soar to build a personal reputation for excellence . . . to live your life as God intended, knowing that He loves you dearly and that He wants the very best for your life? . . . Give up your small ambitions. Believe a big God; remember that 'God is greater'! Get angry with your own mediocrity, and then do something constructive to get yourself out of the same old rut . . . begin living life with a fresh point of view. An exciting life of excellence awaits you—and it can begin today.[6]

We can accept unchangeables and change the changeable in developing a special female self. Through carrying out obligations or duties according to God's blueprint, we'll develop behavior patterns that influence our work ethics.

14 Discerning, Planning, and Providing Wisely

She discerns in decisions, plans for the future, and provides wisely . . . "She considers a field and buys it; From her earnings she plants a vineyard. . . . She is not afraid of the snow for her household, For all her household are clothed with scarlet. . . . She makes coverings for herself; Her clothing is fine linen and purple" (Prov. 31:16,21-22).

*W*omen have been involved in making decisions about marriage, birthing, and rearing children since Eve. But for the most part, the world of business and finance remained outside their control. Christ challenged the traditional perceptions of women's roles.[1] Yet, for centuries women were denied opportunities for education and careers. That's why discerning, planning, and providing in business decisions and investments are relatively new experiences for most women. This attitude has caused much frustration for most of us in both our "residence and work worlds." Helpful changes are developing, though, as males recognize female competence and intellectual ability.

The Proverbs 31 woman showed a great deal of business intelligence. She discerned wisely in business decisions and real estate investments. "She considers a field and buys it; From her earnings she plants a vineyard" (v. 16). In light of her unique model, we might wish all males felt comfortable enough with their masculinity to acknowledge our God-given femininity, like the Proverbs 31 husband. He surely felt comfortable with his masculinity, because he recognized and encouraged his wife's business intelligence. Women make decisions in numerous areas, but, we will only focus on a few.

Discerning that Unlocks a Satisfying Career

In trying to unlock a satisfying career, we must take on Christ's attitude in John 17:4. "I have brought you glory on earth by completing the work you gave me to do" (NIV). Some of us may try six to seven careers during our lifetime. The Proverbs 31 woman gave us a good model of how to unlock a variety of satisfying careers. She became proficient in buying and selling real estate, supervising employees, weaving material, making and selling clothing, and managing her business. She chose marriage, birthed and reared children, and directed her household. She may have agreed with this unknown author's reflection. "The flowers of all the tomorrows are in the seeds of today." Yes, tomorrow's careers rest in today's seeds, awaiting those who will plant and cultivate them.

Unlocking requires initiative, planning, and faith that believes this career encouragement. "For I know the plans I have for you, says the Lord. . . . plans for good and not for evil, to give you a future and a hope" (Jer.29:11, TLB). "All things are possible to him who believes" (Mark 9:23). That's our first choice: Believe there's a "satisfying career" to give a hopeful future. In choosing a career path, we may need other's assistance and expertise. Believing may mean preparing through training or schooling. That's what believing meant for me. Interspersed with rearing my children, I held full- and part-time secretarial jobs to help supplement the family's income. Some challenged me, some didn't.

My mind often played conflicting message-tapes. "Working outside the home neglects your children. You must work for pay, Dick's salary can't stretch far enough for family needs. Go back to college and get your journalism degree." But, I battled seven years before feeling brave enough to walk onto a college campus filled with young adults. When enrollment day arrived, I drove to the community college with both fright and faith fighting inside me. Along with thousands of others, I stood in a waiting line for two hours. Finally, a guidance counselor motioned me to her desk. While showing her my preenrollment sheet, I explained which degree program I wanted. In checking the schedule for class times, she kept telling me the classes I needed were filled. My stomach nerves tied into hard knots. My thoughts whispered a short prayer: *Lord, what am I doing here? I believed You wanted me to enroll and finish my schooling.*

After about thirty minutes of getting nowhere the counselor said, "It's time for my dinner break." My steam valve almost blew off. I didn't know what to do. My emotions said, "Go home and forget this whole thing. You don't belong here." But my mind said, "No! Don't listen to that. God brought you here, and He will open doors somehow for the right classes." So, I looked on my campus map for the snack bar and bought some food. While eating a burrito and drinking a soft drink, I remembered meeting Peggy, one of the guidance counselors, at Suzanne's house. So I prayed something like, "Father, God, I'm not sure what I'm doing here. I really feel foolish. But I believe you want me to enroll and get my degree in journalism. If You *do* want me here, I ask You to guide the registration line so Peggy will have an opening for me."

When the dinner break ended, the long enrollment line started moving again. In a few minutes I reached the registration doorway. Peggy sat at her desk, finishing with a student. I walked over and asked her if she would help me; she answered, "I'll be glad to." She asked all the right questions and guided me into required classes for my journalism program. When we finished the enrollment process, I told Peggy, "Thanks for your patience. You helped me so much." Then, I paid the tuition fees and received my class schedule. The Lord met my college enrollment needs, like only He can. The students' acceptance, plus caring teachers, made my "mid-life schooling" a challenging and stimulating learning experience.

Again the Philippians 4:13 truth became real: "I can do everything God asks me to with the help of Christ who gives me strength and power" (TLB). He helped me unlock a new career through schooling and training in writing skills.

Another choice involves overcoming "roadblocks" that block gifts. To learn about career opportunities check with corporations, adult programs, community colleges, or state employment offices. Call Christian or private schools and organizations like Boy Scouts, Girl Scouts, and InterCristo. Inter-Cristo provides Christians with jobs wherever needed. They're located at 19303 Fremont Avenue, North, Seattle, Washington 98133. For entrepreneur-ing, write Office of Women's Business Ownership, 1441 L Street, Washington, D. C. 20416. They're part of the federal government's Small Business Administration and provide a "Women's Handbook." For a broader scope of career opportunities, check *The Handbook of Labor Statistics* at a library. Helpful books, like *What Color Is Your Parachute?*, can guide you in exploring your interests, talents, and gifts.

Roadblocks are temporary, not permanent; some can be removed with enthusiasm and initiative. Others need stronger tactics in order for us to overcome them.

(1) List all jobs you've held, paid or volunteer, and what you liked best about each. Decide whether you like working with people or machines, sitting at a desk or moving around, supervising or being supervised, or working with detail work or general work. That will help you find a preference pattern in choosing a different type of work to pursue.

(2) Check with a local community college or private counselor for career testing. The Strong-Campbell Interest Inventory helps us understand our work interests and which types of work we may enjoy.

(3) Consider developing interests in arts and crafts or hobbies. Many women hold annual home boutiques to sell items they make.

(4) Compare hours, pay scale, child-care costs and availability, promotion opportunities, transportation availability and costs, creativeness, and taxes.

Sometimes, home entrepreneuring provides the amount of income needed.

(5) Check job limitations. Is travel required and how often? Are travel expenses covered? Is extra schooling or training needed? How long, and is it at night or on the job? Is tuition covered? Is the location safe?

While roadblocks can be removed by hard work, please remember that we cannot do every kind of work well. That's why it's important to evaluate our gifts with reality and honesty.

> Be honest in your estimate of yourselves, . . . for we each have different work to do. . . . God has given each of us the ability to do certain things well. . . . If your gift is that of serving others, serve them well. If you are a teacher do a good job of teaching. . . . If God has given you administrative ability and put you in charge of the work of others, take the responsibility seriously. Those who offer comfort to the sorrowing should do so with Christian cheer. Never be lazy in your work but serve the Lord enthusiastically (Rom. 12:3-8,11, TLB).

Psychologist Rollo May once said, "It is an old and ironic habit of human beings to run faster when we have lost our way." In ignoring God's way for working, many of us are running faster and faster and feeling lost. Some of us have listened to loud, macho feminists proclaim that women cannot enjoy life unless it's lived according to the feminist pattern. Understand that a career is our profession whether or not we receive pay. A paycheck gives us our livelihood. Self-worth, satisfaction, and enjoyment are based on doing what God calls us to do. Feeling self-esteem frees us to unlock and develop both part- or full-time careering in many areas during our life span, including homemaking. We can use the same flexibility as that of the Proverbs 31 woman, when she discerned wisely in business decisions.

Planning that Unlocks Our Limitations

Planning ahead is essential to achieving goals and enjoying work; procrastination is one of our enemies. From procrastinating, we create stressful situations for ourselves as well as others. In contrast, choosing the planning path avoids much confusion and frustration. The Proverbs 31 woman modeled how to plan ahead and unlock limitations. "She is not afraid of the snow for her household, For all her household are clothed with scarlet" (v. 21). This meant that wool and flax had to be bought, woven into material, cut, and sewed into garments long before time to use. This achievement took many months of advance planning.

When my four children were young, we lived in the Chicago area, and wintertime there means *cold*. To stretch a small salary, each fall I bought material to make coats, hats, and outer pants. Making winter garments early meant they were ready before the cold, snowy weather arrived. One year, we started a fad. The frigid winter wind blowing against my children's bare faces while walking to school often caused painful frostbite. So I bought ski masks for them. Many other children quickly followed their example and began wearing them also. Although that's just one example of unlocking limitations, the Proverbs 31 woman developed a wide picture of achievement.

She listened well to Solomon's wisdom. "Take a lesson from the ants. . . . Learn from their ways and be wise! For though they have no king to make them work, yet they labor hard all summer, gathering food for the winter" (Prov. 6:6-8, TLB). He was saying to wipe out limitations with the self-motivation of future planning. Planning helped her chose the work most enjoyable and assign what she didn't like. She hired several maidens for a household staff. Some tutored or watched her children; and some did kitchen work, while the rest worked on all other household chores. This helped her reproduce herself many times with accomplishments. That's why, at first glance, she looks like a perfect, unattainable superwoman. Actually, it was others' assistance that enabled her to unlock time, mind, and energy limitations.

One limitation we have is time. God is omnipresent (everywhere present at the same time), while we can be in just one place—at one time. Life can become over-filled and overwhelming with burdens when we do not use our time well. Anne Ortlund tells women, "Our minutes and hours and days are so precious! But they will be largely wasted unless they flow out of predetermined goals and strategies."[2] Although she kept a busy schedule, the Proverbs 31 woman seemed to balance it well. The writer doesn't say how she scheduled her time, but many of us have learned to use calendars in planning our days. Looking at our calendar before accepting activities outside or inside the residence avoids confusion and embarrassment.

While we have modern appliances for household responsibilities, time is still at a premium. Some families are no longer satisfied with one microwave oven, they need two to get them off to work faster. Many mothers each morning hurry their children to get dressed for school. They hurry one child out the door, speed off to take another to preschool or child care, then rush to work. Out of breath, they run through the work door. Since some of us **over-schedule** our time, we're burning out. Those writing about "burnout" for women, say it occurs at any age and its victims are often described as anyone in a continual state of frustration or fatigue caused from commitment to a cause, way of life, or relationship that fails to give equally in return. This behavior builds in destructive patterns that become addictive.

Dr. Bruce Baldwin, psychologist, calls these patterns "hurry sickness" and says they develop when we choose inappropriate values. For example, instead of enjoying responsibilities or volunteer experiences, receiving our rewards when finished becomes more important. From this off-balance choosing, he says we get into a cycle of go, go, go, but can't seem to stop. We drive faster; get angry when others don't speed up on a green light; spend no time in leisure; make appointments back to back; neglect time for ourselves; and feel people are "out to get me." We set high premiums on getting more and more done. Our self-esteem rests on our accomplishments, like it did with Joy.

She grew up with unloving, nonaccepting parents. At times she felt her father's blows and his scornful, accusing words. In her early teens, she was raped. Since she didn't have a trusting relationship with them, Joy couldn't tell her parents. She feared they would blame her, like they blamed her for other things she didn't do. Consequently, no one ministered to her emotional pain and shame. In adulthood, it's difficult for Joy to trust others or believe anyone can like her for herself. In her job she continues a pattern of overwork; Joy is obsessed with proving she's good enough. By complying with an angry, controlling boss, she works many long hours each week for which she isn't paid.

Each semester at a local college she enrolls in several classes. Joy uses *hurry sickness* to cloud memories so she won't remember and hurt; but she does, nevertheless. Although friends try to share caring concern, she doesn't "feel" worthy of their loving acceptance. Only God's love, power, and perspective—combined with a flexible schedule—can help her turn from this addictive behavior. In designing a flexible schedule, we need the following ingredients:

Time for reading and rest. It's imperative we take time for reading and studying God's truths and talking with Him in prayer. We need time also for reading self-help books and magazines from the Christian perspective. Next, there's rest. Christ respected rest time and encouraged His disciples to do the same. "And He said to them, 'Come away by yourselves to a lonely place and rest a while.' (For there were many people coming and going, and they did not even have time to eat.) And they went away in the boat to a lonely place by themselves" (Mark 6:31-32). Besides getting away from responsibilities, we need daily rest breaks. Resting our emotions remains as important as resting the body.

Time for fun, plus the unexpecteds. Fun times don't have to be expensive. We can walk with others in a park or the mountains or on a beach. We can attend seminars and sports events, go on a picnic or play table games, go bowling or golfing, eat lunch with a friend, play tennis, or work jigsaw or crossword puzzles. Whatever helps us relax, we need to enjoy it for *at least* four consecutive hours each week. In trying to stop a compulsive scheduling of each minute, we must plan for those unexpecteds. If they don't come, we can use the extra time for relaxing and learning to live with ourselves.

Time for work, but not overwork. "Overwork is not the disease itself. It is a symptom of a deeper problem—of tension, inadequacy, a need to achieve—that may have neurotic implications."[3] If we schedule our time out of a "love for work" instead of feelings of guilt, that's a healthy behavior. Whether working outside or inside the residence, we need to make sure we aren't trying to work for self-worth. Self-worth, God's gift to us, is an established fact; we don't need work for something that's already ours. Believing this truth will help us rebuild feelings of self-esteem. Those rebuilt feelings will motivate us to work out God's blueprint in love and perseverance—without overloading.

If you're wondering whether you travel too fast, ask these questions: Can I slow down? Can I stop? Can I relax? If your answer says, "No, I can't control my hurry sickness," you may be burning out. Changing from hurried sickness may require many weeks or months, depending on how firm our patterns are set. Rather than live bound like a cocoon, we can break free. Four suggestions can help us avoid or recover from burnout:

● Take personal responsibility for actions rather than blaming others or work. This does not mean we excuse others' transgressions.

● Be aware of an initial paradox: The need for quick cure-alls to solve all problems. Remember, we're trying to move away from "hurry sickness."

● Confront irrational anger within, such as, "I'm efficient; the world's inefficient." This is an explosive type of stored-up anger we feel toward others because we can't say "no."

● Let yourself enjoy experiences, not just the rewards.[4] That helps us stop accusing ourselves falsely and begin nurturing our damaged inner child.

Setting a realistic schedule we can handle without harming our health honors the Lord. A flexible schedule helps us to develop our intelligence, gifts, ability, and potential. Accepting our God-given femininity puts us in correspondence with God.

Another limitation has to do with the mind. God created us with intellect, but not with His omniscience (all knowingness). "Behold, the [male and female] have become like one of Us, knowing good and evil" (Gen. 3:22). Since then, many have fought word battles over whether God created both sexes with equal intellectual ability. Researchers have sought to discover whether a thinking difference exists between females and males. Some say there is a difference. They say the brain contains right and left hemispheres; working together, they control the way we think or reason. The left hemisphere controls our right side and deals with abstract numbers and language; it processes information with logic and sorts out parts. The right hemisphere controls our left side and grasps things as a whole. It governs mental images of sight, sound, touch, taste, and smell. Thus, it holds our creativeness.[5]

Many believe males' thinking is influenced by the right hemisphere, while females' thinking is influenced by the left. That's why they refer to males as right-brain thinkers and females as left-brain thinkers. However, many overlook the fact that both males and females are designed with limitless ways of creativeness. On the whole, most identify females as being more relational than males because women feel a stronger need for friendship. This conflict causes arguments between couples over issues like frequent telephone conversations and Monday night football.

Some say that males project their thoughts and plans into the future more often than females. For instance, mothers know that little children need food, clothing, and shelter *now*. Fathers, in contrast, know that children grow into teens with costlier needs like schooling or training for their life's work. Men and women do not see the world alike. That doesn't mean women do not plan for the future or that males are not aware of immediate needs. Neither way of thinking is superior to the other. The differences may be cultural or genetic, but God created the differences to complement the two sexes intellect and help us give adequate management to society.

Another limitation rests on physical power. God created us with physical power, but not with His omnipotence (all power). More women than men are known for their emotional strength; whereas, more males than females are known for their physical strength. From the time Eve and Adam chose to sin, humans have wanted to believe the myth that we can become like God. Some women who try to become like God aren't happy unless they are competing with men, and they blame all wrongs or evils on a "male-dominated society." They fight the female-male difference, trying to make themselves "like" men. God equalized male and female in creation; however, *He did not create us alike.* He meant for our created differences to enhance both sexes.

Peter says, "You married men, in the same way, must live with your wives in an intelligent consideration of them; you must show them deference, too, as the weaker sex as they share with you the gracious gift of life, so that your prayers may not be hindered" (1 Pet. 3:7, Williams). Peter was referring to female physical strength. However, some have tried to say that "weaker sex" means weaker mental power, not weaker physical power.

From such an interpretation, many women suffer shame and a squelched intellect. Although God designed us with lesser physical power than males, **He did not design us inferior to males**. God designed us to "discern," "question," and "feel" differently. While males have more physical strength, God did not give them this power to harm and intimidate women or children. Rather, God designed their strength so that with gentleness they could give up, sacrifice, provide for, protect, love, nourish, and preserve others in society (Eph. 5:21-33).

Working in willingness, rather than frenzied hurry sickness, honors God. We are humanity, not Deity. We can work in only one place at a time. Accepting that truth enhances our lives, avoids competition between masculinity and femininity, and unlocks physical limitations.

Providing Wisely for Our Budget

Although she spent and bought much, the Proverbs 31 woman gave good account of her finances. She had to manage money well in order to operate her businesses and residence efficiently. Having available money for transactions meant she had to have a good bookkeeping system. That system enabled her to buy food; clothing (wool, flax, scarlet, linen); investments (land); equipment (distaffs and spindles); and supplies (belt and girdles). The writer doesn't say how she learned to discern so well. But while learning, she may have encountered money-attitude problems like Mark talks about. "But all too quickly the attractions of this world and the delights of wealth, and the search for success and lure of nice things come in and crowd out God's message, . . . so that no crop is produced" (4:19, TLB). Myron Rush describes those four problems as follows:

- *The attractions of this world.* Society is attracted to power, fame, prestige, and control. While unbelievers usually put more emphasis on these things than on God, some believers also spend money and time on the unsatisfying.

- *Delight in wealth.* Acquiring wealth, just to have it, takes so much time and energy that no resources are left for God or others. In contrast, making money, even lots of it, for livelihood and helping to tell the gospel isn't the same as delighting in wealth.

- *Search for success.* Chapters 10 and 11 of 1 Kings show Solomon building a successful kingdom, yet drifting away from God. His misunderstanding of success misguided him. Putting God first, meditating on His truths, and applying them to life can bring success *and* faithfulness to God at the same time (Josh. 1:1-8).

- *The lure of nice things.* The lure of nice things can also keep us from putting God first. Things, regardless of how nice, can never in themselves bring joy, peace, or satisfaction.[5] In contrast, using things to help us or others live out God's blueprint for sharing, gives joy and satisfaction. That's "dedicating things to use" for God's honor instead of just acquiring them for pride or selfish purposes.

Most of us have clashed with money attitude problems at least once. Handling our finances begins in the mind, travels to our willpower, and ends up on paper. That's called budgeting. Dick and I struggled many years before gaining control of our budget. The struggle came because our salary size did not fit our family size. Working for Christian institutions rather than in public education meant a lower salary for Dick. While I had good secretarial skills, we believed I should not work full time outside the residence until our children were older. In addition, my inner struggles kept me from using many other skills to build an entrepreneurship in our home. Many mothers would like to work fewer hours outside the home, but because of inflation they actually have to work more hours.

Designing a budget takes time and energy, but deciding what to put in it may become the biggest battle. Stretching a small, medium, or limited budget doesn't always work without saying "no" to unneeded items or wants. Needs and wants don't always fit into the same category. At times we choose between wants (an expensive car, for instance) and needs—like training or schooling or medical attention for children. The following budget, recommended by a credit union,[7] is one Dick and I have used for many years.

Housing	23%
Food	22%
Transportation	12%
Clothing	10%
Medical Care	5%
Recreation	6%
Education	5%
Savings	7%
Donations	10%

Although that budget helped us eventually gain control of our spending, we believe the secret to "sticking with a budget" is **customizing**. We customized that basic budget many times while our children grew up. Our budget needs are very different from only ten years ago when both our daughters married. With both our sons gone, we're at the stage where education needs have been combined with savings for retirement. While our food, clothing, and medical needs have decreased, other needs have not. The washer, dryer, refrigerator, dishwasher, and two cars seem to take turns needing repairs. The only budget item that has not changed is our donations. Anticipating the unexpecteds, we customize our budget like this:

HOUSING	30%
House payment or rent	
House repairs and redecorating	
House taxes and insurance	
Gas, electricity, garbage, water	
Telephone	
FOOD	9%
Groceries, lunches, entertaining	
TRANSPORTATION	20%
Car payment	
Car licenses, insurance, upkeep	
Car gas and repairs	
CLOTHING	10%

Clothing items
Cleaning
Sewing: material, thread, patterns
Gifts for family and friends
Miscellaneous items

MEDICAL CARE	7%

Regular doctor
Eye doctor, glasses, contacts
Dentist
Health and life insurance

RECREATION	4%

Entertainment activities
Newspapers, magazines, books

SAVINGS AND EXTRAS	10%

Vacation and extras
Savings and Retirement

DONATIONS	10%

TOTAL	100%

Of course, this example is not the best customization for everyone. Each household must decide what percentages to use and then carry through with committed discipline. Paul reminds, "But if any one does not provide for [her] own, and especially for those of [her] household, [she] has denied the faith, and is worse than an unbeliever" (1 Tim 5:8). That principle calls for budget discerning to operate at full capacity, which may make us feel weary and tired. Even though we're intelligent and capable women, some feel incapable of finding challenging, well-paying jobs. Many feel caught in a vicious cycle. If we have children, we want to provide for their needs plus extras; yet, stretching a budget that far can prove impossible.

Conclusion

God doesn't promise to provide *wants*, but "shall supply all [our] needs according to His riches in glory in Christ Jesus" (Phil. 4:19). Supplying for our needs is one way God says, "I love you." Appreciating that love can become difficult, if we compare budgets by looking at differences. But, we can in thankfulness say "no" to careless waste, use God's supplies in carefulness, and spend well His supplies. For those responsibilities, we must discern whether to continue working for pay outside the residence, become better organized and gain control of spending, or develop skills in entrepreneuring. We have a clear model from the Proverbs 31 woman in each area, and we have God's promise to supply our needs. Those choices involve discerning, planning, and providing wisely.

15 Wisdom, Kindness, and Organization Important to Work Ethics

She's wise and kind and organized . . . "She opens her mouth in wisdom, And the teaching of kindness is on her tongue. . . . She looks well to the ways of her household, And does not eat the bread of idleness" (Prov. 31:26-27).

*O*ur potential, abilities, and gifts are designed into many-splendored things by God's wisdom. His wisdom sits above worldly wisdom and "is first of all pure and full of quiet gentleness. Then it is peace-loving and courteous. It allows discussion and is willing to yield to others; it is full of mercy and good deeds. It is wholehearted and straightforward and sincere" (Jas. 3:17, TLB). This wisdom gives the creativity needed to carry out our work. To help us better discern God's wisdom, chapter 8 in Proverbs gives us many descriptive words—*prudence, knowledge, understanding, truth, instruction, listen, discretion, counsel, righteous,* and *power.* In order for us to use wisdom, however, we first must understand its origin.

Solomon said, "The fear of the Lord is the beginning of wisdom" (Prov. 9:10). That *fear* speaks of reverencing the Lord—not feeling afraid of Him. *Reverence* is an attitude of deep respect and esteem mingled with affection. We learn to esteem God the Father, Son, and Holy Spirit through respect and affection. Learning to revere God is a process. Learning about God's attributes, characteristics, and attitudes toward us builds our trust in Him. From that insight we can discern between God's wholesomeness and humankind's unwholesomeness. Thus, revering God will influence our work ethic and communication.

Communicate with Wisdom

It's very apparent from the Proverbs 31 woman's life that she used God's wisdom, rather than the world's. She modeled for us the hardest part about being wise. "She opens her mouth in wisdom" (v. 26). That's a communication model worth following. To speak wisely, she must have prayed this often. "Let the words of my mouth and the meditation of my heart be acceptable in Thy sight, O Lord, my rock and my Redeemer" (Ps. 19:14). She surely agreed with King David when he said, "I will guard my mouth as with a muzzle" (39:1). We have difficulty controlling our words when our emotions dictate our speech because both emotions and speech are controlled by the mind. Hurts and disappointments "store up" in the brain. When not dealt with, they can surface unexpectedly and fill the mouth with wrong words.

In controlling our words, emotions have to work hard because communication covers our work ethics as well as all other areas. *Communication* is described as the interchange or imparting of information, opinions, or thoughts by speech, writing, or signs. However, we impart and interchange with more than just our words. You may have heard the expression, "If you tied her hands, she wouldn't be able to talk." We communicate with body, sign, and eye language—or silence—just as adequately as with words. The key is doing so in wisdom.

One reason we often struggle with this area may stem from the poor communication skills modeled for us in our formative years. Nevertheless, we can change that by identifying our flaws, reprogramming distorted mind-messages, and replacing decayed roots with good roots. While there are many communication flaws, I focus only on three and their root causes.

Fear of femininity. One communication flaw comes from fearing femininity (the quality or nature of the female which distinguishes us from males). Many of us either deny or don't recognize femininity fear. This unhealthy fear comes from a fuzzy self-concept developed from emotional damage and confused thinking. The family is a society's foundation or central unit; it links people to a social structure. Emotional adjustment, intelligence, learning, educational achievement, character, sex role, creativity, industriousness, political affiliation, and religious commitment all spring from the family experience. Next to God, the most important and influential agent on earth is the family.[1]

We see this truth so clearly in connection with parents' failure to give and teach their daughters a healthy view of femininity. Each little girl will follow her own pace of body development, and there is a wide range in the changes associated with sexual maturing. Most girls begin a period of rapid growth around age ten; however, some start as young as eight and others not until fourteen.[2] Many parents feel too embarrassed to talk with their children about biological facts. They fail to assure their daughters that personhood doesn't rest on developing a "curvy" physique. Those who develop slowly aren't as "curvy" as some (like Ann in chapter 2), and they grow up *feeling inferior.* At age eleven, terrifying pain began to rip through my upper chest and rib cage. When the pain would hit, its strength and intensity took away my breath. For some reason I felt shame and could not talk with Mom. Finally I told my sister, JoAnn, and she explained that the pain meant my breasts were developing. Some months later I noticed a red stain on my underwear. I put on a clean pair and washed out the stain, but much to my dismay another red stain appeared. I repeated this pattern several times until my sister noticed me washing and hanging out my underwear on the clothes line. I can't remember what she explained, but her caring concern took away some of my fear.

Parents who fail to teach their children basic biological facts miss the wonderful opportunity of building with them a strong emotional bond of trust. Also, in placing this teaching responsibility on others, parents give up the privilege and opportunity of instilling God's values into their children. That results in children learning biological facts apart from God's moral standards and without hearing or feeling that they are loved and valued by their parents. Consequently, the basis for intimacy and trust is not established between parents and children. Teenagers, then, don't understand the changes going on in their body. They confuse maturing sexual feelings with intimacy needs. They think the two are one and the same. Many become sexually active only to discover too late they've lost their virginity prematurely and foolishly. Some discover they're pregnant. Contrary to what many tell us, most of today's teens want emotional bonding with their parents rather than premarital sexual activity.

Some parents grew up in dysfunctional homes where they suffered different types of abuses and verbal putdowns. They did not grow up with a healthy sense of self-identity and self-esteem; therefore, since they're unable to relate to their children with loving respect, the vicious cycle goes on. These children usually grow up ashamed of their bodies, neglecting their appearance, wearing sloppy clothing, and avoid the use of make-up. Some females adopt a "masculine" style of clothing, walking, and movements; they are trying to make themselves unattractive. Others *feel* unattractive to the opposite sex and avoid establishing meaningful relationships with men. When we suffer abuses or our parents fail to give us "feelings" of worth, importance, and love, we learn to fear our femininity. However, we can teach ourselves a healthy view of self-identity.

(1) Believe that your self-worth rests on being created in God's image.

(2) Accept the fact that you are female and that your female nature was designed by God.

(3) Remind yourself each day that God designed you as a person of worth.

(4) Accept the fact that you are important to God because He created humanity in His image.

(5) Decide that your choice in style is more important than someone else's view, although at times you may need their advice and suggestions.

(6) Remember that your gifts and abilities are equally as important as those of others.

This process takes time, but after a few weeks of applying it, your caterpillar-like self-image will begin to take on the image of a beautiful butterfly. A feeling of self-acceptance will develop as you "believe" that there's nothing about you to fear because God created your femininity or female nature.

Fear of sexuality. Another communication flaw comes from fearing sexuality, the physical and behavioral differences that separate us from males. Because so many parents fail to give their preteens adequate information about sexuality, most boys and girls struggle through their early teen years. While girls mature sexually at an earlier age than boys, their emotional maturity lags behind. Girls who develop quickly are not ready emotionally to deal with the social pressures that follow. Unfortunately, neither are their parents or most boys.

Because most boys aren't taught how to accept their changing bodies or to have a sense of sensitivity for girls, they express their self-consciousness by teasing girls. This adds to the girls' shame and causes them to feel worse about their God-designed bodies. When we don't "feel" that significant others are sensitive toward our privacy while growing up, our emotional needs are damaged. Living with painful memories or excusing others' insensitivity can cause resistance to and denial of healthy sexual feelings. Sexuality needs to be integrated into our character development, value system, and personal relationships.[3] God designed the differences between males and females to complement humanity and enhance the marriage relationship.

When we grow up without appropriate modeling of God's design for sexuality, we may have difficulty relating intimately to our mates. Myrna struggles with this fear. Beginning at age four and lasting three years, she suffered unwanted sexual intrusions. For her, the following years felt like a bundle of nebulous, negative feelings filled with self-hate and guilt. After marriage, her problems multiplied. When making love with her spouse, instead of feeling joy in sharing herself, Myrna felt guilt and shame. After ten years of marriage, Myrna decided she must tell her husband her childhood experiences. Yet she struggled for days, dreading that he might picture her as "dirty" and reject her. So, feeling great fear, she told him. With loving acceptance, he took her in his arms and started crying. Later he said, "To think, you've carried that inside you all these years." He held her close, and they cried together. Telling the terrible secret began a "healing process" for her. Myrna has been married over twenty-five years and remains one of the few who has gotten beyond the 80 percent divorce rate. Reasons for that accomplishment rest on risking to tell the secret, following God's design for sexual expression, and loving acceptance from her spouse. Myrna has had to face the fact that "struggling with sexuality" may last a lifetime. But, with God's insight and others', Myrna is learning to feel compassion toward herself and communicate her life with wisdom.

Fear of sexuality also influences relationships in the workplace. Many misassociate the need for friendship and intimacy with sexual feelings. For that reason, friendly relationships at work may be damaged or destroyed through ignorance or wrong choices. Using God's wisdom rather than the world's helps us in our work ethics. Wisely, we won't join in off-color jokes or conversations; we won't take into the mind obscene pictures, literature, or movies. We will avoid sexual sin or implications, since they "sin" against our body and mind.

Fear of broken trust. A third communication flaw comes from broken trust in meaningful relationships. Severe experiences like a lack of physical safety, an absence of acceptance and emotional nurture, feeling devalued in personhood, or many broken promises damages children's ability to trust. Even in adulthood, it's difficult for them to feel confidence in others. They are thrown into an identity crisis, and having to trust others' decisions or motives creates a dilemma. That's why many adults cannot build strong relationships for friendships or marriage. We need trust in all areas of our lives—including our work ethics. If we suffer from broken trust, our inability to trust shows up in the workplace.

Trust has been most difficult for me to rebuild; at times, I'm still rebuilding. While growing up, my decision making had to fit within a small box designed by Mom and Daddy. Otherwise, I felt their disapproval and mistrust, even after becoming an adult with children of my own. For instance, the summer my daughters were two years old and seven months old, we visited Mom and Daddy. A friend I grew up with was in the same town, also visiting. One hot, humid afternoon, we took her two-year-old boy and my two-year-old girl swimming at one of the creeks. They enjoyed playing in the cool, clear creek water. While watching them play, we sat in the water and talked about when we grew up. Visiting with my friend was wonderful, and after about two hours, we went home.

When I walked into the house, Mom's stare spoke the same judgmental words I grew up with. "You made a bad decision. It doesn't fit into our small box." My friend had made choices in her latter teens that led to birthing a child before marriage and, at times, she misused alcoholic beverages. My parents didn't think I should spend time with someone who acted "that way." They saw me as a little girl making irresponsible choices, instead of seeing me as an adult with stable standards and values. Since they didn't trust themselves, they couldn't trust me. Through not trusting my decisions, they, once again, broke a mind trust.

Since neither of them felt trust, their "decision box" contained mistrust and confusion. Daddy "chose" to assault Mom, rather than love her. Mom "chose" to live with his assaults, rather than leave. Those clear examples of broken-trust confusion show we suffer from letting others "think" for us.

Rebuilding trust in ourselves or others becomes difficult since we often take on victimization patterns without realizing it. Early in life we assume responsibility for others' behavior even when we can do nothing about it. Consequently, because of broken trust, in adulthood we feel the same powerlessness that we felt as children. Our "inner child" needs emotional healing.

That healing, however, comes "not by making a broken thing good enough to work, but by delivering us from the power of that broken thing so that it can no longer rule us. . . . The Holy Spirit does *not* intend to improve us or make us better and better! . . . the Lord heals by leaving the broken part right there in place, overcoming it by His nature."[4] That's how we learn to change *powerless* feelings into *power* feelings. "[We] can do everything God asks [us] to with the help of Christ who gives [us] the strength and power" (Phil. 4:13, TLB). Although it may feel scary, we can throw off powerless feelings to take on His powerful strength. We can switch from others' control to Christ's control.

To offset damage from broken trust, we need to identify areas where we let others "think" for us. After identifying those areas, we can determine how to "think" for ourselves. We can to make our own decisions and take the consequences.

> Yesterday is gone and there is nothing we can do to recall it. Tomorrow is not yet ours because it is not here. Today is the only time we have to profit from yesterday's mistakes and plan toward tomorrow. . . . We may not have control over the circumstance around us but neither do the circumstances have control of us. . . . God so designed us to be in control of ourselves.[5]

Mistakes, whether ours or others, can become learning choices. We can affect our work ethic by reprogramming to go beyond the fear of broken trust.

Teach Kindness Through Speech

How we speak influences all areas of life. Just as we need to communicate with wisdom, we also need to season our speech with kindness. Next to the brain, the tongue probably has the greatest influence on our actions, and James says it is the body member most difficult to control.

> If anyone can control [her] tongue, it proves that [she] has perfect control over [herself] in every other way. The tongue is a small thing, but what enormous damage it can do. . . . The tongue is a flame of fire. . . . and can turn our whole lives into a blazing flame of destruction and disaster. . . . No human being can tame the tongue. . . . And so blessing and cursing come pouring out of the same mouth (Jas. 3:2,5-8,10, TLB).

Since we often speak from our emotions, controlling the tongue proves taxing. Uncontrolled, it can devastate responsibilities and relationships.

We're not told how, but the Proverbs 31 woman "learned" to control her tongue. Not only did she open her mouth in wisdom, but "the teaching of kindness is on her tongue" (v. 26). To teach kindness, though, she must have accepted herself and believed in her choices. We can't teach kindness unless we're, first of all, kind to ourselves. Self-kindness rests on feeling a healthy self-esteem, which rests on accepting God's free gift of self-worth. This frees us to teach kindness. There are numerous ways to do this, but we'll only focus the areas of thoughtful behavior, appreciating others, and responsible behavior.

Teach kindness through thoughtful behavior. How great is the need for thoughtfulness to control our behavior at work! We exhibit thoughtfulness by living carefully, mindfully, and considerately of others; however, this involves risk.

> If you create a life that is always comfortable, always without risk, you have only created a fool's paradise . . . . You would not be where you are now unless you had taken risks, and you will not be where you want to be without risking more. . . . Your life is the direction it takes, not merely the sum of your successes and failures but where you finally decide to go.[6]

Taking the thoughtful route means thinking of others' needs and discerning how or whether we can help. Helping others at work isn't always easy or convenient, and sometimes it involves referring them to someone more qualified.

There are many situations in the workplace that give opportunities to choose between harsh words and kindness. Coworkers may have "bad days" when they lash out at us in uncontrolled anger. Often others may fail to carry out their responsibilities and cause more work for us. We need to be careful about reactions, and we must learn to respond under the Holy Spirit's guidance so we won't belittle or embarrass coworkers. There are times when we need to listen while a fellow worker talks about her frustrations. Listening gives others a sense of value and belonging. Honest praise or helpful suggestions are ways God can minister through us to others. Although thinking of others before ourselves can be risky and involves trust, it helps us show kindness through thoughtful behavior.

Teach kindness through appreciating others. Feeling and showing appreciation for others is a missing link in the workplace and in the church. For some of us, making work decisions or business investments may be new experiences. That attitude may explain the "gift-appreciation lack" so many of us display. Some of us respond with jealousy when we hear of others' achievements. However, to appreciate others gifts, we must feel comfortable with our own gifts. We need an attitude that says, "I'll envy not, so I won't be envied; I'll appreciate, and others can appreciate me." That attitude begins with a strong self-identity, believing we were created in God's image with mind (intelligence), soul (spiritual awareness), and emotions (creative energy). That's the basis for all discerning, developing, and using of our gifts; then we can appreciate others' gifts. This behavior removes "gift-appreciation lack" and teaches kindness.

Recently I studied business management at a southern California university. Several different nationalities and work backgrounds make up our small class of seven women and five men. Few of us were Christians, but week after week, as we met together, I sensed between us a growing dynamic. As we shared job frustrations about employees, salaries, and responsibilities, acceptance and appreciation became the norm. On the last night, our professor dismissed class early so we could share pizza at a nearby pizza parlor. That showed me an new way that Christians can become a "light" for Christ at our workplace. Feeling and showing appreciation for coworkers is important and necessary, for each of us enjoys a sincere "thank you" for a job well done. Although criticism is the norm in the corporate world and, unfortunately, in many Christian organizations, change begins with one person at a time. So, wherever we may be on the organizational chart, we can start a new trend by showing appreciation for our coworkers.

Teach kindness through responsible behavior. Our responsibilities give us an open door to serve the Lord through "doing for others." Matthew tells us that if we're faithful in the areas assigned to us, our responsibilities will grow (25:14-29). The attitude "We can do whatever, whenever, wherever" has brought havoc to our workplaces and all of society. Consequently, many corporations, organizations, and small business owners are reviewing and reestablishing standards for their employees' behavior.

Reports of sexually transmitted diseases (STDs) are the highest in history. The Centers for Disease Control reports that STDs infect an average of **33,000 persons** each day, or one in four Americans between fifteen and fifty-five. Sexually transmitted diseases can cause infertility, tubal pregnancy, blindness in babies born from infected women, cancer, brain damage, heart disease, paralysis, or insanity. Chlamydia, gonorrhea, venerial warts, genital herpes, and syphilis infect about twenty million persons each year. Trichomonaisis and other STDs infect another five million persons yearly.

Acquired immune deficiency syndrome (AIDS) is the STD causing the greatest alarm and confusion. AIDS damages the body's immunity against infection and leaves the victim without defense to fight serious diseases. Researchers continue to debate how AIDS is spread. However, all agree that the disease is spread through sexual contact and intravenous drug use. Although everyone who is exposed does not develop AIDS, it's estimated that **over 15,000** persons each year become victims. Millions have been spend in research, but there is still no cure.

While victims need to be accepted and ministered to, the behavior that causes the spread of AIDS cannot be condoned in the workplace or elsewhere. Doctors say that one casual sex encounter can infect a person with as many as five different diseases.[7] STDs can be transmitted while lying dormant in a person. Yet, people continue to ignore God's clear teaching that sexual sin always brings devastation to the emotions, mind, and body.

Other temptations also confront us in the workplace. Drug and alcohol abuse on the job is multiplying; they take a tremendous toll in lives and money. Legal battles are being fought over both mandatory drug testing and AIDS testing for employees. Bold newspaper headlines and television reports about recent savings and loan scandles show us that stealing goods or money is another temptation for many employees. Some Christians rationalize loafing on the job by handing out gospel tracks and talking about the Bible. They fail to concede that taking money for less than an honest day's work is a subtle form of stealing. Again, God's instructions are clear, "Your body is the temple of the living God; therefore, come out from their midst and do not touch that which is morally wrong" (2 Cor. 6:16-17, author). Paul warns, "Whatever you do, do your work heartily as for the Lord rather than for selfishness" (Col. 3:23, author).

In the workplace and elsewhere, we should choose our friends wisely. While some encourage and strengthen us, others try to weaken us through various temptations. Although we need to see them as persons of worth, like God does, we must not choose their friendship. Rather, we must look for those who see our personalities through God's eyes and cultivate their friendship. Healthy relationships strengthen us in our efforts to teach kindness through thoughtful behavior, appreciating others, and responsible behavior. Those choices will develop our special female self so we can honor the Lord in our residence and in our workplace.

Organizing Ourselves

Organizing ourselves is a necessity in our fast-paced society. We aren't told how she learned, but the Proverbs 31 woman lived out organization. "She looks well to the ways of her household, And does not eat the bread of idleness" (v. 27). One definition for *organize* says "form into a whole from coordinated or interdependent parts." Organizing—forming parts into a whole—is different from inflexibility or trying to control ourselves or others. And neither is it the "perfectionism" many of us suffer from. Molding behavior, schedule, and budget parts into a whole help us live out life with more smoothness and less stress. Unexpected things will come, usually when we want them least, but being organized helps us cope and adapt.

Being organized helps us work efficiently. "Sow your seed in the morning, and do not be idle in the evening, for you do not know whether morning or evening sowing will succeed, or whether both of them alike will be good"

(Eccl. 11:6). Those work ethics please the Lord, because He encourages all able-bodied females—single or married—to participate in work, with or without children, inside or outside the residence. Some of us find organizing others easier than organizing ourselves, but we must do it. At least three areas need our attention as we begin to organize our lives.

Deciding our priorities. We will need to reevaluate our priorities periodically. That process requires motivation, since our priorities change when we take on different responsibilities and roles. A single person without children will have different priorities from someone who is a single person with children. Similarly, a married person without children will have different priorities from someone who is married with children. Our priorities reflect the circumstances of our lives.

What is important to you? Will you take a moment to make a list of the people in your life, the way you spend your time, the use you make of money? What does this list tell you about your priorities? Are you spending too much time on something you really don't value? How will you change your choices? The following suggestions can help you set priorities.

- Use personal pronouns like I, me, my, or mine to personalize your priorities.
- Use short and concise statements. "With God's help, I will break my procrastination habit."
- Keep choices noncompetitive and don't compare them with other friends' choices.
- Set short-range priorities that will move you toward long-range goals.
- Choose areas that need work but are reachable.[8]

Regardless of the areas we choose to work on in organizing ourselves, it's important to seek God's wisdom, grace, and strength. We need those for motivation in deciding our priorities.

Getting rid of clutter. We, of course, must determine for ourselves what is clutter. Many of us make these determinations easier than others. Some of the following suggestions to help in deciding what's necessary and unnecessary clutter come from Jan Dean who teaches seminars on organization. She says, "For everything you bring into the house you should get rid of something. . . . Just about the best thing you can do for yourself is to delete unnecessary objects from your life. If you haven't used something 3-5 years, chances of it coming in handy are pretty slight."[9] Our "unnecessaries" may be needed by those living on low or fixed incomes—another reason to clear out clutter.

The "necessaries" move in and out of a living place each day—car keys, purse, shoes, coats or sweaters, things from work, toys, dirty clothes, and many more. Mom used to say, "A place for everything, and everything in its place." That's the secret to controlling the "necessaries." When you arrive at home, place keys, purse, and coat in their place. The next time they are needed, they will be there waiting for use. Dirty clothes, bedding, and towels need a particular place to wait for laundry, instead of cluttering walking space. Work things and children's toys also need waiting places so others can go right to them. Setting everything not in use in its waiting place prevents many arguments and removes much stress from relationships—two good reasons to organize.

Paying bills at regular intervals. For those who have not formed this habit, switching over can feel frustrating. Designating a particular place to keep bills assures they won't be misplaced or lost. Choosing a drawer or envelope to collect cash receipts and logging them each week helps control unnecessary spending. Storing those items in a large envelope help make "tax-time" less maddening. Also, designating two to four particular days each month for bill paying helps us pay bills on time. All items regarding bills, finances, and records need to be kept in the same place. Organizing our financial responsibilities can lessen stress, help us learn trust in our decisions, and enhance our organization skills.

Conclusion

In the Old Testament, Ruth modeled how organization affects work. She became a willing, industrious worker who lived responsibly. Her father-in-law and husband both died, and she took on the responsibility of caring for herself and her mother-in-law. While she did not carry prestigious credentials, she worked diligently at whatever employment was available. When she met Boaz, her future husband, her work ethic impressed him. Because of her kind and thoughtful actions for others, he felt drawn to Ruth. Her reliable work ethic brought this response from him: "May the Lord reward your work, and your wages be full from the Lord" (Ruth 2:1-12). We who live out reliable work-ethic skills, today, can also expect God's reward with full wages.

Since she didn't waste either time or energy, and did not live idly or lazily, we can say the Proverbs 31 woman felt motivation. Motivation provided perseverance in business responsibilities, and knowing her priorities helped her "look well to the ways of her household." While we organize ourselves, we need to strive for improvement, not perfection—that can damage our self-esteem. Some centuries ago Roman philosopher Seneca said, "Our plans miscarry because they have no aim. When a [woman] does not know what harbor [she] is making for, no wind is the right wind." Believers have an aim, however, and know their ultimate harbor; therefore, using God's wisdom, they can make plans and chart courses. Believers may need schooling and training for work skills in a new field. But through perseverance, in or out of the residence, can in willingness learn how to "work out" our work—the work we enjoy. That choice strengthens our special female self.

Section 5 *Developing Realistic Contentment Skills*

D iscontentment tops the problem list for many females today—discontentment with self, job, circumstances, friends, school, marriage, church, society, children, and even God. One type of woman, the "discontented woman" does not understand when other women express contentment with traditional values and roles. She tells them their lives must be incomplete. Another group of women, committed mainly to traditional values of faith and family, takes issue with these views. Between these two is a third group committed to combining homemaking with meaningful careers. While these groups struggle with each others' views and may never agree totally, finding her way to feelings of contentment is the responsibility of each woman.

Mom and Daddy fought the contentment battle in different ways. Daddy exploded with perpetual motion. He moved from house to house, town to town, and business to business. He couldn't find "whatever" he searched for. Contentment for him was an elusive dream. On the other hand, Mom worked hard giving life from her body and creating beauty with her gifts. She tried to give reality a sense of stability. Daddy painted a drab discontentment picture; whereas, Mom painted a colorful contentment picture. These differences confused me, causing me to struggle with contentment skills. Let me share with you two of my Christmas experiences. They taught me much about contentment.

For my sixth Christmas, one of my older sisters, Jean, gave me a beautiful doll. She had a pink rayon dress with white lace around the neck, sleeves, and hem. Pink rayon bloomers and slip fit underneath the dress. A matching bonnet had ruffles and lace. White dress shoes fit over pink socks. Dolls then were stuffed with cotton. Their head, arms, hands, legs, and feet were made of a glazed chalk. The glazed chalk looked similar to ceramics today, but not as nice. Dampness or water could cause cracking or peeling. So, we had to treat our dolls with care. In addition to the normal features, my doll had open-and-shut eyes, and she cried. Each time I bent her forward, she exclaimed, "Mama!" She was the grandest doll I ever received!

In contrast, my seventh Christmas brought a different experience with dolls. That Christmas painted a different picture of the "acceptable side" of contentment. It's one of the few experiences I remember with delight. World War II battled on, with my two oldest brothers, several cousins, and many family members in its midst. So, my brothers could not spend Christmas with us that year. Also, because of the war, many manufacturers made war supplies instead of their regular products. For that reason, few dolls were available. Many of those had expensive prices, especially for us.

I had few toys, so I kept each one a long time. Living in a small town of less than five hundred people and living on a limited income made shopping difficult. Mom ordered items from either Sears or Montgomery Ward catalogs, or she bought from a traveling salesman. I had heard others talk about "product shortages and expensive things" because of the war. So, I didn't expect to receive a doll for Christmas. Yet, on Christmas morning when I awoke and ran to the Christmas tree, there sat a doll. She wasn't like the one from the Christmas before, but she was a soft, cuddly doll.

Her face was made from glazed chalk, and a few squiggling forehead curls of yellow yarn gave a hairline. All other parts of the doll were covered with blue, fuzzy, cotton flannel and stuffed with cotton. Her arms stuck straight out from the shoulders and were just rounded off—no hands. Likewise, her legs went straight down and rounded off—no feet. Girls today might call her a stuffed toy. But for me, not expecting to receive a doll and not having many toys of any type, she was beautiful. I hugged my doll and played with her like she was the world's most wonderful doll. I couldn't have felt happier. Although my partial doll had no feet, hands, crier, or open-and-shut eyes, I felt contentment.

God, in the Garden of Eden, designed life like the beautiful doll—no flaws. Contentment prevailed as God's gift to humanity. But very quickly, female and male destroyed that contentment by going against God's one command. Contentment is no longer "natural" for us. We must look for it in Christ.

Contentment in adulthood, though, doesn't come easy for me, in part, because of growing up in a very troubled household. Another reason comes from understanding that I must seek contentment; no longer will circumstances be "flawless" in this life. Contentment can become a reality for us, though, especially as we think of one day becoming like Christ, our ultimate contentment.

16 Creativity and Initiative Enrich Contentment

She's creative and shows initiative . . . "She stretches out her hands to the distaff, And her hands grasp the spindle . . . She makes linen garments and sells them, And supplies belts to the tradesmen" (Prov. 31:19,24).

*L*ike *work* became a "smirk" word for some in the sixties, *contentment* has become a "smirk" word for some today and is confusing for others. Since God wants us to feel contentment, He colors life in a different hue from those who complain of discontent. God's kind of contentment, though, is a **learned** behavior, and requires work. Paul worked hard for contentment and spoke about a secret that helped him get along with either much or little. " I have learned to be content in whatever circumstances I am. I know how to get along with humble means, and I also know how to live in prosperity; . . . I have learned the secret of being filled and going hungry. . . . I can do all things through Him who strengthens me" (Phil. 4:11-13).

That's the secret. Using Christ's strength in learning to cope with life's differing circumstances. But Paul didn't imply that life is necessarily an "either-or" situation. He spoke of a flexible balance between the challenge and fulfillment of contentment. That balance calls for a resting or satisfaction of mind without disquiet or craving for something else. In our society, that's quite a feat to accomplish.

Gone are the days when advertisements promoted products, items, churches, produce, schools, cars, jobs, vacations, or clothes on their own merits. Today's advertisements have one purpose. They want people to feel "discontent" with what they have. If people feel discontented, they will spend money or use their charge card to buy what someone has told them they lack. Yet, spending money isn't the problem. The problem is discontentment, which comes from our mind and emotions. That's why Christ cautioned, "For where your treasure is, there will your heart be also" (Matt. 6:21). He, too, spoke of a flexible balance that's needed to help us cope with life's differing circumstances.

Feeling contentment, however, doesn't happen in one week or one month or one year. Continual monitoring is required to get and keep contentment. Like Paul pointed out, whether there's plenty or scarcity, we have to "learn to be content." That's part of developing our special female self and becoming a woman of excellence. That takes hard work—not passivity.

Contentment Doesn't Mean Passivity

Many in the Christian community misunderstand Christ's cautions about a flexible balance between "getting things" and self-worth. His cautions aren't against things as much as they are against basing self-worth on things. Buying things, regardless of their value, can't add to our self-identity. Our self-worth is based on God's worth, His free gift; whereas, contentment must be sought. It's an ongoing process, whether we have little or much or in between. We aren't told how she did, but according to her life-style, the Proverbs 31 woman learned to be content. Yet, she did not learn contentment through a passive detachment *from* life; she learned it through active involvement *with* life. We see her involvement as a busy, industrious willing worker who lived responsibly.

There's an old saying, "God helps those who help themselves." While His help includes material possessions, it covers much more than this. He helps us "get to know ourselves." That takes work and acceptance. Both, working together, can bring contentment. For example, we can evaluate our body before a mirror, looking for spots to trim extra pounds. We can then exercise and change our eating habits. But we must remember that while losing weight may enhance our appearance, weight loss cannot change bone structure, height, facial features, or a traumatic past.

When losing weight for a wrong reason, the pounds usually "crawl" back on quicker than before. Weight loss must be chosen for the right reason: We choose to lose weight for ourselves, not others.

> If you don't know what's important to you, you are much more likely to have trouble getting started. Without knowing it, you may be waiting for someone to tell you what to do. . . . Be sure that the things you do are actually and affirmatively of your own choosing. . . . Please remember, however, that just because your choice may coincide with someone else's, it does not mean that it's not your choice .[1]

Weight loss will become more effective and feel more rewarding when attained because **we** made that choice. This understanding helps us accept limitations that can't be changed. That's flexible balance.

Today's fast-food abundance and our "hurry sickness" which eats up our exercise time causes many of us to struggle with our appearance. The writer doesn't say whether the Proverbs 31 woman battled over her appearance, nor does he give her dress size. But he says she cared about appearance. "She makes coverings for herself; Her clothing is fine linen and purple" (v. 22). Some writers and preachers have given spiritual meanings to "linen and purple." They seem afraid to say the woman liked herself and provided for her appearance. Perhaps they believe spending money to enhance appearance seems unspiritual. Of course, spending indiscriminately or out of proportion to one's needs will discredit our decision making.

It's difficult to describe an "ideal" appearance, because it's as versatile as each colorful sunset or striped rainbow. While we're bombarded with beauty consultants' suggestions, God gives the most helpful ones. "Don't be concerned about the outward beauty that depends on jewelry, or beautiful clothes, or hair arrangement. Be beautiful inside, in your hearts, with the lasting charm of a gentle and quiet spirit which is so precious to God" (1 Pet. 3:3, TLB). Peter wasn't telling us to disregard appearance; rather, he accented the inner beauty that makes outer beauty more beautiful.

Inner beauty provides the first choice for a good appearance.

> Beauty should not be dependent on outer adornment, but outer adornment is not wrong in itself. When outer beauty comes first in your life, it is hollow and displeasing to God, but a beauty that begins from within should . . . influence your outer appearance. When you don't take care of your appearance, you are nonverbally telling others, "I'm not worth it."[2]

It's inner beauty that develops us into women of excellence with a special female self, the self God says to love. Actually, He tells us more than nine times to love and accept ourselves. We love ourselves first by accepting God's free gifts of self-worth and salvation. Next, we love ourselves by accepting both our outer- and inner-selves. Whether or not we choose to accept God's gifts and ourselves will control what we do about our appearance.

Some of us "feel" ugly on the outside and doubt if we can become beautiful inside. "God sees not as [we] see, for [we] look at the outward appearance, but the Lord looks at the heart. The Lord will both bring to light the things hidden in the darkness and disclose the motives of [our] hearts" (1 Sam. 16:7; 1 Cor. 4:5). That is God's love motivation—not guilt motivation—encouraging us to forgive, accept, and love ourselves. When we do, any lack of physical attractiveness slides into the background. That's how this God-designed beauty, which some call character, molds our behavior. "A woman's character can be seen in her appearance, not in a fashionable garment, but in the way she comes across. It is a beauty that surpasses clothing and physical attractiveness. It is that quiet, inner beauty that shows she spends time with God."[3]

Evaluating our outer appearance becomes another choice. Clothes help tell the story of our self-concept: personality, type of work, budget, clothes style, and body language. Basing self-identity on appearance, though, becomes an unhealthy dependency. The basis for evaluating and changing our outward appearance rests on whether or not we like what's there, not on becoming a clone of someone else. Yet, if we block out the mirror, we may be asking for trouble. Slowly, fifteen pounds creeps onto the midsection; our clothes scream, "Take it off!" Lazily, dry blotches crawl onto the face; our thirsty skin cries out, "Give me moisturizer!" Silently, dozens of gray hairs peek their strands through; they yell, "Quick! Cover us with color." Evaluating what we see in our mirror, using others' expertise, and applying needed attention helps "our look."

God tells us to balance concern for our appearance with modesty. "I want the women, on their part, to dress becomingly, that is, modestly and sensibly" (1 Tim. 2:9, Williams). Many women have taken modesty out of their wardrobe, saying it's "out of fashion." One definition for modesty says it's restrained by a sense of propriety; not excessive, extreme, or extravagant. By that definition, modesty is in vogue. The natural look in makeup and the feminine look in clothing have complemented women for quite some time.

Dressing sensibly and modestly shows sensitivity. Because Bathsheba chose to bathe in open view of King David's rooftop, we can say she dressed insensibly and acted immodestly. We might wonder if she knew that David often walked on his rooftop in warm weather. Regardless, her decision did not show sensitivity. Rather, her action set in motion numerous sins which eventually led to her baby's death (2 Sam 11 and 12). We make the same choices today.

God designed males with a chemical makeup that is different from our. Seeing females in low cut tops, short shorts, or bikinis may bring an involuntary emotional response in some males. Choosing to dress modestly may fit under the principle found in Genesis 4. When God confronted Cain about his insensitive attitude toward Abel, he disclaimed his responsibility with "Am I my brother's keeper?" God told Cain that he would suffer because of his wrong toward Abel. With this principle of responsibility in mind, we need to be sensitive to the male chemical makeup. However, our sensitivity does not remove from males their responsibility for controlling their thoughts.

Dr. Laura Mathis says, "The reason God forbids certain actions is not because he enjoys sitting in an ivory tower . . . concocting whimsical ways to restrict us. Certain actions or attitudes are wrong, because they result in natural consequences that are harmful to ourselves or others. . . . All of God's law can be summed up in one word: *love*. Wholesome morality is based on love."[4] Through loving, responsible choices we can become our "brothers' keepers." We can dress with a sense of propriety.

Deciding which areas to change is a third choice. Some of us may not fit society's picture of the "perfect ten" body, but our physical attractiveness isn't God's first concern. God tells us to develop an inner beauty that will permeate the personality and affect our behavior. If we struggle with our appearance, this attitude helps. "Lord, help me *accept* what cannot be changed and *change* what can be changed." Height, age spots, wrinkles, age, frame, or foot size cannot be changed. Weight, hair color, makeup, and clothing style can be changed. Wearing clothes and makeup for our particular skin coloring makes an amazing difference. Correct makeup color gives the skin a softer and more pleasing look. There are a variety of self-help books or consultants that give helpful information about hair and clothing styling.

Changing our physical image doesn't have to become expensive. Solomon gives us a good suggestion: "Have you found honey? Eat only what you need, Lest you have it in excess and vomit it" (Prov. 25:16). In other words to maintain a consistent body weight eat what's needed for nurturing and stop eating before the stomach feels full. If your hair needs styling, go with a style that's manageable and accents your face. When updating your wardrobe, stay within your budget and buy only what's needed; we can wear only one dress or outfit at a time. This same balance applies to shoes, jewelry, and makeup. Our money is spent more wisely when we buy clothes in our right colors that fit and look well. Balanced buying helps us avoid waste, arguments, and selfishness.

Liking our looks is more important than whether another likes or dislikes them. Deciding the look and style that's right for us will help us feel more responsible for ourselves and move us beyond the learned habit of passiveness. As that happens, we feel something new at work in us. This feeling is the opposite of passiveness. It's contentment. We may still feel depressed at times, fear failure sometimes, or have flashbacks of intrusions. We'll still hear Satan ask, "How can God use your imperfections?" Nonetheless, we're learning, changing, and maturing. Even though our job, children, school, friends, church, society, marriage, singleness, or circumstances may not have improved, we're learning contentment.

That's partly what Paul meant when he said, "But godliness actually is a means of great gain, when accompanied by contentment" (1 Tim. 6:6). Paul did not live his life in passivity. He participated actively in life. Yet, regardless of his stressful circumstances—like beatings and unfair imprisonment—he learned contentment. His contentment feelings did not make him weak, though, they made him strong. He didn't sit passively; he looked for ways to improve his circumstances. We can do the same. Going to college or trade school or getting training in other areas may seem risky and scary for women over thirty, especially if we lack healthy self-esteem feelings. But, God has promised to meet our needs, and His provisions always come through, even if they are different from what we had asked or hoped.

Looking back, I can see, now, why the Lord led me to college in "mid life" rather than earlier. If I had added college to my responsibilities of rearing children and working outside the home, there would have been no time or energy for them and Dick. But, the schooling proved challenging and stimulating. At times, the busyness of household responsibilities, church commitments, and studies felt overwhelming. Yet, in their midst I felt God's ongoing peace. His open doors ended the "head-heart gap battle" that I had struggled with for so long, convincing my emotions and mind to agree.

Often, the development of one gift will uncover another gift. While I learned writing skills, speaking and teaching skills began to surface. As my skills and confidence developed, God opened doors for their use. Contentment began to develop as I shared my God-designed gifts. God wants us to use the gifts He gives us. If we don't develop and use them, God doesn't receive honor; others don't receive nurture; and we don't feel contentment. Although developing and using our gifts may feel risky, that activity replaces passivity and leads us into initiative rather than defeatism.

Show Initiative Rather Than Defeatism

God designed us for lives filled with initiative, not defeat. Initiative furnishes us with power or ability to take the lead or initiate action. We can conclude from her life-style that the Proverbs 31 woman took action. "She makes linen garments and sells them, And supplies belts to the tradesmen" (v. 24). Initiative comes in many different colors, like inviting a neighbor for tea or coffee and talk; or volunteering time and gifts at a church, school, hospital, library, or Christian organization. While we can choose initiative rather than defeatism, initiative is the harder to live out. Defeatism involves wrong thinking; whereas, initiative involves *right thinking*.

> It's not what we think we are that holds us back, but what we think we are not. . . . Since 90 per cent of the brain is subconscious, it is . . . important that it be properly programmed. There is awesome power in the subconscious . . . Worry is picturing what we don't want to happen. . . . Knowing that failure pictures tend to reproduce themselves, . . . [they] must be replaced with a success picture. . . . If we picture what we want to happen often enough, it will actualize itself.[5]

Solomon said the same thing in Proverbs 23:7: "For as [she] thinks within [herself], so [she] is." But our inner picture must be developed from thinking right thoughts; that proves harder than drifting in resigned defeat. Right thoughts open up a productive life and free us from wrong thinking.

Paul gives some suggestions on how we can develop right thinking. "Practice thinking on what is true, what is honorable, what is right, what is pure, what is lovable, what is high-toned, yes, on everything that is excellent or praiseworthy" (Phil 4:8, Williams). His right-thinking list covers all areas of life and can steer us away from defeatism into initiative. The following shows us how to coordinate Paul's seven areas of right thinking into our decision making:

• *Right thinking initiates productive action.* Actions are the direct results of our thoughts. Just like we become what we eat, we also become what we think. That's *true*, and believing it will help us conform to this fact. We need right thinking to keep us from conforming to Satan's deceitful lies. "You are not as intelligent as others. You're inferior to others. You're not nice like others; no one likes you now. It was your fault." God wants to free our mind from the devil's deceit and conform us to His fact. "I created you in my image with mind (intelligence), soul (spiritual awareness), and emotions (creative energy). Others' hurts go against my limitations, for I love you. You share my worth."

Believing that truth helps us turn from an emotional, topsy-turvy life. Instead of conforming to Satan's lies, we can learn to think on what is *honorable*, that exemplary sense of personal moral standards and conduct. In reading about Christ's conduct toward others, we can see His honorable behavior. Also, we can read biographies of believers who lived honorably. Both will help initiate productive action.

• *Right thinking initiates productive attitudes.* Our attitudes and thoughts develop from what goes into the mind. Computer people use the acronym GIGO (Garbage In, Garbage Out). Whatever goes into a computer comes out—in the same form that it went in. So, in order to accomplish successful computer output, a person must first learn proper computer input. In like manner, for us to feel productive attitudes (output), we must first think productive thoughts (input). Input depends on what we let in our ear gate or eye gate. Dr. Earl Radmacher talks about this process. "The evil we program into our minds permeates our innermost being, spreading impurity and corruption. Then these things which defile us come gushing out and flood our speech and conduct, thereby defiling others."[6] GIGO.

Since the Proverbs 31 woman related well to others, we can assume she screened well what entered both her eye gate and ear gate. That screening initiated productive attitudes in her thoughts. In other words, she thought on what is *right* conduct (in accordance with what is just or good). James 1:14-15 says we feel tempted by *feeling* lust for people or things. In this regard, if thoughts aren't screened well, they turn into sin. Between an original thought and sin's controlling rests a vast space that we either screen closely or loosely. When the mind's eye gate and ear gate are screened with looseness, GIGO results. In contrast, using God's instructions to screen closely what we think about produces RIRO (Right In, Right Out).

Another attitude comes from thinking about what is *pure*, that which is free from anything that defiles or contaminates. *Pure* was laughed and scoffed at more than most words—until the eighties. Two critical problems brought this change in viewpoint. More and more contamination is being found in our air and drinking water. More and more contamination is found in our bodies through sexually transmitted diseases as well as the abuse of drugs and alcohol. As a result, many are demanding pure air and drinking water. Many who practiced casual sex are rethinking their sexual involvements, choosing marriage and fidelity over the risk of AIDS. Many children and teens are learning to "just say no" to drugs.

While we could not control our past, we can influence our present and future. We can't change our past; yet, we can think on what is pure. We can assume the Proverbs 31 woman lived with right thinking, keeping her free from anything that defiles or contaminates. For "her children . . . bless her; her husband . . . praises her" (v. 28). Pure thinking, from our love for the Lord, produces RIRO.

● *Right thinking initiates lovable thinking. Lovable* means being of the nature to attract love. Although we can be lovable at times, because of our human nature we cannot be lovable all the time. This becomes noticeably clear as we listen to the discordant notes played so loudly in society. We hear this harshness in racial conflicts, male-female conflicts, employer-employee conflicts, parent-child conflicts, Christian-humanist conflicts, and the list goes on. With such a battle going on for the mind, it's difficult to find "lovables" to think on. Even while looking for the lovable, our mind becomes offended over and over again. Television commercials use sex to sell all kinds of products from toothpaste to orange juice. Newspapers and magazines are filled with ads designed to make women discontented with what they have. Since advertisements are "designed" to get our money, few ads are trustworthy; thus, they can't be considered lovable.

Christ's nature, therefore, is the only nature that can attract love and remain pleasing with consistency. For that reason, we can think on His givingness, holiness, purity, love, friendliness, provision, loveliness, and forgiveness. Thinking on Christ initiates motivation toward purifying the mind for productive attitudes.

● *Right thinking initiates productive effect.* Effects in life also result from the thinking process. Thoughts are influenced with both Satan's lies and God's truth. If we believe Satan's lies, we will live the lies. The lies say, "You must work for self-worth for your hurts make you unimportant and unlovable." Listening to Satan's lies keeps us frozen in fear unable to climb out of his slippery-slimy pit of depressing despair. God's truth says, "You are important to me. I love you. I will heal your emotions and open doors for your training. I want to use your gifts." Listening to God's truth rather than Satan's lies develops right thinking, encourages changes, and influences a productive effect.

Thinking on what is *high-toned* is characterized by dignity or high principle, and *praiseworthy* is commendable and deserving of praise. But, many misassociate *high-toned* with self-pride, egotism or a "stuck-up" attitude. In contrast, Christ's life was characterized by dignity and high-principle; thus, His life is deserving of praise. In our society, people with those principles are seldom recognized. The media seems to say, "People don't want to hear the good, just the bad." Television, newspapers, and news magazines cover events that are depraved, destructive, or degrading. Consequently, people's praiseworthy behavior seldom "makes" the news.

In October 1989 Billy Graham was honored for forty years "of presenting a positive message through the media." That made the news. The Hollywood Chamber of Commerce honored Dr. Graham with a "sidewalk star" in front of the famous Mann's Chinese Theater on Hollywood Boulevard. Reading about Ruth and Billy Graham or Mother Teresa of Calcutta, for example, shows us they are characterized by dignity and high principles. These people, in conforming to Christ's image, can motivate us to move away from destructive defeatism toward helpful initiative. From thinking on Christ's high-tone, we see the need for conforming our thoughts to His thoughts. This helps us fight the "continual battle" Satan wages for our mind.

> The devil's top strategy in the battle for your mind is to lower your concept of God. He lowered Eve's concept of God, and the consequences speak for themselves. Don't make the mistake of thinking you can outsmart the devil, because you don't have a ghost of a chance of winning . . . he will knock you out of the contest in the first round.[7]

One way to win the battle with Satan for the mind is reading, studying, and memorizing God's truths. They educate, inform, and teach us about God's plans. They make us aware of Satan's cunning craftiness and strengthen us against his attacks. Another way is by staying in fellowship with a community of believers who will encourage and strengthen us by sharing our struggles, playing with us, and calling us to grow in the Lord.

At times, thinking about what's commendable and deserving of praise helps identify the things that God has done for us. "For as you know him better, he will give you, through his great power, everything you need for living a truly good life" (2 Pet. 1:3, TLB). Identifying God's goodness can motivate us to reach out and do commendable things for others. That's part of the productive effect of right thinking, and it helps us to live more creatively.

How can we carry out Paul's suggestion to practice thinking about things that are true, honorable, right, pure, lovable, high-toned, excellent, and praiseworthy (Phil. 4:8)? With inner strength. Some call this strength the inner locus of control. That's the amount of personal control we perceive we have over events that affect our lives. For instance, those who believe they have no control over their health say, "If we're going to get sick, we will get sick." Yet those who believe doctors control their health say, "Doctors are responsible for keeping us well, no matter what we do to ourselves." Those who believe health control rests on their decisions say, "We feel responsible to develop nutritious eating habits, exercise, take vitamins, get adequate rest and sleep, and see a doctor for regular checkups."[8]

This third group has a healthy inner locus of control. Believers have the Holy Spirit to help us develop a strong self-identity. We can do all things through Christ who strengthens us (Phil. 4:13). **Doing** takes time and hard work, getting us beyond harmful mind-messages that destroy our self-identity. Yet, unresolved emotional struggles take away the initiative, motivation, and will power we need to develop our gifts and abilities. We must first identify the struggles and then rely on the Holy Spirit and God's resources to work them through. That helps us to see ourselves as persons of value. This new picture, or healthy inner locus of control, is the Holy Spirit giving us the initiative to develop our special female self.

We Can Live Life Creatively

God designed us with the ability to bring things or projects into reality. That's what it means to be creative. Looking at the Proverbs 31 woman through wide-angle lens, we can see she modeled a variety of creativity. Verse 19 shows one picture of her initiative. "She stretches out her hands to the distaff, And her hands grasp the spindle." Distaffs and spindles were used in the process of spinning flax into thread, then into cloth, and then into clothing. In contrast, women today have many more options in arranging for clothing. Some of us create our own, while some pay others to create theirs. Clothing, though, covers only one area of creative initiative.

For much of history professional endeavor were closed to women. Thus, our creativity was limited to the "home setting." Today, men and women are realizing that *creativity* for either sex means developing God-given gifts for use. While fear, doubt, and damaged emotions seem to be limitations which hold us back, often, all we need is the initiative to get busy and use our gifts.

Those perceived limitations cannot keep us from living a creative life when we *settle* the self-worth question, *accept* our value to God, and *believe* we have gifts. These choices give the strong initiative needed in discerning and developing gifts. This, however, is a process, and going through it can feel discouraging at times. One reason is that some who haven't developed their gifts feel jealousy. Another reason is that some don't understand the importance of encouraging those who are going through the process. Although we need encouragement, we cannot put onto others our responsibility to use our gifts. That motivation must come from within. "For God has not given us a spirit of timidity, but of power and love and discipline" (2 Tim. 1:7). With God's strength, there are countless ways we can turn strong initiative into creativeness.

● *Using creative talents and gifts means expanding and broadening many areas.* Mom did that. From her creativeness I learned to take worn out and torn furniture and reupholster it with beautiful new fabric. I also learned to sew drapes, curtains, and bedspreads. She also taught me to take a man's coat and make a coat for my small son. I learned how to remodel houses from her. I feel as competent with hammer, nails, screwdriver, and screws as I feel with cloth, patterns, scissors, thread, and a sewing machine. From Mom's creativeness I learned about God, church, and giving. Mom loved helping others; she always gave her best efforts whether teaching the Bible, upholstering, sewing, or cooking. Her creativity also included playing the piano or organ and singing about God's love with her strong alto voice.

Through the years many other women have become challenging models for me. Some teach creatively from God's word; some write, produce, and perform music; others play all types of musical instruments. Many create beautiful crafts like handmade quilts, crocheted bedspreads, tablecloths, or doilies and sell them in home boutiques. Some teach aerobic exercise classes and proper nutrition. Many are creative counselors, teachers, and administrators. Others are real estate agents, doctors, writers, and lawyers. When we use the Proverbs 31 woman's model of creative initiative for motivation, we find ourselves moving towards contentment. Using our God-given gifts removes emptiness from the inner-female self.

● *Using gifts to create calls for faith and perseverance in pain.*

> God is the promoter of . . . creative thinking. He . . . is pleased when you use your mind constructively. . . . Creativity is not idle dallying. In most cases it emerges after hard work and awesome resistance. Sometimes the greatest friction comes from inside oneself. . . . It is painful to create . . . Anyone whose aim in life is to avoid pain will not create. Those who are afraid of failing will not create. . . . Creative thinking is what some authorities call adventurous thinking. . . . Creativity is the happy expectation of life.[9]

Creative thinking can be painful. I've lost count of the times when confusion and frustration almost kept me from writing. Each time, though, God would minister to me through the Holy Spirit or an individual, offering His loving encouragement. That would revive my faith and hope and enable me to keep going. That's what the writer of Hebrews meant when he said, "Now faith is being sure of what we hope for and certain of what we do not see" (11:1, NIV). Thus, both faith and perseverance are needed to help us live creatively.

● *Using gifts to create calls for dreaming that will open our imagination.* Dreaming has gotten a bad name from those who didn't learn how to carry through. Think of where we would be if Edison hadn't "envisioned" the light bulb. Think about how dull life would be if musicians didn't daydream and "hear" the beautiful music they write and perform. If teachers didn't daydream about better ways of teaching; if speakers didn't daydream to "think up" better ways of communicating God's truths; society would be much poorer. What if architects didn't dream and "draw" practical, livable houses; if scientists and doctors didn't dream and "discover" needed medications? If Henry Ford hadn't dreamed and designed the automobile or if the Wright brothers hadn't dreamed into reality their "flying machine," we would still be walking.

During my teens, fantasizing enabled me to cope with my pain-filled reality. That kind of daydreaming is not what I'm referring to. That kind of daydreaming denies reality. Dreaming with the intent to create is important, although it often seems valueless and unproductive. If we've received criticism because of creative daydreaming, it becomes harder to create. That's why faith and perseverance are such important features of creating. When others reject our dreams, hopes, and plans, we feel emotional pain. But when we communicate with God and He whispers, "Go ahead, I'm with you. I want to use your creative initiative," we must persevere. Working under God's guidance, faith and hard work become reality.

● *Using gifts calls for increasing knowledge and seeking opposite viewpoints.* Learning how to listen and when to talk proves hard for many, but it's a must for creating. In creating, we need to learn all we can about what we want to do. At times, we must receive new information from an opposite viewpoint to develop clearer pictures. To get new, needed information we must ask questions and then listen. Listening helps broaden our perspective and gives more insight. That helps us use our gifts because living life with creativity doesn't just happen. I saw a billboard that read, "Necessity may change some circumstances, but never a goal." A creative mind must look for new material and even change directions at times.

To be creative, we need to be informed. We can obtain input from several sources. (1) Information. We can find many facts from doing research in a library, talking with others, and taking trips. (2) Isolation. We need "time" to think through input to form our ideas well. (3) Imagination. Our mind must have liberty to roam and explore the possibilities. (4) Investigation. Know the market and search to see if your dream is different or if others have already dreamed it. (5) Integration. What's the overview? Our idea must fit together well. (6) Implementation. Carry through and don't quit, even if it seems impossible. God can't receive honor and we can't achieve if we don't persevere in faith to completion.[10]

Completion is important to any creative initiative, including development of realistic contentment skills. Contentment isn't laziness, unconcern, or doubt. However, many wear masks and imitate contentment; when in reality, they cover up disappointment. Many believers deny their feelings of discontent since they believe God says, "Be happy and contented at all times." And if they aren't, someone will say, "Something must be wrong with your spiritual life." But masking or denying true feelings cannot change what's going on inside. Discontentment shows up on the outside—on our sad face or drooped shoulders. Yet, we need some discontentment in order to remember what happiness is. Thus, God can use discontentment to urge us toward initiative and growth.

Conclusion

Remember, we must work for contentment; we don't find it by sitting passively on the sidelines. It comes in the midst of being involved with life. We can, at any age, begin the process of discerning and developing gifts. We can settle the self-worth question by receiving God's free gift of self-worth. We can believe God gave us gifts to develop and search Scripture for guidance in using them. We can expect confirmation from others when using our gifts, although contentment doesn't depend on others' confirmation. Unleashing our creativity shreds cocoon strands, frees a special female self, and builds contentment.

17 Confirmation of Self-worth Enhances Contentment

Others confirm her self-worth . . . "Her children rise up and bless her; Her husband also, and he praises her" (Prov. 31:28).

How we picture ourselves—not how others picture us—is the most significant part of learning contentment. We interchange many words like self-image, female-self, self-identity, or self-worth to speak about how we picture ourselves. Many people confuse salvation with self-worth. The two, though, aren't the same; they are separate. When God created Adam and Eve in His image, they felt strong self-identity. They felt good about themselves. "Although the man and his wife were both naked, neither of them was embarrassed or ashamed" (Gen. 2:25, TLB). They were naked in mind, body, and soul. Thus they enjoyed an uninhibited and transparent relationship with each other—and God.

God told them they could eat any garden fruit except from the knowledge tree. In going against God's command they sinned, destroying their uninhibited relationship with Him. And yet, their sin did not destroy their self-worth. They still shared God's immeasurable worth. But, their sin put them in need of something that could wash out sin and restore the relationship. The "something" became God's free salvation gift through Christ's death on a cross. *Salvation covers sin; self-worth covers inferiority*. Both help develop our self-picture and give basis for contentment.

In that sense, others' approval gives good feelings and confirms our self-identity. The Proverbs 31 woman modeled how her self-worth was confirmed by others. "Her children rise up and bless her; Her husband also, and he praises her" (v. 28). While creativity and initiative enriched her life, approval and encouragement enhanced the contentment process.

We Can Confirm Each Other

Whether we are single or married, we have people who are important to us, even if they aren't family. Some relatives live at an emotional distance from us and don't love or confirm. This was Judy's experience. She never knew her birth parents and was adopted when she was nine months old by a couple who had lost three children through death. It was her adoptive mother's second marriage. But by the time Judy was three, her parents divorced. Then when Judy was five, her mother married again. Her new father had problems with alcohol dependency and killed himself two years later.

After about four years, her mother married for a fourth time. This behavior pattern showed Judy and others that her adopted mother had problems sustaining a marital relationship. This succession of broken relationships made it difficult for her to trust others. Even though Judy tried to like her new father, she wondered how long he would last. When Judy was twelve, her stepfather started incestuous intrusions. Judy told her mother, but her mother would not intervene. Then Judy told her adoptive father, whom she considered to be her real father. About two years later, he asked her to live with him. He lived alone, but Judy felt safe with him. They shared a helpful, respectful relationship. Later, she began to "feel" some confirmation of her self-identity.

Though living with her adopted father improved her situation, she was troubled by his compulsive gambling. After high school she attended and graduated from a Christian college. There she received helpful insight from competent Christian counselors, who helped her see that broken relationships and violations had destroyed her feeling of self-worth. With their help, Judy began changing her self-picture. Their loving acceptance helped her feel cared for and valued; they confirmed her self-worth.

Acceptance and encouragement help us feel worthwhile. Even if we can't verbalize the words, we feel "I have worth; I'm important. Someone listens to me without condemning or criticizing or asking in return." Those feelings confirm the worth we received from God and show the importance of Paul's instructions. "Practice bearing one another's burdens, and in this way carry out the law of Christ" (Gal. 6:2, Williams). Lila is known for helping bear others' burdens. At age sixteen, Lila married Dawson Trotman. While encouraging and assisting Dawson to build a group called The Navigators into an international Christian organization, she birthed and reared six children. When she was only forty-three, Dawson drowned after saving another person from drowning. Using God's strength and grace, she carried on with parenting and helping meet other women's emotional needs. Few women have been called to bear what Lila has carried on her shoulders. She has shown that bearing each other's burdens helps verify and strengthen our self-esteem.

Bearing each other's burdens includes spending time together, listening, and talking without condemning or criticizing. It means giving care without asking in return or offering help without controlling. When we bear another's burdens, we encourage without overinflating hope, approve without necessarily agreeing, and accept without asking for change. Sounds easy? Not to me. Yet, how wonderful confirmation of my self-identity feels and how damaging lack of confirmation feels. We may not be always successful; but relating with this attitude helps others. "Do for others what you want them to do for you" (Matt. 7:12,TLB). That's giving "OKness."

In Christ, You're OK, and I'm OK

"OKness," though, doesn't rest on working for self-worth. Rather, it rests on God's finished work of creating us in His image and on Christ's finished work of salvation. Self-worth gives us freedom from inferiority; salvation gives us freedom from sin. Both bring about a complementary (not competitive) and corresponding relationship with God. Being in correspondence with God is accepting His free gift of self-worth. In contrast, competing with Him is working for self-esteem through status, position, or "doing unto others" so they'll think we're nice. While we cannot "work" for OKness, we can "accept" OKness. God's OKness restores our damaged feelings of self-esteem.

When we picture ourselves as persons of worth, love for God fills us and spills over onto others. We can then see them as persons of worth. In this way God enables us to live out His instruction. "Love your neighbor as yourself" (Matt. 19:19; see Matt. 22:39; Mark 12:31; Luke 10:27; Rom. 13:9; Gal. 5:14; Jas. 2:8; Lev. 19:18). In Christ, you're OK and I'm OK. OKness wipes out totem-pole importance, removes the need for competing, and places us "equal in value to" others. That truth helps us understand why Martin Luther said, "God's love does not love that which is worthy of being loved, but it creates that which is worthy of being loved."

While we can never do anything to *make* us worthy of God's love, being worthy and *feeling* God's worth aren't the same. Feeling worth relates both to belonging and love, two primary elements in developing our self-picture. Feeling loved makes us *feel* like we belong. We're both loved by God and belong to God through His acts of creation and salvation, which give us OKness.

Christ said, "It makes one happier to give than to get" (Acts 20:35, Williams). For us to know "how" to give, we must know "how" to receive. Receiving involves trust and risk, since it's giving of ourselves. It's the idea, "I receive with willingness this gift from you to use in some way best for me." That's risky. Some *gift givers* want something and do not care whether the receiver wants to give something back in return. Paul says, "Each must give what [she] has purposed in [her] heart to give, not sorrowfully or under compulsion, for it is the happy giver that God loves" (2 Cor. 9:7, Williams). Therefore, we must distinguish between some who are compelled to give in order to receive and those who give with no strings attached. Remembering how we felt when we received assistance helps us give with sensitivity.

God models well the dual role of giving and receiving. He gave His only begotten Son to die for our sin. Yet, God also receives. His Word says, "And you shall love the Lord your God with all your heart and with all your soul and with all your might" (Deut. 6:5). He gave us life; yet, at the same time wants our love and receives our praise. He knows how to receive; He knows how to give. He doesn't give to get something in return or to impress others; rather, He gives with no strings attached.

The Proverbs 31 woman also models the dual role of giving and receiving. She extends acts of goodwill; she's a willing, industrious worker. She's organized, creative, and shows initiative. Yet, in all that giving she allowed others to give to her through receiving from them. The writer doesn't give any details about how those closest to this woman confirmed her self-esteem. But they gave her confirmation through their blessings or praises, and in her receiving she confirmed their self-worth and hers. In living out the dual role of giving and receiving, the Proverbs 31 woman told others, "You're OK, and I'm OK."

Confirmation Needs Healthy Interdependence

Learning the difference between interdependence, dependence, and independence is uppermost in importance for confirming self-worth. These three patterns of living work in separate directions and have no connection. Understanding that difference will help us learn the value of healthy interdependence.

Dependence

One definition for *dependence* says it's being dependent or relying on another for support for existence. God planned for children to "depend" on adults for their livelihood. When children become adults and still depend on other adults for their livelihood, that's not OK. They're following a learned behavior that can lead only to destruction. (However, there are times when mental, physical, or emotional exceptions must be considered.) Those of us struggling with an unhealthy dependence must become free. This means commitment to changing our behavior.

Stop denying the dependence. Some of us have not identified our pattern of relying on parents, spouse, or friends for support. We may think, *I can't do things like others. My parents didn't help or encourage me to attend college. I'm overweight. I'm not good in math or English.* Even if those things are true, dwelling on them compounds dependency. Staying in the state of relying on another for emotional or financial support, when we are capable of supporting ourselves, is unacceptable. We need to learn to rely on ourselves. Identifying dependency areas (depending on others for decision making instead of using *our* ability) will enable us to go beyond an unhealthy dependence.

Stop covering up the dependence. For many of us, the dependency pattern covers all our life areas. Some cover up dependency on alcohol, drugs (prescribed or illicit), sex, or running too fast. We must acknowledge our need to "uncover." Since God has promised to meet our needs, uncovering is possible. In doing that, we may need to seek professional help at a hospital, rehabilitation center, or counseling center, because He usually meets our needs through others. There are many private, state, and county institutions that help others "uncover" from addictive behaviors.[1] Similarly, competent Christian counselors can give insight and perspective on learning how to slow down and live with ourselves without unhealthy dependence.

Independence

One definition for *independence* is freedom from subjection to the influence or control of others. If we've lived with intrusive and controlling others, we want freedom from that. And in trying to get away, some of us developed "independence" as a protection. We feel a strong need to be in control of our lives. Often not aware of our behavior, we communicate messages like, "I don't need your friendship or trust your judgment. I can get along fine without your help and acceptance; I'm sufficient in myself." Those messages, though, suggest the opposite of our needs. Because we are often unaware of these attitudes, it's difficult for us to understand why trust and closeness don't develop in relationships. Yet, we can learn how to go beyond a learned behavior pattern of destructive independence.

Stop the deception of self-sufficiency. God designed for believers the dual role of bearing others' burdens and bearing personal burdens. (Gal. 6:2,5). Self-sufficiency goes against that role and says, "I can get along by myself. I don't need anyone else." That is Satan's lie. We need encouragement, friendship, and burden bearers. At the same time, we need to develop a healthy kind of self-reliance; but not to shut out others, not to live independently of others. We need this type of self-reliance to help us first bear our burdens and then bear the burdens of others.

In a sense, self-sufficiency is self-punishment. It prevents us from feeling good about ourselves or others and adds to our fear of closeness. Closeness fear encourages a false feeling of emotional safety built upon independence. Self-sufficiency says, "I can go it alone. I won't get hurt again." To overcome this attitude, we can begin to place small trust stones one on top of another and glue them together with closeness. By trusting in small things, we begin moving toward a healthy interdependence. We're beginning to feel, "I do need friendship and others. I can't go it alone. I'm willing to share more of my thoughts and feelings with others."

In a sense, self-sufficiency is self-punishment. It prevents us from felling good about ourselves or others and adds to our fear of closeness. This fear encourages a false feeling of emotional safety built upon independence. Self-sufficiency says, "I can go it alone. I won't get hurt again." To overcome this attitude, we can begin to place small trust stones one on top of another and glue them together with closeness. By trusting in small things, we begin moving toward a healthy interdependence. We're beginning to feel, "I do need friendship and others."

In allowing others to help bear our burdens, we're moving beyond the self-sufficiency deception of trying to carry heavy emotional loads by ourselves. The independent do not want to admit that they may need help; they don't want to appear "weak." However, God did not create us to live as lonely islands; He created us to share our lives with others so that through them He can share His strength with us.

Stop avoiding a responsibility to others. Self-sufficiency says, "I take care of myself; let others take care of themselves." Responsibility to others says, "When I am with those whose consciences bother them easily, I don't act as though I know it all and don't say they are foolish; the result is that they are willing to let me help them" (1 Cor. 9:22, TLB). Paul suffered extreme physical and emotional pain, yet he learned to maintain trust. He remained vulnerable so that he could reach out and minister to others.

While responsibility to others takes commitment and time, it doesn't mean living their lives for them. Neither does it mean having guilt feelings for others' indiscretions nor making them dependent on us for support or existence. *Responsibility to others* means a willingness to share our life through friendship, encouragement, and bearing burdens. At times, that involvement might feel like a sacrifice; it may even result in disappointments. Sharing our lives will carry us from a damaging independence toward healthy interdependence.

Interdependence

One definition for *interdependence* is mutually and reciprocally dependent. Interdependence calls for a two-way response from two or more individuals who want mature relationships. This requires risk and trust because interdependence cannot function without "trust." However, those of us suffering from damaged emotions find mutual and reciprocal response in relationships most difficult. Nevertheless, trust helps us work together, decide together, offer friendship together, and bear burdens together. Dependence and independence run contrary to trust. Dependent people do not trust themselves; independent people do not trust others. Interdependence means we trust ourselves and others, and it works in us to enhance contentment skills.

Learning to console. We grow through cheering or comforting others during times of distress or depression. Giving consolation isn't always easy, especially if we've never received consolation. But, consolation confirms others' self-worth when we go beyond ourselves to reach out and show them concern. Billy Graham gives some suggestions for consoling. First, ask God to give you a tender heart; next, use the gift of listening. Don't register shock at what the person may say. Let the person decide if she wants you to read the Bible or pray. Anticipate needs without being told and don't stop being a comforter when the wounds seem to be healed.[2]

Cheering or comforting others gives us the opportunity to encourage rather than criticize. We cannot schedule others' healing; their pain must heal according to their timetable. After her husband died, our friend Jeri wrote this about her healing process.

> I couldn't understand all that was going on. . . . [But] slowly I began to find answers to some of my immediate questions. . . . Even though I doubted God's plan for me, I was sorting through the small pieces of the pattern. I held on to the promise that as I let God's Word lead me, the jigsaw of life would one day fit together.[3]

Encouraging others to be themselves and express their deepest pain is part of consolation.

Learning to confront. Unhealthy passivity changes as we bring together our views and those of others for comparison or examination. Confronting others, though, can feel scary and can keep us from initiating healthy behavior. We may fear being overpowered mentally because of unwanted verbal intrusions. We may misunderstand confrontation because we have been taught that confronting is "un-Christian." We may also not know how to confront.[4] Comparing and examining views must take place constructively and in love for the purpose of building interdependence. We have the right to be listened to in seriousness. Yet, as much as possible, confrontation needs to address a particular behavior or attitude for the purpose of edifying and building up (1 Cor. 10:23).

"Confrontation invites another to change but does not demand it [and] does not make continuation of the friendship hang on a change of life. . . . Acceptance of the other person is not connected to agreement or disagreement."[5] Jesus gives the best way to achieve and keep balance in confronting others: "Practice dealing with others as you would like for them to deal with you" (Matt. 7:12, Williams). In showing us how to do that, David Augsburger tells us to confront with care, expressing concern for the other. Confront in gentleness, not taking more than you give. Confront constructively to avoid blame or shame. Confront with acceptance to avoid judging others' motives. Confront clearly, stating your facts, feelings, and conclusions.[6]

Conclusion

Interdependence is the most helpful of these three ways of relating to others, and it requires the most time and work to develop. Actually, there's a strong similarity between interdependence and mutual submission. Both are needed for males and females to respect one another. Both are needed in order for us to confront in love with an uncritical attitude. Connecting mutual submission with a mutual, reciprocal interdependence helps us confirm others' worth and value. Interdependence connected to mutual submission also helps us work with "responsive others" to build a mature relationship. That confirms we're equal in value and enhancing our contentment.

18 *Achievement and Fulfillment Encourage Contentment*

She experiences achievement and feels fulfillment . . . "Many daughters have done nobly, But you excel them all. . . . Give her the product of her hands, And let her works praise her in the gates" (Prov. 31:29,31).

*T*he overemphasis on achievement and fulfillment in today's society comes from selfishness. Many suffer from compulsive behaviors that drive them to "work for self-esteem feelings." While strong, vocal feminists call loudly for women to find achievement and self-identity, their goals for women do not always encourage contentment. On the other hand, lack of commitment, initiative, and creativity do not equal contentment. Neither do laziness, passivity, or unconcern. We don't find contentment from careers, children, single life, or married life. And yet, life choices and responsibilities help color different shades of contentment.

Working out "contentment" depends on how we see ourselves. For too long, some women have pictured themselves as lacking ability, personality, and achievement. That fuzzy picture doesn't portray the Proverbs 31 woman. She's creative, shows initiative, and feels achievement and fulfillment with her self-worth confirmed. Incompetence, passivity, or unfulfillment have no part in her life. In fact, the Canon portrays her with contentment: "Many daughters have done nobly, But you excel them all" (v. 29).

Establishing a Contentment Foundation

How do you picture contentment? Everyone develops a mental picture of contentment; some are more clear while others are blurred or fuzzy. Helen Andelin's picture of what she believes women need in order to be content is blurred.

> There is one need which is fundamental, and it is for woman to be loved and cherished by her man. Without this one ingredient woman is unfulfilled. . . .

> Love is not reserved for the young, the single, nor the beautiful. It is reserved for those who arouse it in man. . . . . It isn't necessary for the man to know or do anything about the matter. In fact, it is an advantage if he does not. The art is to arouse his feelings. This is not a difficult accomplishment for woman, because it is based upon her natural instincts.[1]

This blurred photograph places contentment on a foundation of manipulation. Our fulfillment does not rest on whether or not we succeed in deceiving, manipulating, or seducing a man into marrying us. That kind of marriage would become despicable and unbearable, with concentration only on the physical side of the relationship. When we tired of such an endless and demeaning emptiness, we would fail because, according to *Fascinating Womanhood,* "If man does not love with heart and soul, it is entirely the woman's fault."[2] It's clear that Andelin's contentment rests on manipulation and selfishness. Her contentment foundation is unstable, unreliable, filled with deceit, and will damage our special female self.

Betty Friedan provides another example of an inadequate basis for contentment. "For women to have . . . identity and freedom, they must have economic independence. . . . Equality and human dignity are not possible for women if they are not able to earn . . . .[3] Friedan's fuzzy photograph contradicts the Bible's image of women. God created us with full identity, dignity, and freedom; we do not have to "work" for them. Also, He created us to cooperate rather than compete. Cooperation enhances a healthy interdependence.

Friedan goes on to link economic independence with the right to abortion on demand. Placing economic independence on the same level with power to end babies' lives degrades and destroys our full identity, freedom, and dignity. Our need to provide a livelihood cannot be linked with abortion. The body and emotions deserve proper care which covers saying "no" to indiscriminate sex and saying "yes" to discriminate abstinence. (While aborting may be necessary to save a mother's life, it cannot become a contraceptive.) Friedan's contentment foundation is unstable with constant change, unreliable and unlasting, and filled with deceit, damaging our special female self.

Dr. Mary Jo Bane defines a third way for some people to seek "contentment" in the midst of turmoil. Bane says divorce should remain a useful safety valve for families and improves marriage quality. Going even further, she sees no merit in holding families together.

> What happens to children depends not only on what happens in the homes, but what happens in the outside world. We really don't know how to raise children. If we want to talk about equality of opportunity for children, then the fact that children are raised in families means there's no equality. It's a dilemma. In order to raise children with equality, we must take them away from families and communally raise them.[4]

This improves family life? Stripping children away from parents to put them in communals is as off-center as advocating divorce for a safety valve. Couples can't live together for long without problems. Divorcing simply because problems develop does not meet God's standards. His solutions for problems do not rest on ripping and tearing apart families; rather, the solutions lie in working together to solve them. Sharing interdependence, giving and receiving, mutual compromise, loving and accepting, and receiving competent counsel help us solve problems and avoid divorce. Thus, God and His standards remain the only "safety valve." God's wisdom cuts across the ignorance of those who fail to seek truth from His instructions.

> The philosophy of rebellion and hatred underlying modern-day feminism has been largely responsible for the destruction of the American nuclear family. The feminist movement has drawn many restless women into its ranks—women who . . . have legitimate gripes about the way they've been treated by men, but who are seeking answers to their problems in the wrong places.[5]

In this light, Beverly LaHaye says a selfishness cult has grown up in America, trying to destroy not just the family, but our whole civilization. Taking children away from their families and rearing them communally certainly fits into the description of ignorance and selfishness. Dr. Bane's contentment foundation is unstable, unreliable, and deceitful.

In seeking contentment we must choose our foundations carefully and renew our commitment again and again. At different times in our lives, we may be tempted to seek contentment in possessions or relationships. However, contentment cannot rest on things, careers, sex, or people, since they are unstable and change continually. We must remember that contentment comes only as we are "in Christ." Placing contentment on any other foundation than faith in Christ becomes sin. And all sin offers is ". . . excessive or inappropriate gratification of impulses ('lust of the flesh'), . . . accumulation, by wrongful means or motives, of things that leave the inner person hollow ('lust of the eyes'), . . . inflated self-estimation created by . . . comparing one's money, power, prestige, or fortune to others ('Pride of life')."[6] There's only one who is *stable and unchanging.* "Jesus Christ is the same yesterday and today, yes and forever" (Heb. 13:8). "But Thou [God] art the same" (Ps. 102:27). Only God's immeasurable worth and Christ's salvation give us contentment, worthwhileness, and stability.

Overcoming Emptiness with Achievement

How we view personal achievement depends on how we see ourselves.

> I love being a woman! Not because it suits my emotion, which it does; not because it matches my physical characteristics, which it does; but because I am assured that this was God's choice and design for me. . . . When a woman does

not like her sex, she lives in conflict with her purpose and potential for life. [We] need to recognize and accept the truth that God did not create [us] inferior. . . . By God's design, [we] have a definite purpose to follow and fulfill.[7]

In accepting ourselves, we feel strong self-identity and emotional health within our special female self. We, then, can relate to others as persons of worth, since we relate to others in the same way we feel about ourselves.

The Proverbs 31 woman accepted herself, because she portrays a healthy self-identity. Looking at her photograph, we see a track record of achievement. **She is not a superwoman, though.** Her track record is attainable to all of us.

Mom modeled achievement, but it was all work—no play. So, the model I gave my children was one of work. When I felt sick, I worked; even during my four pregnancies there was only work, no rest or play. But, my work was for self-esteem. When I wasn't working, I sensed a huge guilt cloud hovering over me. I didn't know it was OK to rest or play with my children; neither did I recognize that through "my work" I was seeking good feelings about me. Behind the continual working lingered a turbulent confusion. At times I felt envy and anger towards women who took time to use speaking or teaching gifts. I thought, *If I can stay at home to take care of my house and children, so can they*. This shows how far I was from understanding that contentment comes from developing and using spiritual gifts.

When we moved to California, our house in Illinois didn't sell for fourteen months. Because we were also purchasing a house here, I had to either work for pay or lose the house. For days, words battled inside my mind, *If you go out of the home to work, leaving your children, you're a failure. . . . But if I don't, we'll have to sell the house and move into an apartment. . . . After all, God, You made us come out here. Couldn't You have sold our house?* I felt He had tricked and deceived us. So, amidst feelings of confusion and anger I acknowledged my need to work for pay. At the same time, my emotions said I had failed the children and Dick. Feeling like a failure, I slipped into a confining depression and felt no motivation to get out of bed each day. I felt worthless.

Dick wanted to get me out of the house, so he suggested we go to a museum which was about one hour's drive from us. Getting out of the house and away from responsibilities for a few hours helped turn my depression around. Slowly, I returned to my daily schedule; a few weeks later I accepted a secretarial position. During that time Dick supervised breakfast while our teenage girls shared starting dinner and helping with the laundry. All four children helped clean the kitchen, wash dishes, and clean their rooms. Years later, I see how that difficult time helped me allow the children to become more responsible for themselves.

The six of us working together helped solve a problem we couldn't avoid.

Like many other people, we were victims of a housemarket-price dropout. The Lord blessed our frugal living and efforts, enabling us to pay off our financial indebtedness and keep our house. Because we looked for and used problem solutions, we didn't need to follow Dr. Bane's suggestion of "safety-valve" divorce. The experience gave me a sense of achievement.

With all the achieving, though, I felt an emptiness. It had been many years since I taught Junior Sunday School and Vacation Bible School. Working both inside and outside the home and caring for the children left no time for other responsibilities. Yet, I couldn't work enough to "feel good" about me. The guilt cloud hovered lower and lower. Busyness does not end emptiness; neither does achievement—if sought for its own sake. If busyness and achievement leave us feeling empty, we need to reevaluate with questions like: "Am I running too fast and leaving no time for the Lord? Have I failed to discern and use my spiritual gifts? Are they being neglected?" Since "yes" was my answer to those questions, I had to redirect my busyness.

In chapter fourteen I told how the Lord directed me to go back to school and get my degrees in secretarial science and journalism. Developing my gifts wasn't easy or glamorous and using them is even frustrating at times, like when I deal with "difficult people." But, life now feels more meaningful and worthwhile since I know that my gifts are not being neglected. Like many others, I've found that achieving from using spiritual gifts both fills emptiness and encourages contentment.

Feeling Contentment with Fulfillment

Our lives are canvasses on which we paint different pictures of contentment. What seems grand to you may not appeal to me. What seems grand to me may not interest you. That difference illustrates a small portion of God's magnitude in creating our uniqueness.

Nevertheless, some don't appreciate God's creative design.

> Macho feminism despises anything which seeks to interfere with the desires of Number One. It is intrinsically anti-family . . . anti-men . . . even lesbianism is exalted by some . . . as the ultimate form of feminism. . . . The ideology which regards the existence of human beings as the world's greatest problem finds a natural sympathy with the view that procreation is beneath a woman's dignity. . . . Feminism . . . projected . . . a new image of women: a drab, macho feminism of hard-faced and hard-hearted women who were bound and determined to carve their place in the world, no matter whose bodies they have to climb over to do it.[8]

A sense of futility comes from seeking fulfillment in this way. Those who believe God's design for contentment doesn't work experience confusion. To find fulfillment, we need to remember to do three things: *Receive God's worth* for our self-worth; *put God first,* in proper perspective; *live out God's blueprint.* With those choices intact, self-identity, achievement, and expression of unique individuality *are recognized* for both sexes. In our unique differences we share "equal access" to His immeasurable worth.

God also gave us *choice*; using God's wisdom, we choose our contentment and fulfillment. Since God blueprints us, we can trust His judgment. The Proverbs 31 woman used God's wisdom to help her achieve and feel contentment. That's why this statement could be made in confidence. "Give her the product of her hands, And let her works praise her in the gates" (v. 31). Since her husband, a city hall elder, sat in the gates and helped carry on the city's business, her life was identified with his. Of course, people also identified the Proverbs 31 woman by their business dealings with her. Thus, as we paint our self-image, we can fill our palette with vibrant colors, whether we are single or married. However, we must remember that painting fulfillment comes from *feeling* self-identity, not in trying to *get* self-identity.

Paint from Christ's view. "The more we begin to see life from Christ's view, the broader our creative living will become. Creative thinking and activity are a by-product of His direct influence."[9] Since our human intelligence comes from being created in His image, seeing ourselves as persons of worth motivates us to work hard in painting fulfillment. Discontentment is like a worm that eats the meat out of a nut and then, when the nut is opened, there is nothing left but an empty shell. Circumstances in our lives, like that worm, sometimes eat the blessing out of the mercy we've received. Even though we may have felt some comfort, the overall experience left us feeling like an empty shell.

Nevertheless, we don't have to allow a painful past to hold us back. We can break away from whatever keeps us from creative expression. Reading and studying God's Word and getting insight into Christ's thinking help us break away. One example is looking at the way He pictures our worth and value to society. His view enhances our self-esteem.

Paint from choice. We don't paint life by guessing; we paint by discriminate choice. Almost four hundred years ago, Jeremiah Burroughs penned these words about fulfillment.

> What a foolish thing is this, that because I have not got what I want, I will not enjoy the comfort of what I have. . . . God gives you many mercies, but you see others have more mercies than you and therefore you cry for more; but God does not give you what you want and because of that you throw away what you have—is this not folly in your hearts? It is unthankfulness.[10]

A large part of learning to feel content is to concern ourselves with others' needs. Many times I've felt sorry for "me" while tunneling through difficult circumstances until I learned of someone else's heavy burden. Learning to give of our compassion helps us to feel fulfillment.

In deciding where to create, decide on a focus. For instance, we may choose from administrating, nursing, writing, teaching, parenting, singing, acting, or counseling. After we determine a focus, we need to identify three or more things to do in getting started. Check with your church, for example, to see where your gifts are needed. Private groups like hospitals or schools can always use your volunteer service. Another possibility is to inquire with your city about "senior" groups which need help. Reaching out to create can feel painful and discouraging at times. But choosing with God's wisdom helps to build contentment.

Paint from expectation. Anticipation and an expectant mental attitude require faith and trust. Everyone, then, can create, communicate, design, and build "things or events" never done before. In looking for our creative area, an opportunity may look fulfilling. But after awhile, we find that what we've chosen really doesn't fit our gifts. The need to try another type of creative opportunity becomes apparent. That's OK because it's part of discerning our interests and gifts. Using an expectant attitude of faith and trust, we can continue looking ways to serve creatively. Grandma Moses didn't begin painting until she became a senior. Colonel Sanders didn't start his "finger-licking good" chicken business until after he retired at age sixty-five. With perseverance, these individuals and others like them accepted the unpleasant along with the pleasant. While both chose a different area, they chose expectantly. Their attitude helped them paint fulfillment with vibrant colors.

Conclusion

Many unbelievers say we use God for a crutch. They don't understand the attitude, "My Father, I need you. I can't go it alone." They fail to see the strength needed to acknowledge our weakness. Seeking God's help and guidance is a mutual giving and taking. God, in willingness, gives; we, in willingness, receive. Our receiving, in turn, enables us to give to others. That's healthy interdependence—not a crutch—and cuts through damaging dependence or destructive independence, enhancing contentment. We can learn contentment whether we are single or married, with career or without career. Contentment from God's perspective cuts out the "superwoman syndrome" and brings in the "satisfied-woman syndrome."

That's what makes the difference in whether or not we can say with Paul, "I have learned the secret of contentment in every situation" (Phil. 4:12, TLB). The secret isn't that our problems have disappeared. The secret is that Christ stays with us, giving hope; that's the interdependence of two working together to solve problems. Using this God-designed process, our achievements and fulfillments create feelings of contentment within us.

One More Choice

*W*hile writing this book, I've recognized more fully my damaged emotions and serious, intense personality. Although I know my self-worth is settled, I still struggle sometimes to prove myself. Sometimes I still grieve over my lost childhood and envy those who grew up in constructive atmospheres with loving, calm fathers. While I'm working toward change and growth, I have to cope with reality. At this time and place, each of us live at different life-road intersections. Although our choices aren't the same, we're all "equal in value" with God's immeasurable worth. We're created in His image with mind (intelligence), emotions (creative energy), and soul (spiritual awareness). We have His power to use, His love to feel, and His truths to choose. They're ours to use in seeking to go beyond our emotional losses and become all we can be in Christ Jesus.

In light of that, I share a poem Ruth Graham prayed years ago. Some of us are single; some are married. But, regardless of differences, my emphasis rests on God the Father's **leading** in our lives.

> "Dear God," I prayed, all unafraid,
> (As girls are wont to be)
> "I do not want a handsome man—
> But let him be like Thee.
>
> "I do not need one big and strong,
> Nor one so very tall,
> Nor need he be some genius,
> Or wealthy, Lord, at all.
>
> "But let his head be high, dear God,
> And let his eye be clear,
> His shoulders straight, whate'er his state,
> Whate'er his earthy sphere.

"And let his face have character,
A ruggedness of soul
And let his whole life show, dear God,
A singleness of goal.

"And when he comes, *as he will come,*
With quiet eyes aglow—
I'll understand that he's the man
I prayed for long ago."[1]

Ruth expected to be single, not married. "As a young girl, out there in China," she says, "I committed my life to the Lord. And I got exactly the opposite of what I'd expected. I thought the Lord wanted me in Tibet, isolated and obscure, and I was happy at the prospect. Instead, what I've got are publicity and the spotlight. Maybe you won't believe it, but in some ways that's harder."[2] Ruth has lived through many lonely, hard experiences. She still feels great physical pain from a broken hip and its replacement. Life hasn't been without problems, frustrations; or emotional pain, but God's love, truth, and power have never left or forsaken her.

Many times I've felt, "God doesn't care. He's skipped out on me." Perhaps you've also felt those feelings. The life of faith, however, rests on *trust* not **feelings**. When Satan uses old mind-messages against us, we can pray something like this: "My loving Father, although I'm discouraged and feel forsaken, I believe You're here. I believe You're working in me, although I can't see any results. Help me use Your power to break those destructive mind-tapes. I love You and trust You." Physical and emotional healing takes time. That's why comparing our progress with others can feel discouraging.

Those of us who struggle with damaged emotions have God the Father's love, God the Son's healing, and God the Holy Spirit's power. They shred cocoon strands to free us from an ugly "caterpillar" self-image and release within us a beautiful butterfly. As that inner butterfly gains strength and learns to fly, our special female self will develop into a woman of excellence. Will you choose to work out God's process for growth? I pray you will answer "yes."

Notes

Introduction
    1. Myrna White, "This Butterfly Called Me," (Wheaton, Ill.: Special Way, Ltd; Wheaton-Fox Productions), side A, song 4.

Section 1—Developing a Strong Self-Image
Chapter 1
    1. Ira J. Tanner, *Loneliness: The Fear of Love* (New York: Harper and Row Publishers, 1973), xiv.
    2. Maurice E. Wagner, *The Sensation of Being Somebody* (Grand Rapids, Mich.: Zondervan Publishing House, 1975), 118.
    3. Ibid., 28-30.
    4. James Dobson, *Hide or Seek* (Old Tappan, N.J.: Fleming H. Revell Co., 1974), 23-26.
    5. Wagner, 29.
    6. Bruce Narramore, *You're Someone Special* (Grand Rapids, Mich.: Zondervan Publishing House, 1978), 128-29.
    7. Patti Roberts, *Ashes to Gold* (New York: Jove Publications, 1985), 96, 110-11.
    8. Wagner, 30.
    9. Joan Winmill Brown, *No Longer Alone* (Minneapolis: World Wide Publications, 1975), 37, 44, 51-53, 60-61, 64-65, 67.
    10. Vernard Eller, *The Language of Canaan and the Grammar of Feminism* (Grand Rapids, Mich.: Wm. B. Eerdmans Publishing Co., 1982), 38.
    11. John and Paula Sandford, *The Transformation of the Inner Man* (South Plainfield, N.J.: Bridge Publishing, 1982), 15.

Chapter 2
    1. W. D. Robson-Scott, *The Future of an Illusion* (Garden City, N. Y.: Anchor Books, Doubleday & Co., 1961), 40-50.
    2. David A. Seamands, *Healing of Memories* (Wheaton, Ill.: Victor Books, 1985), 12.
    3. Gary Collins, *You Can Profit from Stress* (Santa Ana, Calif.: Vision House Publishers, 1977), 13.
    4. Seamands, 15.
    5. Ibid., 72. Also, the basic ideas of defense mechanisms came from Dr. David A. Seamands.

6. David Augsburger, *Caring Enough to Forgive* (Ventura, Calif.: Regal Books, 1981), 52. Some of the basic ideas for forgiveness came from Dr. Augsburger. Others are mine.

Chapter 3

1. David A. Seamands, *Healing for Damaged Emotions* (Wheaton, Ill.: Victor Books, 1981), 61.

2. James Dobson, *Hide or Seek* (Old Tappan, N. J.: Fleming H. Revell Co., 1974), 151.

3. Seamands, 68.

4. Dick Wolf, *Find Yourself, Give Yourself* (Colorado Springs, Colo.: NavPress, 1983), 158.

5. Dick is Dr. Richard J. Mohline, Administrative Dean of Rosemead School of Psychology, Biola University, La Mirada, California.

6. Seamands, 61, 70.

7. The basic ideas for defiant, compliant, withdrawing personalities come from Maurice E. Wagner.

8. Seamands, 61, 70.

Chapter 4

1. Bruce Narramore, *You're Someone Special* (Grand Rapids, Mich.: Zondervan Publishing House, 1978), 126.

2. Mildred Newman and Bernard Berkowitz, *How to Take Charge of Your Life* (New York: Bantam Books, 1978), 5-6.

3. Walter Trobisch, *Love Yourself* (Downers Grove, Ill.: InterVarsity Press, 1976), 8-9.

4. Ibid., 16, 18.

5. Ibid., 23.

6. Dick Wulf, *Find Yourself, Give Yourself* (Colorado Springs, Colo.: Navpress, 1983), 111.

7. Don Baker, *Acceptance* (Portland, Oreg.: Multnomah Press, 1985), 59, 76.

8. John Powell, *Why Am I Afraid to Tell You Who I Am* (Allen, Tex.: Tabor Publishing, 1969), 8-9, 12.

9. Florence Littauer, *How to Get Along with Difficult People* (Eugene, Oreg. Harvest House Publishers, 1984), 8-9.

10. Ibid., 161-63.

Chapter 5

1. Nancy Anne Smith, *Winter Past* (Downers Grove, Ill.: InterVarsity Press, 1977), 20, 25-26, 68.

2. Susan Forward, *Betrayal of Innocence* (New York, N. Y.: Penguin Books, 1984) 3-4.

3. Abuse statistics came from: Maxine Rock, "How Could This Happen to My Friend?," *McCall's*, April 1983, 58; "Rage Turns to Rape," *Ladies' Home Journal*, September 1983, 144; Carole S. Dunning, "Helping and Healing the Sexually Abused" seminar, January 1985 (Dunning is a licensed marriage, family, and child counselor); *The World Almanac* (New York: Newspaper Enterprise Association, 1986), 792.

4. David A. Stoop, *Selftalk—Key to Personal Growth* (Old Tappan, N. J.: Fleming H. Revell, 1982), 30.

5. Ibid., 33, 38, 40-41, 44.

6. David A. Seamands, *Healing for Damaged Emotions* (Wheaton, Ill.: Victor Books, 1981), 56, 72.

7. Paul Tournier, *Creative Suffering* (New York: Harper and Row, Publishers, 1982), 112.

Section 2—Developing Sensitive Serving Skills

1. Dr. James Dobson quoted in "Focus on the Family" monthly newsletter, January 1987.

Chapter 6

1. Credit for the Greek research regarding submission and obedience goes to my husband, Dr. Richard J. Mohline.

2. Richard J. Foster, *Celebration of Discipline* (San Francisco: Harper and Row, Publishers, 1978), 97-98, 102.

3. Dawn Bethe Frankfort, "Women Don't Want, or Need, to Suffer," *USA Today*, December 19, 1985, 13A. She interviewed and quoted Paula Caplan.

Chapter 7

1. Penelope Russianoff, *Why Do I Think I Am Nothing Without a Man?* (New York: Bantam Books, 1981), xvi.

2. Luci Swindoll, *Wide My World, Narrow My Bed* (Portland, Oreg.: Multnomah Press, 1982), 39.

3. Some of the basic ideas about sexual sin came from Gary Collins, *You Can Profit from Stress* (Santa Ana, Calif.: Vision House Publishers, 1977), 108-9.

4. Mary Vespa, "In Their Own Words," *People's Magazine*, May 4, 1981, 56-60. She interviewed Joy Dryfoos and Richard Lincoln who researched facts for New York's Alan Guttmacher Institute.

5. David R. Carlin, "Suicide and Private Morality," *America*, June 9, 1984, 438.

6. Paul Brand and Philip Yancey, *In His Image* (Grand Rapids, Mich.: Zondervan Publishing House, 1984), 185, 196, 199.

Chapter 8

1. The four reasons why males choose passivity in relationships is from Dr. Richard J. Mohline.

2. Kenneth S. Wuest, "Four Greek Words for Love," *Bibliotheca Sacra* 116 (July 1959): 242.

3. Ibid., 243.

4. Neil Clark Warren, *Make Anger Your Ally* (Garden City, N. Y.: Doubleday and Co., 1983), 17, 19, 21, 23.

5. Ibid., 29-30.

6. *The Document: Declaration of Feminism,* 10-11 quoted from the leaflet, "Do These Women Speak for You?" Prepared by Concerned Women for America, 122 C. Street NW, Washington, D.C. 20001.

7. Some book suggestions to read regarding emotional healing are as follows:

David Augsburger, *Caring Enough to Forgive,* Regal Books
Rich Buhler, *Love No Strings Attached,* Thomas Nelson Publishers
Dwight L. Carlson, *When Life Isn't Fair,* Harvest House Publishers
Richard J. Foster, *Celebration of Discipline,* Harper and Row, Publishers
Sara Hines Martin, *Healing for Adult Children of Alcholoics* and *Shame on You!*, Broadman Press
Laura A. Mathis, *The Road to Wholeness,* Tyndale House Publishers
Harold Morris, *Twice Pardoned,* Focus on the Family Publishing
Bruce Narramore, *You're Someone Special,* Zondervan Publishing House
David Seamands, *Healing for Damaged Emotions* and *Healing of Memories,* Victor Books
Neil Warren, *Make Anger Your Ally,* Doubleday and Co.

Chapter 9

1. Donald M. Joy, *Lovers—Whatever Happened to Eden?* (Waco, Tex.: Word Books, 1987), 91-92.

2. Charles R. Swindoll, *Improving Your Serve* (Waco, Tex.: Word Books, 1981), 189, 191.

3. David Augsburger, *Caring Enough to Confront* (Ventura, Calif.: Regal Books, 1981), 94.

4. Ibid., 90, 98, 101.

5. The breakdown of percentages came from Jerrold S. Greenberg, *Comprehensive Stress Management* (Dubuque, Iowa: Wm. C. Brown Co. Publishers, 1983), 297.

6. The three sub-titles in this section came from Mary Stewart Van Leeuwen, "The End of Female Passivity," *Christianity Today*, January 17, 1986, 13-I.

7. The five "E's" came from Dr. Dan Baumann in April 1979, as senior pastor of Whittier Area Baptist Fellowship, Whittier, California. He's now Executive Director of Church and Pastoral Services for the General Baptist Conference and has written several books.

8. Joy, 140-42.

9. Ibid., 135.

Section 3—Developing Sensible Relational Skills
Chapter 10

1. Paul W. Swets, *Talking So That People Will Listen* (Englewood Cliffs, N.J.: Prentice-Hall, 1983), 47.

2. The basic ideas for passive and perceptive listening came from Myron D. Rush, *Richer Relationships* (Wheaton, Ill.: Victor Books, 1983), 166-69.

3. Ted W. Engstrom with Robert C. Larson, *The Fine Art of Friendship* (New York: Thomas Nelson Publishers, 1985), 57.

4. Swets, 5.

5. Ibid., 75.

6. Cecil G. Osborne, *The Art of Getting Along with People* (Grand Rapids, Mich.: Zondervan Publishing House, 1985), 169.

7. Bernard Berkowitz and Mildred Newman, *How to Take Charge of Your Life* (New York: Bantam Books, 1978), 24, 35.

Chapter 11

1. Dorothy R. Pape, *In Search of God's Ideal Woman* (Downers Grove, Ill.: InterVaristy Press, 1976), 81-83.

2. Jean Lush with Patricia H. Rushford, *Emotional Phases of a Woman's Life* (Old Tappan, N. J.: Fleming H. Revell, 1986), 77. (Quoted Gillian Ford, "Premenstrual Syndrome Relief," PMS Relief, P. O. Box 10, Newcastle, CA 95658).

3. Basic ideas regarding PMS in this section are from Dr. Carol Ann Francis, Christian Psychologist, Los Angeles.

4. Lush and Rushford, 212.

5. Ibid., 94, 96.

6. Ibid., 76.

7. Cecil G. Osborne, *The Art of Getting Along with People* (Grand Rapids, Mich.: Zondervan Publishing House, 1980), 9.

8. Kathy Narramore and Alice Hill, *Kindred Spirits* (Grand Rapids, Mich.: Zondervan Publishing House, 1985), 28.

9. Paul Tournier, *To Understand Each Other* (Old Tappan, N. J.: Fleming H. Revell, 1967), 37, 42.

10. J. B. Phillips, *Your God Is too Small* (New York: Macmillan Publishing Co., 1961), 19.

Chapter 12

1. *1980 Census of Population*, United States Summary, U. S. Department of Commerce, vol. 1 General, (U.S. Government Printing Office, Issued May 1983), Figure 16, 15.

2. Cecil Osborne, *The Art of Understanding Yourself* (Grand Rapids, Mich.: Zondervan Publishing House, 1967), 94.

3. Lawrence J. Crabb, Jr. and Dan B. Allender, *Encouragement* (Grand Rapids, Mich.: Zondervan Publishing House, 1984), 29-30, 32-33.

4. Paul Tournier, *To Understand Each Other* (Old Tappan, N. J.: Fleming H. Revell Co., 1967), 52, 59.

5. Suggested books giving insight and perspective regarding unwanted intrusions and how to cope:

Janet Congo, *Finding Inner Security*, Regal Books

Jim and Sally Conway, *Your Marriage Can Survive Mid-Life Crisis*, Thomas Nelson

Lawrence Crabb, Jr., *Inside Out*, NavPress

Lawrence Crabb, Jr., and Dan B. Allender, *Encouragement*, Zondervan

William and Kristi Gualtiere, *Mistaken Identity*, Fleming H. Revell

Jan Frank, *A Door of Hope*, Here's Life Publishers

Maxine Hancock and Karen Mains, *Child Sexual Abuse: A Hope for Healing*, Harold Shaw

Stormie Omartian, *Stormie*, Harvest House Publishers

David B. Peters, *A Betrayal of Innocence*, Word Publishers

Deborah Roberts, *Raped*, Zondervan Publishing House

Section 4—Developing Reliable Work-Ethic Skills
Chapter 13

1. Betty Friedan, *The Feminine Mystique* (New York: Dell Publishing Co., 1983), 384.

2. Connaught C. Marshner, *The New Traditional Woman* (Washington, D. C.: Free Congress Research and Education Foundation, 1982), 3-4.

3. Basic ideas came from John S. Morgan and J. R. Philip, *You Can't Manage Alone* (Grand Rapids, Mich.: Zondervan Publishing House, 1985), 21-22.

4. Ted W. Engstrom, *The Pursuit of Excellence*, (Grand Rapids, Mich.: Zondervan Publishing House, 1982), 63, 65.

5. Dorothy L. Sayers, *Are Women Human?* (Grand Rapids, Mich.: William B. Eerdmans Publishing Co., 1971), 14-15.

6. Engstrom, 18-20.

Chapter 14

1. Mark 15:37-41; Luke 10:38-42; 23:49-56; 24:1-10; John 4:7-29; 20:1-18; Acts 1:12-14. These Scriptures make a significant statement about female importance and position being equal with male.

2. Anne Ortlund, *Disciplines of the Beautiful Woman* (Waco, Tex.: Word Books, Publishers, 1977), 60.

3. Ted W. Engstrom, *The Pursuit of Excellence* (Grand Rapids, Mich.: Zondervan Publishing House, 1982), 91. Quoted John Catoir from *What a Day This Can Be* (New York: The Christophers).

4. Basic ideas for "Hurry Sickness" came from Dr. Bruce Baldwin, guest speaker, "Focus on the Family," aired over KKLA, Los Angeles, Calif., November 7, 1986.

5. Basic ideas regarding the functions of the brain came from Roger Sperry, "Probing the Two Minds of Man," in *THE HUMAN BODY The Brain: Mystery of Matter and Mind* (Washington, D.C.: U. S. News Books)

6. Myron Rush, *Lord of the Marketplace* (Wheaton, Ill.: Victor Books, 1986) 170-72.

7. Original budget came from the Conservative Baptist Credit Union in Anaheim, California.

Chapter 15

1. Basic information regarding family structure came from W. Peter Blitchington, *Sex Roles and the Christian Family* (Wheaton, Ill.: Tyndale, 1984), 16, 49.

2. Basic information regarding physical development can be found in the booklet by Marion O. Lerrige and Michael A. Cassidy, *Your Child from 9 to 12* (Chicago: Budlong Press, 1965), 1,4.

3. Basic ideas regarding sexuality came from Lewis B. Smedes, *Love Within Limits* (Grand Rapids, Mich.: Wm. B. Eerdmans Publishing Co., 1978), 67.

4. John and Paula Sandford, *The Transformation of the Inner Man* (South Plainfield, N.J.: Bridge Publishing, 1982), 10, 11.

5. Betty J. Coble, *Woman—Aware and Choosing* (Nashville, Tenn.: Broadman Press, 1975), 40, 42.

6. David Viscott, *Risking* (New York: Pocket Books, 1977), 27, 32.

7. Lewis J. Lord with Jeannye Thornton and Joseph Carey, "Sex with Care" *U.S. News & World Report*, June 2, 1986, 53-57.

8. Denis Waitley, *Seeds of Greatness* (Old Tappan, N.J.: Fleming H. Revell, 1983), 141-42, 144-45.

9. Yvonne G. Baker, *Successfully Single* (Denver, Colo.: Accent Books, 1985), 166.

Section 5—Developing Realistic Contentment Skills
Chapter 16

1. Bernard Berkowitz and Mildred Newman, *How to Take Charge of Your Life* (New York: Bantam Books, 1978), 100.

2. Joanne Wallace, *The Confident Woman* (Old Tappan, N.J.: Fleming H. Revell, 1985), 21.

3. Gien Karssen, *The Best of All* (Colorado Springs, Colo.: Navpress, 1982), 29.

4. Laura A. Mathis, *The Road to Wholeness* (Eugene, Oreg.: Tyndale House Publishers, 1987), 195.

5. Bill Glass, *Expect to Win* (Waco, Tex.: Word Books, 1981), 24-25.

6. Earl D. Radmacher, *You & Your Thoughts* (Wheaton, Ill.: Tyndale House Publishers, 1977, 1982), 16.

7. Ibid., 44.

8. Basic ideas for Locus of Control came from Jerrold S. Greenberg, *Comprehensive Stress Management* (Dubuque, Iowa: Wm. C. Brown Co. Publishers, 1983).

9. William Coleman, *You Can Be Creative* (Eugene, Oreg.: Harvest House Publishers, 1983), 13, 22-23, 33, 130.

10. Ibid., 36-41, 128-30.

Chapter 17

1. Overcomers Outreach, 2290 West Whittier Blvd., Suite D, La Habra, CA 90631; (a Christian

ministry addressing alcoholism and drug dependency); Betty Ford Center, 39000 Bob Hope Drive, Rancho Mirage, CA 92270; Sexaholics Anonymous (SA), P. O. Box 300, Simi Valley, CA 93062 (a fellowship to share experiences, strength, and hope to help solve a common problem and help others to recover); S-ANON, 2303 North 44th Street, Suite 279, Phoenix, AZ 85008. For local A. A. chapters and other support groups, check the yellow pages.

2. Billy Graham, *Facing Death and the Life After* (Minneapolis: Grason, 1987), 174-76.

3. Jeri Krumroy, *Grief Is Not Forever* (Elgin, Ill.: Brethren Press, 1985), 68, 70.

4. Dwight L. Carlson, *Overcoming Hurts and Anger* (Eugene, Oreg.: Harvest House Publishers, 1981), 79-80.

5. David Augsburger, *Caring Enough to Confront* (Ventura, Calif.: Regal Books, 1985), 53.

6. Ibid., 58-59.

Chapter 18

1. Helen B. Andelin, *Fascinating Womanhood* (San Luis Obispo, Calif.: Pacific Press, 1963), introduction

2. Ibid.

3. Betty Friedan, *The Feminine Mystique* (New York: Dell Publishing Co., 1983), 384-85.

4. Quoted from the leaflet, "Do These Women Speak For You?" Prepared by Concerned Women for America.

5. Beverly LaHaye, *The Restless Woman* (Grand Rapids, Mich.: Zondervan Publishing House, 1984), 78, 89.

6. Laura A. Mathis, *The Road to Wholeness* (Wheaton, Ill.: Tyndale House Publishers, 1987), 80-81.

7. Beverly LaHaye, *I Am a Woman by God's Design* (Old Tappan, N. J.: Fleming H. Revell Co., 1980) 18.

8. Connaught C. Marshner, *The New Traditional Woman* (Washington, D. C.: The Free Congress Research and Education Foundation, 1982), 3.

9. William Coleman, *You Can Be Creative* (Eugene, Oreg.: Harvest House Publishers, 1983), 44.

10. Quoted from "More than Money," a publication of Evangelical Christian Credit Union, Fall 1990, 6.

One More Choice

1. Stanley High, *Billy Graham* (New York: McGraw-Hill Book Co., 1956), 115.

2. Ibid., 122.